SCIENCE AND MYTH:
ARE THEY
ONE AND THE SAME?

- **Was Adam the first test-tube baby? And was Eve the original beneficiary of organ transplant surgery?**

- **Did nuclear fission destroy Sodom and Gomorrah?**

- **Did computer printouts exist 5,000 years ago?**

- **How were the ancients able to describe accurately details about our solar system that are only *now* being revealed by deep space probes?**

The incredible answers are all here—
fully documented with the latest scientific
findings—in an important and fascinating
new work by the respected author of
THE EARTH CHRONICLES.

Other Avon Books by
Zecharia Sitchin

THE EARTH CHRONICLES

GENESIS REVISITED

IS MODERN SCIENCE CATCHING UP WITH ANCIENT KNOWLEDGE?

ZECHARIA SITCHIN

AVON BOOKS
An Imprint of HarperCollins*Publishers*

Dedicated to my wife,
Frieda (Rina) *née* Regenbaum
who encouraged me to "stop talking
and start writing" about the *Nefilim*.

AVON BOOKS
An Imprint of HarperCollins*Publishers*
10 East 53rd Street
New York, New York 10022-5299

Copyright © 1990 by Zecharia Sitchin
Uranus photo (p. 8) © Finley Holiday Films
Published by arrangement with the author
Library of Congress Catalog Card Number: 90-92997
ISBN: 0-380-76159-9
www.avonbooks.com

First Avon Books Printing: October 1990

Avon Trademark Reg. U.S. Pat. Off. and in Other Countries, Marca Registrada, Hecho en U.S.A.
HarperCollins® is a trademark of HarperCollins Publishers Inc.

Printed in the U.S.A.

OPM   20   19   18   17   16   15   14   13

TABLE OF CONTENTS

FOREWORD

The last decades of the twentieth century have witnessed an upsurge of human knowledge that boggles the mind. Our advances in every field of science and technology are no longer measured in centuries or even decades but in years and even months, and they seem to surpass in attainments and scope anything that Man has achieved in the past.

But is it possible that Mankind has come out of the Dark Ages and the Middle Ages; reached the Age of Enlightenment; experienced the Industrial Revolution; and entered the era of high-tech, genetic engineering, and space flight—only to catch up with ancient knowledge?

For many generations the Bible and its teachings have served as an anchor for a searching Mankind, but modern science appeared to have cast us all adrift, especially in the confrontation between Evolution and Creationism. In this volume it will be shown that the conflict is baseless; that the Book of Genesis and its sources reflect the highest levels of scientific knowledge.

Is it possible, then, that what our civilization is discovering today about our planet Earth and about our corner of the universe, the heavens, is only a drama that can be called "Genesis Revisited"—only a *re*discovery of what had been known to a much earlier civilization, on Earth and on another planet?

The question is not one of mere scientific curiosity; it goes to the core of Mankind's existence, its origin, and its destiny. It involves the Earth's future as a viable planet because it concerns events in Earth's past; it deals with where we are going because it reveals where we have come from. And the answers, as we shall see, lead to inevitable conclusions that some consider too incredible to accept and others too awesome to face.

1

1

The Host of Heaven

> In the beginning
> God created the Heaven and the Earth.

The very concept of a beginning of all things is basic to modern astronomy and astrophysics. The statement that there was a void and chaos before there was order conforms to the very latest theories that chaos, not permanent stability, rules the universe. And then there is the statement about the bolt of light that began the process of creation.

Was this a reference to the Big Bang, the theory according to which the universe was created from a primordial explosion, a burst of energy in the form of light, that sent the matter from which stars and planets and rocks and human beings are formed flying in all directions and creating the wonders we see in the heavens and on Earth? Some scientists, inspired by the insights of our most inspiring source, have thought so. But then, how did ancient Man know the Big Bang theory so long ago? Or was this biblical tale the description of matters closer to home, of how our own little planet Earth and the heavenly zone called the Firmament, or "hammered-out bracelet," were formed?

Indeed, how did ancient Man come to have a cosmogony at all? How much did he really know, and how did he know it?

It is only appropriate that we begin the quest for answers where the events began to unfold—in the heavens; where also, from time immemorial, Man has felt that his origins, higher values—God, if you will—are to be found. As thrilling as discoveries made by the use of microscopes are, it is what telescopes enable us to see that fills us with the realization of the grandeur of nature and the universe. Of all recent advances, the most impressive have undoubtedly been the discoveries in the heavens surrounding our planet. And what staggering ad-

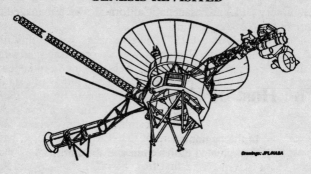

Figure 1

vances they have been! In a mere few decades we Earthlings have soared off the face of our planet; roamed Earth's skies hundreds of miles above its surface; landed on its solitary staellite, the Moon; and sent an array of unmanned spacecraft to probe our celestial neighbors, discovering vibrant and active worlds dazzling in their colors, features, makeup, satellites, rings. For the first time, perhaps, we can grasp the meaning and feel the scope of the Psalmist's words:

> The heavens bespeak the glory of the Lord
> and the vault of heaven reveals His handiwork.

A fantastic era of planetary exploration came to a magnificent climax when, in August 1989, the unmanned spacecraft designated *Voyager 2* flew by distant Neptune and sent back to Earth pictures and other data. Weighing just about a ton but ingeniously packed with television cameras, sensing and measuring equipment, a power source based on nuclear decay, transmitting antennas, and tiny computers (Fig. 1), it sent back whisperlike pulses that required more than four hours to reach Earth even at the speed of light. On Earth the pulses were captured by an array of radiotelescopes that form the Deep Space Network of the U.S. National Aeronautics and Space Administration (NASA); then the faint signals were translated by electronic wizardry into photographs, charts, and other forms of data at the sophisticated facilities of the Jet Propulsion

Laboratory (JPL) in Pasadena, California, which managed the project for NASA.

Launched in August 1977, twelve years before this final mission—the visit to Neptune—was accomplished, *Voyager 2* and its companion, *Voyager 1*, were originally intended to reach and scan only Jupiter and Saturn and augment data obtained earlier about those two gaseous giants by the *Pioneer 10* and *Pioneer 11* unmanned spacecraft. But with remarkable ingenuity and skill, the JPL scientists and technicians took advantage of a rare alignment of the outer planets and, using the gravitational forces of these planets as "slingshots," managed to thrust *Voyager 2* first from Saturn to Uranus and then from Uranus to Neptune (Fig. 2).

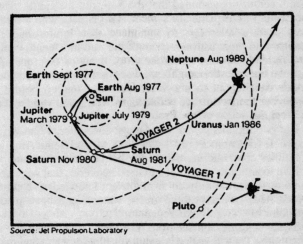

Source: Jet Propulsion Laboratory

Figure 2

Thus it was that for several days at the end of August 1989, headlines concerning another world pushed aside the usual news of armed conflicts, political upheavals, sports results, and market reports that make up Mankind's daily fare. For a few days the world we call Earth took time out to watch another world; we, Earthlings, were glued to our television sets, thrilled by closeup pictures of another planet, the one we call Neptune.

As the dazzling images of an aquamarine globe appeared on our television screens, the commentators stressed repeatedly that this was the first time that Man on Earth had ever really been able to see this planet, which even with the best Earth-based telescopes is visible only as a dimly lit spot in the darkness of space almost three billion miles from us. They reminded the viewers that Neptune was discovered only in 1846, after perturbations in the orbit of the somewhat nearer planet Uranus indicated the existence of another celestial body beyond it. They reminded us that no one before that—neither Sir Isaac Newton nor Johannes Kepler, who between them discovered and laid down the laws of celestial motion in the seventeenth and eighteenth centuries; neither Copernicus, who in the sixteenth century determined that the Sun, not the Earth, was in the center of our planetary system, nor Galileo, who a century later used a telescope to announce that Jupiter had four moons—no great astronomer until the mid-nineteenth century and certainly no one in earlier times knew of Neptune. And thus not only the average TV viewer but the astronomers themselves were about to see what had been unseen before—it would be the first time we would learn the true hues and makeup of Neptune.

But two months *before* the August encounter, I had written an article for a number of U.S., European, and South American monthlies contradicting these long-held notions: Neptune *was* known in antiquity, I wrote; and the discoveries that were about to be made would only confirm ancient knowledge. Neptune, I predicted, would be blue-green, watery, and have patches the color of "swamplike vegetation"!

The electronic signals from *Voyager 2* confirmed all that and more. They revealed a beautiful blue-green, aquamarine planet embraced by an atmosphere of helium, hydrogen, and methane gases, swept by swirling, high-velocity winds that make Earth's hurricanes look timid. Below this atmosphere there appear mysterious giant "smudges" whose coloration is sometimes darker blue and sometimes greenish yellow, perhaps depending on the angle at which sunlight strikes them. As expected, the atmospheric and surface temperatures are below freezing, but unexpectedly Neptune was found to emit heat that emanates from within the planet. Contrary to the previous consideration of Neptune as being a "gaseous" planet, it was determined by *Voyager 2* to have a rocky core above which there floats, in the words of the JPL scientists, "a slurry mixture of water ice." This watery layer, circling the rocky core as the planet revolves in its sixteen-hour day, acts as a dynamo that creates a sizable magnetic field.

This beautiful planet (see Neptune, page 8) was found to be encircled by several rings made up of boulders, rocks, and dust and is orbited by at least eight satellites, or moons. Of the latter, the largest, Triton, proved no less spectacular than its planetary master. *Voyager 2* confirmed the retrograde motion of this small celestial body (almost the size of Earth's Moon): it orbits Neptune in a direction opposite to that of the coursing of Neptune and all other known planets in our Solar System, not anticlockwise as they do but clockwise. Besides its very existence, its approximate size, and its retrograde motion, astronomers knew nothing else of Triton. *Voyager 2* revealed it to be a "blue moon," an appearance resulting from methane in Triton's atmosphere. The surface of Triton showed through the thin atmosphere—a pinkish gray surface with rugged, mountainous features on one side and smooth, almost craterless features on the other side. Close-up pictures suggested recent volcanic activity but of a very odd kind: what the active, hot interior of this celestial body spews out is not molten lava but jets of slushy ice. Even preliminary assessments indicated that Triton had flowing water in its past, quite possibly even lakes that may have existed on the surface until relatively recent times, in geological terms. The astronomers had no immediate explanation for "double-tracked ridge lines" that run straight for hundreds of miles and, at one or even two points, intersect at what appears to be right angles, suggesting rectangular areas (Fig. 3).

The discoveries thus fully confirmed my prediction: Neptune is indeed blue-green; it is made up in great part of water; and it does have patches whose coloration looks like "swamplike vegetation." This last tantalizing aspect may bespeak more than a color code if the full implication of the discoveries on Triton is taken into consideration: there, "darker patches with brighter halos" have suggested to the scientists of NASA the existence of "deep pools of *organic* sludge." Bob Davis re-

Figure 3

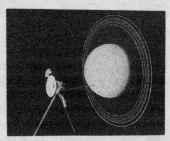

Neptune *Uranus*

ported from Pasadena to *The Wall Street Journal* that Triton, whose atmosphere contains as much nitrogen as Earth's, may be spewing out from its active volcanoes not only gases and water ice but also "organic material, carbon-based compounds which apparently coat parts of Triton."

Such gratifying and overwhelming corroboration of my prediction was not the result of a mere lucky guess. It goes back to 1976 when *The 12th Planet*, my first book in The Earth Chronicles series, was published. Basing my conclusions on millennia-old Sumerian texts, I had asked rhetorically: "When we probe Neptune someday, will we discover that its persistent association with waters is due to the watery swamps" that had once been seen there?

This was published, and obviously written, a year *before* Voyager 2 was even launched and was restated by me in an article two months before the Neptune encounter.

How could I be so sure, on the eve of *Voyager*'s encounter with Neptune, that my 1976 prediction would be corroborated—how dared I take the chance that my predictions would be disproved within weeks after submitting my article? My certainty was based on what happened in January 1986, when *Voyager 2* flew by the planet Uranus.

Although somewhat closer to us—Uranus is "only" about two billion miles away—it lies so far beyond Saturn that it cannot be seen from Earth with the naked eye. It was discovered in 1781 by Frederick Wilhelm Herschel, a musician turned amateur astronomer, only after the telescope was perfected. At the time of its discovery and to this day, Uranus has been hailed as the first planet *un*known in antiquity to be discovered in modern times; for, it has been held, the ancient peoples knew of and venerated the Sun, the Moon, and only five planets (Mercury, Venus, Mars, Jupiter, and Saturn), which they believed moved around the Earth in the "vault of heaven"; nothing could be seen or known beyond Saturn.

But the very evidence gathered by *Voyager 2* at Uranus proved the opposite: that at one time a certain ancient people did know about Uranus, and about Neptune, and even about the more-distant Pluto!

Scientists are still analyzing the photographs and data from Uranus and its amazing moons, seeking answers to endless

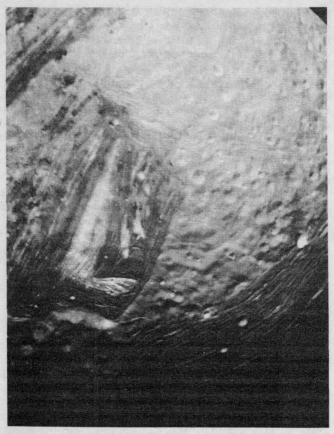

Plate A

puzzles. Why does Uranus lie on its side, as though it was hit by another large celestial object in a collision? Why do its winds blow in a retrograde direction, contrary to what is normal in the Solar System? Why is its temperature on the side that is hidden from the Sun the same as on the side facing the Sun? And what shaped the unusual features and formations on some of the Uranian moons? Especially intriguing is the moon called Miranda, ''one of the most enigmatic objects in the solar sys-

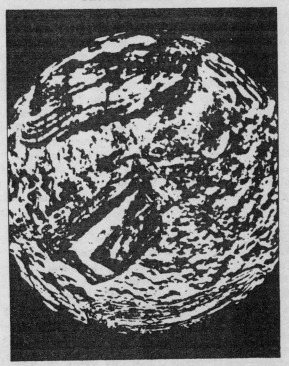

Figure 4

tem,'' in the words of NASA's astronomers, where an elevated, flattened-out plateau is delineated by 100-mile-long escarpments that form a right angle (a feature nicknamed ''the Chevron'' by the astronomers), and where, on both sides of this plateau, there appear elliptical features that look like racetracks ploughed over by concentric furrows (Plate A and Fig. 4).

Two phenomena, however, stand out as the major discoveries regarding Uranus, distinguishing it from other planets. One is its color. With the aid of Earth-based telescopes and unmanned spacecraft we have become familiar with the graybrown of Mercury, the sulphur-colored haze that envelops Venus, the reddish Mars, the multihued red-brown-yellow Jupiter and Saturn. But as the breathtaking images of Uranus began to appear on television screens in January 1986, its most striking feature was its *greenish blue color*—a color totally different from that of all the previous planets seen (see Uranus, page 8).

The other different and unexpected finding had to do with what Uranus is made of. Defying earlier assumptions by astronomers that Uranus is a totally "gaseous" planet like the giants Jupiter and Saturn, it was found by *Voyager 2* to be covered not by gases but by *water*; not just a sheet of frozen ice on its surface but an *ocean of water*. A gaseous atmosphere, it was found, indeed enshrouds the planet; but below it there churns an immense layer—6,000 miles thick!—of "super-heated water, its temperature as high as 8,000 degrees Fahrenheit" (in the words of JPL analysts). This layer of liquid, hot water surrounds a molten rocky core where radioactive elements (or other, unknown processes) produce the immense internal heat.

As the images of Uranus grew bigger on the TV screen the closer *Voyager 2* neared the planet, the moderator at the Jet Propulsion Laboratory drew attention to its unusual green-blue color. I could not help cry out loud, "Oh, my God, it is exactly as the Sumerians had described it!" I hurried to my study, picked up a copy of *The 12th Planet*, and with unsteady hands looked up page 269 (in the Avon paperback edition). I read again and again the lines quoting the ancient texts. Yes, there was no doubt: though they had no telescopes, the Sumerians had described Uranus as MASH.SIG, a term which I had translated "bright greenish."

A few days later came the results of the analysis of *Voyager 2*'s data, and the Sumerian reference to water on Uranus was also corroborated. Indeed, there appeared to be water all over the place: as reported on a wrap-up program on the television series NOVA ("The Planet That Got Knocked on Its Side"), "*Voyager 2* found that all the moons of Uranus are made up of rock and ordinary water ice." This abundance, or even the mere presence, of water on the supposed "gaseous" planets and their satellites at the edges of the Solar System was totally unexpected.

Yet here we had the evidence, presented in *The 12th Planet*, that in their texts from millennia ago the ancient Sumerians had not only known of the existence of Uranus but had accurately described it as greenish blue and watery!

What did all that mean? It meant that in 1986 modern science did not discover what had been unknown; rather, it *re*discovered and caught up with ancient knowledge. It was, therefore, because of that 1986 corroboration of my 1976 writings and thus of the veracity of the Sumerian texts that I felt confident enough to predict, on the eve of the *Voyager 2* encounter with Neptune, what it would discover there.

The *Voyager 2* flybys of Uranus and Neptune had thus confirmed not only ancient knowledge regarding the very existence of these two outer planets but also crucial details regarding them. The 1989 flyby of Neptune provided still more corroboration of the ancient texts. In them, Neptune was listed before Uranus, as would be expected of someone who is coming into the Solar System and sees first Pluto, then Neptune, and then Uranus. In these texts or planetary lists Uranus was called *Kakkab shanamma*, "Planet Which Is the Double" of Neptune. The *Voyager 2* data goes far to uphold this ancient notion. Uranus is indeed a look-alike of Neptune in size, color, and watery content; both planets are encircled by rings and orbited by a multitude of satellites, or moons. An unexpected similarity has been found regarding the two planets' magnetic fields: both have an unusually extreme inclination relative to the planets' axes of rotation—58 degrees on Uranus, 50 degrees on Neptune. "Neptune appears to be almost a magnetic twin of Uranus," John Noble Wilford reported in *The New York Times*. The two planets are also similar in the lengths of their days: each about sixteen to seventeen hours long.

The ferocious winds on Neptune and the water ice slurry layer on its surface attest to the great internal heat it generates, like that of Uranus. In fact, the reports from JPL state that initial temperature readings indicated that "Neptune's temperatures are similar to those of Uranus, which is more than a billion miles closer to the Sun." Therefore, the scientists assumed "that Neptune somehow is generating more of its internal heat than Uranus does"—somehow compensating for its greater distance from the Sun to attain the same temperatures as Uranus generates, resulting in similar temperatures on both planets—and thus adding one more feature "to the size and other characteristics that make Uranus a near twin of Neptune."

"Planet which is the double," the Sumerians said of Uranus in comparing it to Neptune. "Size and other characteristics that make Uranus a near twin of Neptune," NASA's scientists announced. Not only the described characteristics but even the terminology—"planet which is the double," "a near twin of Neptune"—is similar. But one statement, the Sumerian one, was made circa 4,000 B.C., and the other, by NASA, in A.D. 1989, nearly 6,000 years later. . . .

In the case of these two distant planets, it seems that modern science has only caught up with ancient knowledge. It sounds incredible, but the facts ought to speak for themselves. Moreover, this is just the first of a series of scientific discoveries in the years since *The 12th Planet* was published that corroborate its findings in one instance after another.

Those who have read my books (*The Stairway to Heaven, The Wars of Gods and Men,* and *The Lost Realms* followed the first one) know that they are based, first and foremost, on the knowledge bequeathed to us by the Sumerians.

Theirs was the first known civilization. Appearing suddenly and seemingly out of nowhere some 6,000 years ago, it is credited with virtually all the "firsts" of a high civilization: inventions and innovations, concepts and beliefs, which form the foundation of our own Western culture and indeed of all other civilizations and cultures throughout the Earth. The wheel and animal-drawn vehicles, boats for rivers and ships for seas, the kiln and the brick, high-rise buildings, writing and schools and scribes, laws and judges and juries, kingship and citizens' councils, music and dance and art, medicine and chemistry, weaving and textiles, religion and priesthoods and temples— they all began there, in Sumer, a country in the southern part of today's Iraq, located in ancient Mesopotamia. Above all, knowledge of mathematics and astronomy began there.

Indeed, all the basic elements of modern astronomy are of Sumerian origin: the concept of a celestial sphere, of a horizon and a zenith, of the circle's division into 360 degrees, of a celestial band in which the planets orbit the Sun, of grouping stars into constellations and giving them the names and pictorial images that we call the zodiac, of applying the number 12 to this zodiac and to the divisions of time, and of devising a calendar that has been the basis of calendars to this very day. All that and much, much more began in Sumer.

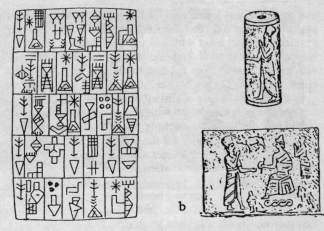

a   b

Figure 5

The Sumerians recorded their commercial and legal trans-
actions, their tales and their histories, on clay tablets (Fig. 5a);
they drew their illustrations on cylinder seals on which the
depiction was carved in reverse, as a negative, that appeared
as a positive when the seal was rolled on wet clay (Fig. 5b).
In the ruins of Sumerian cities excavated by archaeologists in
the past century and a half, hundreds, if not thousands, of the
texts and illustrations that were found dealt with astronomy.
Among them are lists of stars and constellations in their correct
heavenly locations and manuals for observing the rising and
setting of stars and planets. There are texts specifically dealing
with the Solar System. There are texts among the unearthed
tablets that list the planets orbiting the Sun in their correct
order; one text even gives the distances between the planets.
And there are illustrations on cylinder seals depicting the Solar
System, as the one shown in Plate B that is at least 4,500 years
old and that is now kept in the Near Eastern Section of the
State Museum in East Berlin, catalogued under number
VA/243.

If we sketch the illustration appearing in the upper left-hand
corner of the Sumerian depiction (Fig. 6a) we see a complete
Solar System in which the Sun (not Earth!) is in the center,

Plate B

orbited by all the planets we know of today. This becomes
clear when we draw these known planets around the Sun in
their correct relative sizes and order (Fig. 6b). The similarity
between the ancient depiction and the current one is striking;
it leaves no doubt that the twinlike Uranus and Neptune were
known in antiquity.

The Sumerian depiction also reveals, however, some differences. These are not artist's errors or misinformation; on
the contrary, the differences—two of them—are very significant.

The first difference concerns Pluto. It has a very odd orbit—
too inclined to the common plane (called the Ecliptic) in which
the planets orbit the Sun, and so elliptical that Pluto sometimes
(as at present and until 1999) finds itself not farther but closer
to the Sun than Neptune. Astronomers have therefore speculated, ever since its discovery in 1930, that Pluto was originally
a satellite of another planet; the usual assumption is that it was
a moon of Neptune that "somehow"—no one can figure out
how—got torn away from its attachment to Neptune and attained its independent (though bizarre) orbit around the Sun.

This is confirmed by the ancient depiction, but with a significant difference. In the Sumerian depiction Pluto is shown
not near Neptune but between Saturn and Uranus. And Sumerian cosmological texts, with which we shall deal at length,
relate that Pluto was a satellite of Saturn that was let loose to

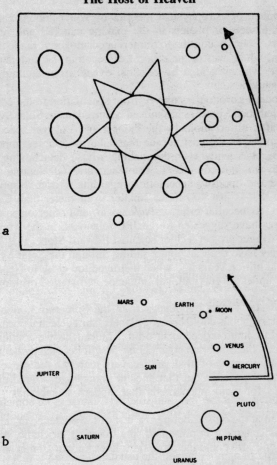

Figure 6

eventually attain its own "destiny"—its independent orbit around the Sun.

The ancient explanation regarding the origin of Pluto reveals not just factual knowledge but also great sophistication in matters celestial. It involves an understanding of the complex forces that have shaped the Solar System, as well as the development of astrophysical theories by which moons can become planets or planets in the making can fail and remain moons. Pluto, according to Sumerian cosmogony, made it; our Moon, which was in the process of becoming an independent planet, was prevented by celestial events from attaining the independent status.

Modern astronomers moved from speculation to the conviction that such a process has indeed occurred in our Solar System only after observations by the Pioneer and Voyager spacecraft determined in the past decade that Titan, the largest moon of Saturn, was a planet-in-the-making whose detachment from Saturn was not completed. The discoveries at Neptune reinforced the opposite speculation regarding Triton, Neptune's moon that is just 400 miles smaller in diameter than Earth's Moon. Its peculiar orbit, its volcanism, and other unexpected features have suggested to the JPL scientists, in the words of the Voyager project's chief scientist Edward Stone, that "Triton may have been an object sailing through the Solar System several billion years ago when it strayed too close to Neptune, came under its gravitational influence and started orbiting the planet."

How far is this hypothesis from the Sumerian notion that planetary moons could become planets, shift celestial positions, or fail to attain independent orbits? Indeed, as we continue to expound the Sumerian cosmogony, it will become evident that not only is much of modern discovery merely a rediscovery of ancient knowledge but that ancient knowledge offered explanations for many phenomena that modern science has yet to figure out.

Even at the outset, before the rest of the evidence in support of this statement is presented, the question inevitably arises: How on Earth could the Sumerians have known all that so long ago, at the dawn of civilization?

The answer lies in the second difference between the Sumerian depiction of the Solar System (Fig. 6a) and our present knowledge of it (Fig. 6b). It is the inclusion of a large planet in the empty space between Mars and Jupiter. We are not aware of any such planet; but the Sumerian cosmological, astronomical, and historical texts insist that there indeed exists one more planet in our Solar System—its twelfth member: they included the Sun, the Moon (which they counted as a celestial body in its own right for reasons stated in the texts), and ten, not nine, planets. It was the realization that a planet the Sumerian texts called NIBIRU ("Planet of the Crossing") was neither Mars nor Jupiter, as some scholars have debated, but another planet that passes between them every 3,600 years that gave rise to my first book's title, *The 12th Planet*—the planet which is the "twelfth member" of the Solar System (although technically it is, as a *planet*, only the tenth).

It was from that planet, the Sumerian texts repeatedly and persistently stated, that the ANUNNAKI came to Earth. The term literally means "Those Who from Heaven to Earth Came." They are spoken of in the Bible as the *Anakim*, and in Chapter 6 of Genesis are also called *Nefilim*, which in Hebrew means the same thing: Those Who Have Come Down, from the Heavens to Earth.

And it was from the Anunnaki, the Sumerians explained— as though they had anticipated our questions—that they had learnt all they knew. The advanced knowledge we find in Sumerian texts is thus, in effect, knowledge that was possessed by the Anunnaki who had come from Nibiru; and theirs must have been a very advanced civilization, because as I have surmised from the Sumerian texts, the Anunnaki came to Earth about 445,000 years ago. Way back then they could already travel in space. Their vast elliptical orbit made a loop—this is the exact translation of the Sumerian term—around all the outer planets, acting as a moving observatory from which the Anunnaki could investigate all those planets. No wonder that what we are discovering now was already known in Sumerian times.

Why anyone would bother to come to this speck of matter we call Earth, not by accident, not by chance, not once but repeatedly, every 3,600 years, is a question the Sumerian texts have answered. On their planet Nibiru, the Anunnaki/Nefilim were facing a situation we on Earth may also soon face: ecological deterioration was making life increasingly impossible. There was a need to protect their dwindling atmosphere, and the only solution seemed to be to suspend gold particles above it, as a shield. (Windows on American spacecraft, for example, are coated with a thin layer of gold to shield the astronauts from radiation). This rare metal had been discovered by the Anunnaki on what they called the Seventh Planet (counting from the outside inward), and they launched Mission Earth to obtain it. At first they tried to obtain it effortlessly, from the waters of the Persian Gulf; but when that failed, they embarked on toilsome mining operations in southeastern Africa.

Some 300,000 years ago, the Anunnaki assigned to the African mines mutinied. It was then that the chief scientist and the chief medical officer of the Anunnaki used genetic manipulation and in-vitro fertilization techniques to create "primitive workers"—the first *Homo sapiens* to take over the backbreaking toil in the gold mines.

The Sumerian texts that describe all these events and their condensed version in the Book of Genesis have been extensively dealt with in *The 12th Planet*. The scientific aspects of those developments and of the techniques employed by the Anunnaki are the subject of this book. Modern science, it will be shown, is blazing an amazing track of scientific advances— but the road to the future is replete with signposts, knowledge, and advances from the past. The Anunnaki, it will be shown, have been there before; and as the relationship between them and the beings they had created changed, as they decided to give Mankind civilization, they imparted to us some of their knowledge and the ability to make our own scientific advances.

Among the scientific advances that will be discussed in the ensuing chapters will also be the mounting evidence for the existence of Nibiru. If it were not for *The 12th Planet*, the discovery of Nibiru would be a great event in astronomy but no more significant for our daily lives than, say, the discovery in 1930 of Pluto. It was nice to learn that the Solar System has one more planet "out there," and it would be equally gratifying to confirm that the planetary count is not nine but ten; that would especially please astrologers, who need twelve celestial bodies and not just eleven for the twelve houses of the zodiac.

But after the publication of *The 12th Planet* and the evidence therein—which has not been refuted since its first printing in 1976—and the evidence provided by scientific advances since then, the discovery of Nibiru cannot remain just a matter involving textbooks on astronomy. If what I have written is so—

if, in other words, the Sumerians were correct in what they were recording—the discovery of Nibiru would mean not only that there is one more planet out there but that there is Life out there. Moreover, it would confirm *that there are intelligent beings out there*—people who were so advanced that, almost half a million years ago, they could travel in space; people who were coming and going between their planet and Earth every 3,600 years.

It is *who* is out there on Nibiru, and not just its existence, that is bound to shake existing political, religious, social, economic, and military orders on Earth. What will the repercussions be when—not if—Nibiru is found?

It is a question, believe it or not, that is already being pondered.

GOLD MINING—HOW LONG AGO?

Is there evidence that mining took place, in southern Africa, during the Old Stone Age? Archaeological studies indicate that it indeed was so.

Realizing that sites of abandoned ancient mines may indicate where gold could be found, South Africa's leading mining corporation, the Anglo-American Corporation, in the 1970s engaged archaeologists to look for such ancient mines. Published reports (in the corporation's journal *Optima*) detail the discovery in Swaziland and other sites in South Africa of extensive mining areas with shafts to depths of fifty feet. Stone objects and charcoal remains established dates of 35,000, 46,000, and 60,000 B.C. for these sites. The archaeologists and anthropologists who joined in dating the finds believed that mining technology was used in southern Africa "during much of the period subsequent to 100,000 B.C."

In September 1988, a team of international physicists came to South Africa to verify the age of human habitats in Swaziland and Zululand. The most modern techniques indicated an age of 80,000 to 115,000 years.

Regarding the most ancient gold mines of Monotapa in southern Zimbabwe, Zulu legends hold that they were worked by "artificially produced flesh and blood slaves created by the First People." These slaves, the Zulu legends recount, "went into battle with the Ape-Man" when "the great war star appeared in the sky" (see *Indaba My Children*, by the Zulu medicine man Credo Vusamazulu Mutwa).

2

IT CAME FROM OUTER SPACE

"It was Voyager [project] that focused our attention on the importance of collisions," acknowledged Edward Stone of the California Institute of Technology (Caltech), the chief scientist of the Voyager program. "The cosmic crashes were potent sculptors of the Solar System."

The Sumerians made clear, 6,000 years earlier, the very same fact. Central to their cosmogony, worldview, and religion was a cataclysmic event that they called the Celestial Battle. It was an event to which references were made in miscellaneous Sumerian texts, hymns, and proverbs—just as we find in the Bible's books of Psalms, Proverbs, Job, and various others. But the Sumerians also described the event in detail, step by step, in a long text that required seven tablets. Of its Sumerian original only fragments and quotations have been found; the mostly complete text has reached us in the Akkadian language, the language of the Assyrians and Babylonians who followed the Sumerians in Mesopotamia. The text deals with the formation of the Solar System prior to the Celestial Battle and even more so with the nature, causes, and results of that awesome collision. And, with a single cosmogonic premise, it explains puzzles that still baffle our astronomers and astrophysicists.

Even more important, whenever these modern scientists have come upon a satisfactory answer—it fits and corroborates the Sumerian one!

Until the Voyager discoveries, the prevailing scientific viewpoint considered the Solar System as we see it today as the way it had taken shape soon after its beginning, formed by immutable laws of celestial motion and the force of gravity. There have been oddballs, to be sure—meteorites that come from somewhere and collide with the stable members of the

Solar System, pockmarking them with craters, and comets that zoom about in greatly elongated orbits, appearing from somewhere and disappearing, it seems, to nowhere. But these examples of cosmic debris, it has been assumed, go back to the very beginning of the Solar System, some 4.5 billion years ago, and are pieces of planetary matter that failed to be incorporated into the planets or their moons and rings. A little more baffling has been the asteroid belt, a band of rocks that forms an orbiting chain between Mars and Jupiter. According to Bode's law, an empirical rule that explains why the planets formed where they did, there should have been a planet, at least twice the size of Earth, between Mars and Jupiter. Is the orbiting debris of the asteroid belt the remains of such a planet? The affirmative answer is plagued by two problems: the total amount of matter in the asteroid belt does not add up to the mass of such a planet, and there is no plausible explanation for what might have caused the breakup of such a hypothetical

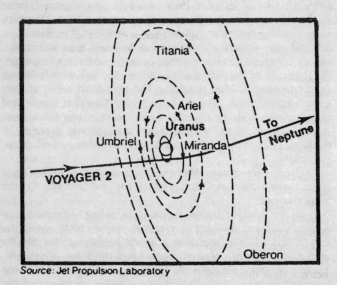

Source: Jet Propulsion Laboratory

Figure 7

planet; if a celestial collision—when, with what, and why? The scientists had no answer.

The realization that there had to be one or more major collisions that changed the Solar System from its initial form became inescapable after the Uranus flyby in 1986, as Dr. Stone has admitted. That Uranus was tilted on its side was already known from telescopic and other instrumental observations even before the Voyager encounter. But was it formed that way from the very beginning, or did some external force—a forceful collision or encounter with another major celestial body—bring about the tilting?

The answer had to be provided by the closeup examination of the moons of Uranus by *Voyager 2*. The fact that these moons swirl around the equator of Uranus *in its tilted position*—forming, all together, a kind of bull's-eye facing the Sun (Fig. 7)—made scientists wonder whether these moons were there at the time of the tilting event, or whether they formed after the event, perhaps from matter thrown out by the force of the collision that tilted Uranus.

The theoretical basis for the answer was enunciated, prior to the encounter with Uranus, among others by Dr. Christian Veillet of the French Centre d'Etudes et des Recherches Geodynamiques. If the moons formed at the same time as Uranus, the celestial "raw material" from which they agglomerated should have condensed the heavier matter nearer the planet; there should be more of heavier, rocky material and thinner ice coats on the inner moons and a lighter combination of materials (more water ice, less rocks) on the outer moons. By the same principle of the distribution of material in the Solar System—a larger proportion of heavier matter nearer the Sun, more of the lighter matter (in a "gaseous" state) farther out—the moons of the more distant Uranus should be proportionately lighter than those of the nearer Saturn.

But the findings revealed a situation contrary to these expectations. In the comprehensive summary reports on the Uranus encounter, published in *Science*, July 4, 1986, a team of forty scientists concluded that the densities of the Uranus moons (except for that of the moon Miranda) "are significantly heavier than those of the icy satellites of Saturn." Likewise, the *Voyager 2* data showed—again contrary to what "should have been''—that the two larger inner moons of Uranus, Ariel and Umbriel, are lighter in composition (thick, icy layers; small, rocky cores) than the outer moons Titania and Oberon, which were discovered to be made mostly of heavy rocky material and had only thin coats of ice.

These findings by *Voyager 2* were not the only clues suggesting that the moons of Uranus were not formed at the same time as the planet itself but rather some time later, in unusual circumstances. Another discovery that puzzled the scientists was that the rings of Uranus were pitch-black, ''blacker than coal dust,'' presumably composed of ''carbon-rich material, a sort of primordial tar *scavenged from outer space*'' (the emphasis is mine). These dark rings, warped, tilted, and ''bizarrely elliptical,'' were quite unlike the symmetrical bracelets of icy particles circling Saturn. Pitch-black also were six of the new moonlets discovered at Uranus, some acting as ''shepherds'' for the rings. The obvious conclusion was that the rings and moonlets were formed from the debris of a ''violent event in Uranus's past.'' Assistant project scientist at JPL Ellis Miner stated it in simpler words: ''A likely possibility is that an interloper from outside the Uranus system came in and struck a once larger moon sufficiently hard to have fractured it.''

The theory of a catastrophic celestial collision as the event that could explain all the odd phenomena on Uranus and its moons and rings was further strengthened by the discovery that the boulder-size black debris that forms the Uranus rings circles the planet once every eight hours—a speed that is twice the speed of the planet's own revolution around its axis. This raises the question, how was this much-higher speed imparted to the debris in the rings?

Based on all the preceding data, the probability of a celestial collision emerged as the only plausible answer. ''We must take into account the strong possibility that satellite formation conditions were affected by the event that created Uranus's large obliquity,'' the forty-strong team of scientists stated. In simpler words, it means that in all probability the moons in question were created as a result of the collision that knocked Uranus on its side. In press conferences the NASA scientists were more audacious. ''A collision with something the size of Earth, traveling at about 40,000 miles per hour, could have done it,'' they said, speculating that it probably happened about four billion years ago.

Astronomer Garry Hunt of the Imperial College, London, summed it up in seven words: "Uranus took an almighty bang early on."

But neither in the verbal briefings nor in the long written reports was an attempt made to suggest what the "something" was, where it had come from, and how it happened to collide with, or bang into, Uranus.

For those answers, we will have to go back to the Sumerians. . . .

Before we turn from knowledge acquired in the late 1970s and 1980s to what was known 6,000 years earlier, one more aspect of the puzzle should be looked into: Are the oddities at Neptune the result of collisions, or "bangs," unrelated to those of Uranus—or were they all the result of a single catastrophic event that affected all the outer planets?

Before the *Voyager 2* flyby of Neptune, the planet was known to have only two satellites, Nereid and Triton. Nereid was found to have a peculiar orbit: it was unusually tilted compared with the planet's equatorial plane (as much as 28 degrees) and was very eccentric—orbiting the planet not in a near-circular path but in a very elongated one, which takes the moon as far as six million miles from Neptune and as close as one million miles to the planet. Nereid, although of a size that by planetary-formation rules should be spherical, has an odd shape like that of a twisted doughnut. It also is bright on one side and pitch-black on the other. All these peculiarities have led Martha W. Schaefer and Bradley E. Schaefer, in a major study on the subject published in *Nature* magazine (June 2, 1987) to conclude that "Nereid accreted into a moon around Neptune or another planet and that both it and Triton were knocked into their peculiar orbits by some large body or planet." "Imagine," Brad Schaefer noted, "that at one time Neptune had an ordinary satellite system like that of Jupiter or Saturn; then some massive body comes into the system and perturbs things a lot."

The dark material that shows up on one side of Nereid could be explained in one of two ways—but both require a collision in the scenario. Either an impact on one side of the satellite swept off an existing darker layer there, uncovering lighter material below the surface, or the dark matter belonged to the impacting body and "went splat on one side of Nereid." That the latter possibility is the more plausible is suggested by the discovery, announced by the JPL team on August 29, 1989, that all the new satellites (six more) found by *Voyager 2* at Neptune "are very dark" and "all have irregular shapes," even the moon designated 1989N1, whose size normally would have made it spherical.

The theories regarding Triton and its elongated and retrograde (clockwise) orbit around Neptune also call for a collision event.

Writing in the highly prestigious magazine *Science* on the eve of the *Voyager 2* encounter with Neptune, a team of Caltech scientists (P. Goldberg, N. Murray, P. Y. Longaretti, and D. Banfield) postulated that "Triton was captured from a heliocentric orbit"—from an orbit around the Sun—"as a result of a collision with what was then one of Neptune's regular satellites." In this scenario the original small Neptune satellite "would have been devoured by Triton," but the force of the collision would have been such that it dissipated enough of Triton's orbital energy to slow it down and be captured by Neptune's gravity. Another theory, according to which Triton was an original satellite of Neptune, was shown by this study to be faulty and unable to withstand critical analysis.

The data collected by *Voyager 2* from the actual flyby of Triton supported this theoretical conclusion. It also was in accord with other studies (as by David Stevenson of Caltech) that showed that Triton's internal heat and surface features could be explained only in terms of a collision in which Triton was captured into orbit around Neptune.

"Where did these impacting bodies come from?" rhetorically asked Gene Shoemaker, one of NASA's scientists, on the NOVA television program. But the question was left without an answer. Unanswered too was the question of whether the cataclysms at Uranus and Neptune were aspects of a single event or were unconnected incidents.

It is not ironic but gratifying to find that the answers to all these puzzles were provided by the ancient Sumerian texts, and that all the data discovered or confirmed by the Voyager flights uphold and corroborate the Sumerian information and my presentation and interpretation thereof in *The 12th Planet*.

The Sumerian texts speak of a single but comprehensive event. Their texts explain more than what modern astronomers have been trying to explain regarding the outer planets. The ancient texts also explain matters closer to home, such as the origin of the Earth and its Moon, of the Asteroid Belt and the comets. The texts then go on to relate a tale that combines the credo of the Creationists with the theory of Evolution, a tale that offers a more successful explanation than either modern conception of what happened on Earth and how Man and his civilization came about.

It all began, the Sumerian texts relate, when the Solar System was still young. The Sun (APSU in the Sumerian texts, meaning "One Who Exists from the Beginning"), its little companion MUM.MU ("One Who Was Born," our Mercury) and farther away TI.AMAT ("Maiden of Life") were the first members of the Solar System; it gradually expanded by the "birth" of three planetary pairs, the planets we call Venus and Mars between Mummu and Tiamat, the giant pair Jupiter and Saturn (to use their modern names) beyond Tiamat, and Uranus and Neptune farther out (Fig. 8).

Into this original Solar System, still unstable soon after its formation (I estimated the time about four billion years ago), an Invader appeared. The Sumerians called it NIBIRU; the Babylonians renamed it *Marduk* in honor of their national god. It appeared from outer space, from "the Deep," in the words of the ancient text. But as it approached the outer planets of our Solar System, it began to be drawn into it. As expected, the first outer planet to attract Nibiru with its gravitational pull was Neptune—E.A ("He Whose House Is Water") in Sumerian. "He who begot him was Ea," the ancient text explained.

Nibiru/Marduk itself was a sight to behold; alluring, sparkling, lofty, lordly are some of the adjectives used to describe it. Sparks and flashes bolted from it to Neptune and Uranus as it passed near them. It might have arrived with its own satellites already orbiting it, or it might have acquired some as a result

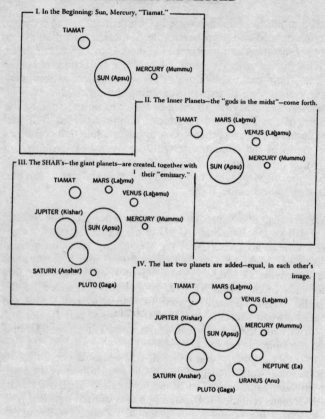

I. In the Beginning: Sun, Mercury, "Tiamat."

TIAMAT

SUN (Apsu)   MERCURY (Mummu)

II. The Inner Planets—the "gods in the midst"—come forth.

TIAMAT   MARS (Laḫmu)
VENUS (Laḫamu)
SUN (Apsu)   MERCURY (Mummu)

III. The SHAR's—the giant planets—are created, together with their "emissary."

TIAMAT   MARS (Laḫmu)
VENUS (Laḫamu)
JUPITER (Kishar)   SUN (Apsu)   MERCURY (Mummu)
SATURN (Anshar)
PLUTO (Gaga)

IV. The last two planets are added—equal, in each other's image.

TIAMAT   MARS (Laḫmu)
VENUS (Laḫamu)
JUPITER (Kishar)   SUN (Apsu)   MERCURY (Mummu)
NEPTUNE (Ea)
SATURN (Anshar)   URANUS (Anu)
PLUTO (Gaga)

Figure 8

of the gravitational pull of the outer planets. The ancient text speaks of its "perfect members . . . difficult to perceive"— "four were his eyes, four were his ears."

As it passed near Ea/Neptune, Nibiru/Marduk's side began to bulge "as though he had a second head." Was it then that the bulge was torn away to become Neptune's moon Triton? One aspect that speaks strongly for this is the fact that Nibiru/Marduk entered the Solar System in a retrograde (clockwise) orbit, counter to that of the other planets (Fig. 9). Only

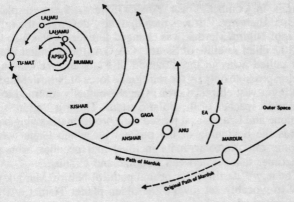

Figure 9

this Sumerian detail, according to which the invading planet was moving counter to the orbital motion of all the other planets, can explain the retrograde motion of Triton, the highly elliptical orbits of other satellites and comets, and the other major events that we have yet to tackle.

More satellites were created as Nibiru/Marduk passed by *Anu*/Uranus. Describing this passing of Uranus, the text states that "Anu brought forth and begot the four winds"—as clear a reference as one could hope for to the four major moons of Uranus that were formed, we now know, only during the collision that tilted Uranus. At the same time we learn from a later passage in the ancient text that Nibiru/Marduk himself gained three satellites as a result of this encounter.

Although the Sumerian texts describe how, after its eventual capture into solar orbit, Nibiru/Marduk revisited the outer planets and eventually shaped them into the system as we know it today, the very first encounter already explains the various puzzles that modern astronomy faced or still faces regarding Neptune, Uranus, their moons, and their rings.

Past Neptune and Uranus, Nibiru/Marduk was drawn even more into the midst of the planetary system as it reached the immense gravitational pulls of Saturn (AN.SHAR, "Foremost of the Heavens") and Jupiter (KI.SHAR, "Foremost of the Firm Lands"). As Nibiru/Marduk "approached and stood as though in combat" near Anshar/Saturn, the two planets "kissed their lips." It was then that the "destiny," the orbital path, of Nibiru/Marduk was changed forever. It was also then that the chief satellite of Saturn, GA.GA (the eventual Pluto), was pulled away in the direction of Mars and Venus—a direction possible only by the retrograde force of Nibiru/Marduk. Making a vast elliptical orbit, Gaga eventually returned to the outermost reaches of the Solar System. There it "addressed" Neptune and Uranus as it passed their orbits on the swing back. It was the beginning of the process by which Gaga was to become our Pluto, with its inclined and peculiar orbit that sometimes takes it between Neptune and Uranus.

The new "destiny," or orbital path, of Nibiru/Marduk was now irrevocably set toward the olden planet Tiamat. At that time, relatively early in the formation of the Solar System, it was marked by instability, especially (we learn from the text) in the region of Tiamat. While other planets nearby were still wobbling in their orbits, Tiamat was pulled in many directions by the two giants beyond her and the two smaller planets between her and the Sun. One result was the tearing off her, or the gathering around her, of a "host" of satellites "furious with rage," in the poetic language of the text (named by scholars the *Epic of Creation*). These satellites, "roaring monsters," were "clothed with terror" and "crowned with halos," swirling furiously about and orbiting as though they were "celestial gods"—planets.

Most dangerous to the stability or safety of the other planets was Tiamat's "leader of the host," a large satellite that grew to almost planetary size and was about to attain its independent "destiny"—its own orbit around the Sun. Tiamat "cast a spell for him, to sit among the celestial gods she exalted him." It was called in Sumerian KIN.GU—"Great Emissary."

Now the text raised the curtain on the unfolding drama; I have recounted it, step by step, in *The 12th Planet*. As in a Greek tragedy, the ensuing "celestial battle" was unavoidable as gravitational and magnetic forces came inexorably into play, leading to the collision between the oncoming Nibiru/Marduk with its seven satellites ("winds" in the ancient text) and Tiamat and its "host" of eleven satellites headed by Kingu.

Although they were headed on a collision course, Tiamat orbiting counterclockwise and Nibiru/Marduk clockwise, the

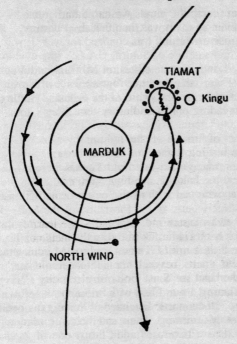

Figure 10

two *planets* did not collide—a fact of cardinal astronomical importance. It was the satellites, or "winds," (literal Sumerian meaning: "Those that are by the side") of Nibiru/Marduk that smashed into Tiamat and collided with her satellites.

In the first such encounter (Fig.10), the first phase of the Celestial Battle,

> The four winds he stationed
> that nothing of her could escape:
> The South Wind, the North Wind,
> the East Wind, the West Wind.
> Close to his side he held the net,
> the gift of his grandfather Anu who brought forth
> the Evil Wind, the Whirlwind and the Hurricane. . . .

He sent forth the winds which he had created,
the seven of them; to trouble Tiamat within
they rose up behind him.

These "winds," or satellites, of Nibiru/Marduk, "the seven of them," were the principal "weapons" with which Tiamat was attacked in the first phase of the Celestial Battle (Fig. 10). But the invading planet had other "weapons" too:

In front of him he set the lightning,
with a blazing flame he filled his body;
He then made a net to enfold Tiamat therein. . . .
A fearsome halo his head was turbaned,
He was wrapped with awesome terror as with a cloak.

As the two planets and their hosts of satellites came close enough for Nibiru/Marduk to "scan the inside of Tiamat" and "perceive the scheme of Kingu," Nibiru/Marduk attacked Tiamat with his "net" (magnetic field?) to "enfold her," shooting at the old planet immense bolts of electricity ("divine lightnings"). Tiamat "was filled with brilliance"—slowing down, heating up, "becoming distended." Wide gaps opened in its crust, perhaps emitting steam and volcanic matter. Into one widening fissure Nibiru/Marduk thrust one of its main satellites, the one called "Evil Wind." It tore Tiamat's "belly, cut through her insides, splitting her heart."

Besides splitting up Tiamat and "extinguishing her life," the first encounter sealed the fate of the moonlets orbiting her—all except the planetlike Kingu. Caught in the "net"—the magnetic and gravitational pull—of Nibiru/Marduk, "shattered, broken up," the members of the "band of Tiamat" were thrown off their previous course and forced into new orbital paths in the *opposite direction*: "Trembling with fear, they turned their backs about."

Thus were the comets created—thus, we learn from a 6,000-year-old text, did the comets obtain their greatly elliptical and retrograde orbits. As to Kingu, Tiamat's principal satellite, the text informs us that in that first phase of the celestial collision Kingu was just deprived of its almost-independent orbit. Nibiru/Marduk took away from him his "destiny." Nibiru/Marduk made Kingu into a DUG.GA.E, "a mass of lifeless clay,'' devoid of atmosphere, waters and radioactive matter and shrunken in size; and "with fetters bound him,'' to remain in orbit around the battered Tiamat.

Having vanquished Tiamat, Nibiru/Marduk sailed on on his new "destiny.'' The Sumerian text leaves no doubt that the erstwhile invader orbited the Sun:

> He crossed the heavens and surveyed the regions,
> and Apsu's quarter he measured;
> The Lord the dimensions of the Apsu measured.

Having circled the Sun (Apsu), Nibiru/Marduk continued into distant space. But now, caught forever in solar orbit, it had to turn back. On his return round, Ea/Neptune was there to greet him and Anshar/Saturn hailed his victory. Then his new orbital path returned him to the scene of the Celestial Battle, "turned back to Tiamat whom he had bound.''

> The Lord paused to view her lifeless body.
> To divide the monster he then artfully planned.
> Then, as a mussel, he split her into two parts.

With this act the creation of "the heaven'' reached its final stage, and the creation of Earth and its Moon began. First the new impacts broke Tiamat into two halves. The upper part, her "skull,'' was struck by the Nibiru/Marduk satellite called North Wind; the blow carried it, and with it Kingu, "to places that have been unknown''—to a brand-new orbit where there had not been a planet before. The Earth and our Moon were created (Fig. 11)!

The other half of Tiamat was smashed by the impacts into bits and pieces. This lower half, her "tail,'' was "hammered together'' to become a "bracelet'' in the heavens:

> Locking the pieces together,
> as watchmen he stationed them. . . .
> He bent Tiamat's tail to form the Great Band
> as a bracelet.

Thus was "the Great Band,'' the Asteroid Belt, created. Having disposed of Tiamat and Kingu, Nibiru/Marduk once

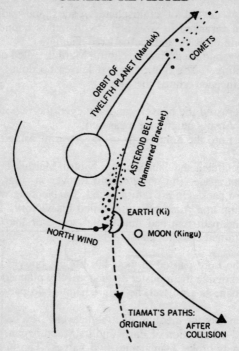

Figure 11

again "crossed the heavens and surveyed the regions." This time his attention was focused on the "Dwelling of Ea" (Neptune), giving that planet and its twinlike Uranus their final makeup. Nibiru/Marduk also, according to the ancient text, provided Gaga/Pluto with its final "destiny," assigning to it "a hidden place"—a hitherto unknown part of the heavens. It was farther out than Neptune's location; it was, we are told, "in the Deep"—far out in space. In line with its new position as the outermost planet, it was granted a new name: US.MI—"He Who Shows the Way," the first planet encountered coming *into* the Solar System—that is, from outer space toward the Sun.

Thus was Pluto created and put into the orbit it now holds. Having thus "constructed the stations" for the planets, Ni-

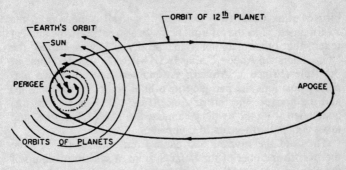

Figure 12

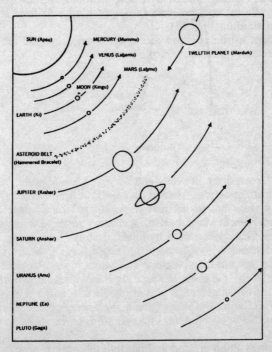

Figure 13

biru/Marduk made two "abodes" for itself. One was in the "Firmament," as the asteroid belt was also called in the ancient texts; the other far out "in the Deep" was called the "Great/Distant Abode," alias E.SHARRA ("Abode/Home of the Ruler/Prince"). Modern astronomers call these two planetary positions the perigee (the orbital point nearest the Sun) and the apogee (the farthest one) (Fig. 12). It is an orbit, as concluded from the evidence amassed in *The 12th Planet*, that takes 3,600 Earth-years to complete.

Thus did the Invader that came from outer space become the twelfth member of the Solar System, a system made up of the Sun in the center, with its longtime companion Mercury; the three olden pairs (Venus and Mars, Jupiter and Saturn, Uranus and Neptune); the Earth and the Moon, the remains of the great Tiamat, though in a new position; the newly independent Pluto; and the planet that put it all into final shape, Nibiru/Marduk (Fig. 13).

Modern astronomy and recent discoveries uphold and corroborate this millennia-old tale.

WHEN EARTH HAD NOT BEEN FORMED

In 1766 J. D. Titius proposed and in 1772 Johann Elert Bode popularized what became known as "Bode's law," which showed that planetary distances follow, more or less, the progression 0, 2, 4, 8, 16, etc., if the formula is manipulated by multiplying by 3, adding 4, and dividing by 10. Using as a measure the astronomical unit (AU), which is the distance of Earth from the Sun, the formula indicates that there should be a planet between Mars and Jupiter (the asteroids are found there) and a planet beyond Saturn (Uranus was discovered). The formula shows tolerable deviations up until one reaches Uranus but gets out of whack from Neptune on.

Planet	Distance (AU)	Bode's Law Distance	Bode's Law Deviation
Mercury	0.387	0.400	3.4%
Venus	0.723	0.700	3.2%
Earth	1.000	1.000	
Mars	1.524	1.600	5.0%
Asteroids	2.794	2.800	
Jupiter	5.203	5.200	
Saturn	9.539	10.000	4.8%
Uranus	19.182	19.600	2.1%
Neptune	30.058	38.800	36.3%
Pluto	39.400	77.200	95.9%

Bode's law, which was arrived at empirically, thus uses Earth as its arithmetic starting point. But according to the Sumerian cosmogony, at the beginning there was Tiamat between Mars and Jupiter, whereas Earth had not yet formed.

Dr. Amnon Sitchin has pointed out that if Bode's law is stripped of its arithmetical devices and only the geometric progression is retained, the formula works just as well *if Earth is omitted*—thus confirming Sumerian cosmogony:

Planet	Distance from Sun (miles)	Ratio of Increase
Mercury	36,250,000	—
Venus	67,200,000	1.85
Mars	141,700,000	2.10
Asteroids (Ti.Amat)	260,400,000	1.84
Jupiter	484,000,000	1.86
Saturn	887,100,000	1.83
Uranus	1,783,900,000	2.01

3

IN THE BEGINNING

In the beginning
God created the heaven and the earth.
And the earth was without form and void
and darkness was upon the face of the deep,
And the Spirit of God moved upon the face of the waters.
And God said, Let there be light; and there was light.

For generations this majestic outline of the manner in which
our world was created has been at the core of Judaism as well
as of Christianity and the third monotheistic religion Islam,
the latter two being outgrowths of the first. In the seventeenth
century Archbishop James Ussher of Armagh in Ireland calculated from these opening verses of Genesis the precise day
and even the moment of the world's creation, in the year 4004
B.C. Many old editions of the Bible still carry Ussher's chronology printed in the margins; many still believe that Earth
and the Solar System of which it is a part are indeed no older
than that. Unfortunately, this belief, known as Creationism,
has taken on science as its adversary; and science, firmly wed
to the Theory of Evolution, has met the challenge and joined
the battle.

It is regrettable that both sides pay little heed to what has
been known for more than a century—that the creation tales
of Genesis are edited and abbreviated versions of much more
detailed Mesopotamian texts, which were in turn versions of
an original Sumerian text. The battle lines between the Creationists and Evolutionists—a totally unwarranted demarcation,
as the evidence herewith presented will show—are undoubtedly more sharply etched by the principle of the separation
between religion and state that is embodied in the U.S. Con-
stitution. But such a separation is not the norm among the

Earth's nations (even in enlightened democracies such as England), nor was it the norm in antiquity, when the biblical verses were written down.

Indeed, in ancient times the king was also the high priest, the state had a national religion and a national god, the temples were the seat of scientific knowledge, and the priests were the savants. This was so because when civilization began, the gods who were worshipped—the focus of the act of being "religious"—were none other than the Anunnaki/Nefilim, who were the source of all manner of knowledge, alias science, on Earth.

The merging of state, religion, and science was nowhere more complete than in Babylon. There the original Sumerian *Epic of Creation* was translated and revised so that Marduk, the Babylonian national god, was assigned a celestial counterpart. By renaming Nibiru "Marduk" in the Babylonian versions of the creation story, the Babylonians usurped for Marduk the attributes of a supreme "God of Heaven and Earth." This version—the most intact one found so far—is known as *Enuma elish* ("When in the heights"), taken from its opening words. It became the most hallowed religious-political-scientific document of the land; it was read as a central part of the New Year rituals, and players reenacted the tale in passion plays to bring its import home to the masses. The clay tablets (Fig. 14) on which they were written were prized possessions of temples and royal libraries in antiquity.

The decipherment of the writing on the clay tablets discovered in the ruins of ancient Meospotamia more than a century ago led to the realization that texts existed that related biblical creation tales millennia before the Old Testament was compiled. Especially important were texts found in the library of the Assyrian king Ashurbanipal in Nineveh (a city of biblical renown); they recorded a tale of creation that matches, in some parts word for word, the tale of Genesis. George Smith of the British Museum pieced together the broken tablets that held the creation texts and published, in 1876, *The Chaldean Genesis*; it conclusively established that there indeed existed an Akkadian text of the Genesis tale, written in the Old Babylonian dialect, that preceded the biblical text by at least a thousand years. Excavations between 1902 and 1914 uncovered tablets

Figure 14

with the Assyrian version of the creation epic, in which the name of Ashur, the Assyrian national god, was substituted for that of the Babylonian Marduk. Subsequent discoveries established not only the extent of the copying and translation, in antiquity, of this epic text, but also its unmistakable Sumerian origin.

It was L. W. King who, in 1902, in his work *The Seven Tablets of Creation*, showed that the various fragments add up to seven tablets; six of them relate the creation process; the seventh tablet is entirely devoted to the exaltation of "the Lord"—Marduk in the Babylonian version, Ashur in the Assyrian one. One can only guess that this seven-tablet division somehow is the basis of the division of the biblical story into a seven-part timetable, of which six parts involve divine handiwork and the seventh is devoted to a restful and satisfactory look back at what had been achieved.

It is true that the Book of Genesis, written in Hebrew, uses the term *yom*, commonly meaning and translated as "day," to denote each phase. Once, as a guest on a radio talk show in a "Bible Belt" city, I was challenged by a woman who called in about this very point. I explained that by "day" the Bible does not mean our term of twenty-four hours on Earth but rather conveys the concept of a phase in the process of creation. No, she insisted, that is exactly what the Bible means: twenty-four hours. I then pointed out to her that the text of the first chapter of Genesis deals not with a human timetable but with that of the Creator, and we are told in the Book of Psalms (90:4) that in God's eyes "a thousand years are like yester-Day." Would she concede, at least, that Creation might have taken six thousand years? I asked. To my disappointment, there was no concession. Six days means six *days*, she insisted.

Is the biblical tale of creation a religious document, its contents to be considered only a matter of faith to be believed or disbelieved; or it is a scientific document, imparting to us essential knowledge of how things began, in the heavens and on Earth? This, of course, is the core of the ongoing argument between Creationists and Evolutionists. The two camps would have laid down their arms long ago were they to realize that what the editors and compilers of the Book of Genesis had done was no different from what the Babylonians had done: using the only scientific source of their time, those descendants of Abraham—scion of a royal-priestly family from the Sumerian capital Ur—also took the *Epic of Creation*, shortened and edited it, and made it the foundation of a national religion glorifying Yahweh "who is in the Heavens and on Earth."

In Babylon, Marduk was a dual deity. Physically present, resplendent in his precious garments (Fig. 15), he was worshipped as *Ilu* (translated "god" but literally meaning "the Lofty One"); his struggle to gain supremacy over the other Anunnaki gods has been detailed in my book *The Wars of Gods and Men*. On the other hand, "Marduk" was a celestial deity,

Figure 15

a planetary god, who in the heavens assumed the attributes, role, and credit for the primordial creations that the Sumerians had attributed to Nibiru, the planet whose most frequent symbolic depiction was that of a winged disc (Fig. 16). The Assyrians, replacing Marduk with their national god Ashur, combined the two aspects and depicted Ashur as a god within the winged disc (Fig. 17).

The Hebrews followed suit but, preaching monotheism and recognizing—based on Sumerian scientific knowledge—the universality of God, ingeniously solved the problem of duality and of the multitude of Anunnaki deities involved in the events on Earth by concocting a singular-but-plural entity, not an *El* (the Hebrew equivalent of *Ilu*) but *Elohim*—a Creator who is plural (literally "Gods") and yet One. This departure from the Babylonian and Assyrian religious viewpoint can be explained only by a realization that the Hebrews were aware that the deity who could speak to Abraham and Moses and the celestial Lord whom the Sumerians called Nibiru were not one and the same scientifically, although all were part of a universal, ev-

Figure 16

Figure 17

erlasting, and omnipresent God—Elohim—in whose grand design for the universe the path of each planet is its predetermined "destiny," and what the Anunnaki had done on Earth was likewise a predetermined mission. Thus was the handiwork of a universal God manifest in Heaven and on Earth.

These profound perceptions, which lie at the core of the biblical adoption of the creation story, *Enuma elish*, could be arrived at only by bringing together religion and science while retaining, in the narrative and sequence of events, the scientific basis.

But to recognize this—that Genesis represents not just religion but also science—one must recognize the role of the Anunnaki and accept that the Sumerian texts are not "myth" but factual reports. Scholars have made much progress in this respect, but they have not yet arrived at a total recognition of the factual nature of the texts. Although both scientists and theologians are by now well aware of the Mesopotamian origin of Genesis, they remain stubborn in brushing off the scientific value of these ancient texts. It cannot be science, they hold, because "it should be obvious by the nature of things that none of these stories can possibly be the product of human memory" (to quote N. M. Sarna of the Jewish Theological Seminary in *Understanding Genesis*). Such a statement can be challenged only by explaining, as I have repeatedly done in my writings, that the information of how things began—including how Man himself was created—indeed did not come from the memory of the Assyrians or Babylonians or Sumerians but from the knowledge and *science* of the Anunnaki/Nefilim. They too, of course, could not "remember" how the Solar System was created or how Nibiru/Marduk invaded the Solar System, because they themselves were not yet created on their planet. But just as our scientists have a good notion of how the Solar System came about and even how the whole universe came into being (the favorite theory is that of the Big Bang), the Anunnaki/Nefilim, capable of space travel 450,000 years ago, surely had the capacity to arrive at sensible scenarios of creation; much more so since their planet, acting as a spacecraft that sailed past all the outer planets, gave them a chance at repeated close looks that were undoubtedly more extensive than our Voyager "peeks."

Several updated studies of the *Enuma elish*, such as *The Babylonian Genesis* by Alexander Heidel of the Oriental Institute, University of Chicago, have dwelt on the parallels in theme and structure between the Mesopotamian and biblical narratives. Both indeed begin with the statement that the tale takes its reader (or listener, as in Babylon) to the primordial time when the Earth and "the heavens" did not yet exist. But whereas the Sumerian cosmogony dealt with the creation of the Solar System and only then set the stage for the appearance of the celestial Lord (Nibiru/Marduk), the biblical version skipped all that and went directly to the Celestial Battle and its aftermath.

With the immensity of space as its canvas, here is how the Mesopotamian version began to draw the primordial picture:

> When in the heights Heaven had not been named
> And below earth had not been called,
> Naught but primordial Apsu, their Begetter,
> Mummu, and Tiamat, she who bore them all.
> Their waters were mingled together.
> No reed had yet been formed,
> No marshland had appeared.

Even in the traditional King James version, the biblical opening is more matter-of-fact, not an inspirational religious opus but a lesson in primordial science, informing the reader that there indeed was a time when Heaven and the Earth did not yet exist, and that it took an act of the Celestial Lord, his "spirit" moving upon the "waters," to bring Heaven and Earth about with a bolt of light.

The progress in biblical and linguistic studies since the time of King James has moved the editors of both the Catholic *The New American Bible* and *The New English Bible* of the churches in Great Britain to substitute the word "wind"—which is what the Hebrew *ru'ach* means—for the "Spirit of God," so that the last verse now reads "a mighty wind swept over the waters." They retain, however, the concept of "abyss" for the Hebrew word *Tehom* in the original Bible; but by now even theologians acknowledge that the reference is to no other entity than the Sumerian *Tiamat*.

With this understanding, the reference in the Mesopotamian version to the mingling "waters" of Tiamat ceases to be allegorical and calls for a factual evaluation. It goes to the question of the plentiful waters of Earth and the biblical assertion (correct, as we shall soon realize) that when the Earth was formed it was completely covered by water. If water was so abundant even at the moment of Earth's creation, then only if Tiamat was also a watery planet could the half that became Earth be watery!

The watery nature of Tehom/Tiamat is mentioned in various biblical references. The prophet Isaiah (51:10) recalled "the primeval days" when the might of the Lord "carved the Haughty One, made spin the watery monster, drained off the waters of the mighty Tehom." The psalmist extolled the Lord of Beginnings who "by thy might the waters thou didst disperse, the leader of the watery monsters thou didst break up."

What was the "wind" of the Lord that "moved upon the face of the waters" of Tehom/Tiamat? Not the divine "Spirit" but the satellite of Nibiru/Marduk that, in the Mesopotamian texts, was called by that term! Those texts vividly described the flashes and lightning strokes that burst off Nibiru/Marduk as it closed in on Tiamat. Applying this knowledge to the biblical text, its correct reading emerges:

> When, in the beginning,
> The Lord created the Heaven and the Earth,
> The Earth, not yet formed, was in the void,
> and there was darkness upon Tiamat.
> Then the Wind of the Lord swept upon its waters
> and the Lord commanded, "Let there be lightning!"
> and there was a bright light.

The continuing narrative of Genesis does not describe the ensuing splitting up of Tiamat or the breakup of her host of satellites, described so vividly in the Mesopotamian texts. It is evident, however, from the above-quoted verses from Isaiah and Psalms, as well as from the narrative in Job (26:7–13), that the Hebrews were familiar with the skipped-over portions of the original tale. Job recalled how the celestial Lord smote "the helpers of the Haughty One," and he exalted the Lord

who, having come from the outer reaches of space, cleaved
Tiamat (Tehom) and changed the Solar System:

> The hammered canopy He stretched out
> in the place of *Tehom*,
> The Earth suspended in the void;
> He penned waters in its denseness,
> without any cloud bursting. . . .
>
> His powers the waters did arrest,
> His energy the Haughty One did cleave.
> His wind the Hammered Bracelet measured out,
> His hand the twisting dragon did extinguish.

The Mesopotamian texts continued from here to describe
how Nibiru/Marduk formed the asteroid belt out of Tiamat's
lower half:

> The other half of her
> he set up as a screen for the skies;
> Locking them together
> as watchmen he stationed them. . . .
> He bent Tiamat's tail
> to form the Great Band as a bracelet.

Genesis picks up the primordial tale here and describes the
forming of the asteroid belt thus:

> And Elohim said:
> Let there be a firmament in the midst of the waters
> and let it divide the waters from the waters.
> And Elohim made the Firmament,
> dividing the waters which are under the Firmament
> from the waters which are above the Firmament.
> And Elohim called the Firmament "Heaven."

Realizing that the Hebrew word *Shama'im* is used to speak
of Heaven or the heavens in general, the editors of Genesis
went into some length to use two terms for "the Heaven"
created as a result of the destruction of Tiamat. What separated

the "upper waters" from the "lower waters," the Genesis text stresses, was the *Raki'a*; generally translated "Firmament," it literally means "Hammered-out Bracelet." Then Genesis goes on to explain that Elohim then called the *Raki'a*, the so-called Firmament, *Shama'im*, "the Heaven"—a name that in its first use in the Bible consists of the two words *sham* and *ma'im*, meaning literally "where the waters were." In the creation tale of Genesis, "the Heaven" was a specific celestial location, where Tiamat and her waters had been, where the asteroid belt was hammered out.

That happened, according to the Mesopotamian texts, when Nibiru/Marduk returned to the Place of Crossing—the second phase of the battle with Tiamat: "Day Two," if you wish, as the biblical narrative does.

The ancient tale is replete with details each of which is amazing by itself. Ancient awareness of them is so incredible that its only plausible explanation is the one offered by the Sumerians themselves—namely, that those who had come to Earth from Nibiru were the source of that knowledge. Modern astronomy has already corroborated many of these details; by doing so, it indirectly confirms the key assertions of the ancient cosmogony and astronomy: the Celestial Battle that resulted in the breakup of Tiamat, the creation of Earth and the asteroid belt, and the capture of Nibiru/Marduk into permanent orbit around our Sun.

Let us look at one aspect of the ancient tale—the "host" of satellites, or "winds," that the "celestial gods" had.

We now know that Mars has two moons, Jupiter sixteen moons and several more moonlets, Saturn twenty-one or more, Uranus as many as fifteen, Neptune eight. Until Galileo discovered with his telescope the four brightest and largest satellites of Jupiter in 1610, it was unthinkable that a celestial body could have more than one such companion—evidence Earth and its solitary Moon.

But here we read in the Sumerian texts that as Nibiru/Marduk's gravity interacted with that of Uranus, the Invader "begot" three satellites ("winds") and Anu/Uranus "brought forth" four such moons. By the time Nibiru/Marduk reached Tiamat, it had a total of seven "winds" with which to attack Tiamat, and Tiamat had a "host" of eleven—among them the "leader of the host," which was about to become an independently orbiting planet, our eventual Moon.

Another element of the Sumerian tale, of great significance to the ancient astronomers, was the assertion that the debris from the lower half of Tiamat was stretched out in the space where she had once existed.

The Mesopotamian texts, and the biblical version thereof in Genesis, are emphatic and detailed about the formation of the asteroid belt—insisting that such a "bracelet" of debris exists and orbits the Sun between Mars and Jupiter. But our astronomers were not aware of that until the nineteenth century. The first realization that the space between Mars and Jupiter was not just a dark void was the discovery by Giuseppe Piazzi on January 1, 1801, of a small celestial object in the space between the two planets, an object that was named Ceres and that has the distinction of being the first known (and named) asteroid. Three more asteroids (Pallas, Juno, and Vesta) were discovered by 1807, none after that until 1845, and hundreds since then, so that almost 2,000 are known by now. Astronomers believe that there may be as many as 50,000 asteroids at least a mile in diameter, as well as many more pieces of debris, too small to be seen from Earth, which number in the billions.

In other words, it has taken modern astronomy almost two centuries to find out what the Sumerians knew 6,000 years ago.

Even with this knowledge, the biblical statement that the "Hammered-out Bracelet," the *Shama'im*—alias "*the* Heaven," divided the "waters which are below the Firmament" from the "waters which are above the Firmament" remained a puzzle. What, in God's name, was the Bible talking about?

We have known, of course, that Earth was a watery planet, but it has been assumed that it is uniquely so. Many will undoubtedly recall science-fiction tales wherein aliens come to Earth to carry off its unique and life-giving liquid, water. So even if the ancient texts had in mind Tiamat's, and hence Earth's, waters, and if this was what was meant by the "water which is below the Firmament," what water was there to talk about regarding that which is "above the Firmament"?

We know—don't we?—that the asteroid belt had, indeed, as the ancient text reported, divided the planets into two groups.

"Below" it are the Terrestrial, or inner, Planets; "above" it the gaseous, or Outer, Planets. But except for Earth the former had barren surfaces and the latter no surfaces at all, and the long-held conventional wisdom was that neither group (again, excepting Earth) had any water.

Well, as a result of the missions of unmanned spacecraft to all the other planets except Pluto, we now know better. Mercury, which was observed by the spacecraft *Mariner 10* in 1974/75, is too small and too close to the Sun to have retained water, if it ever had any. But Venus, likewise believed to be waterless because of its relative proximity to the Sun, surprised the scientists. It was discovered by unmanned spacecraft, both American and Soviet, that the extremely hot surface of the planet (almost 900 degrees Fahrenheit) was caused not so much by its proximity to the Sun as by a "greenhouse" effect: the planet is enshrouded in a thick atmosphere of carbon dioxide and clouds that contain sulphuric acid. As a result the heat of the Sun is trapped and does not dissipate back into space during the night. This creates an ever-rising temperature that would have vaporized any water that Venus might have had. But did it ever have such water in its past?

The careful analysis of the results of unmanned probes led the scientists to answer emphatically, yes. The topographical features revealed by radar mapping suggested erstwhile oceans and seas. That such bodies of water might have indeed existed on Venus was indicated by the finding that the "hell-like atmosphere," as some of the scientists termed it, contained traces of water vapor.

Data from two unmanned spacecraft that probed Venus for an extended period after December 1978, *Pioneer-Venus 1* and *2*, convinced the team of scientists that analyzed the findings that Venus "may once have been covered by water at an average depth of thirty feet"; Venus, they concluded (*Science*, May 7, 1982), once had "at least 100 times as much water in liquid form as it does today in the form of vapor." Subsequent studies have suggested that some of that ancient water was used up in the formation of the suphuric acid clouds, while some of it gave up its oxygen to oxidize the rocky surface of the planet.

"The lost oceans of Venus" can be traced in its rocks; that was the conclusion of a joint report of U.S. and Soviet scientists

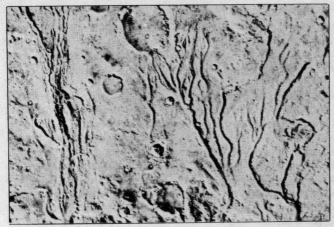

Plate C

published in the May 1986 issue of *Science*. There was indeed water "below the Firmament," not only on Earth but also on Venus.

The latest scientific discoveries have added Mars to the list of inner planets whose waters corroborate the ancient statement.

At the end of the nineteenth century the existence of enigmatic "canals" on Mars was popularized by the telescopic observations of the Italian astronomer Giovanni Schiaparelli and the American Percival Lowell. This was generally laughed off; and the conviction prevailed that Mars was dry and barren. The first unmanned surveys of Mars, in the 1960s, seemed to confirm the notion that it was a "geologically lifeless planet, like the Moon." This notion was completely discredited when the spacecraft *Mariner 9* launched in 1971, went into orbit around Mars and photographed its entire surface, not just the 10 percent or so surveyed by all the previous probes. The results, in the words of the astronomers managing the project, "were astounding." *Mariner 9* revealed that volcanoes, canyons, and *dry river beds* abound on Mars (Plate C). "Water has played an active role in the planet's evolution," stated Harold Masursky of the U.S. Geological Survey, who headed the team analyzing the photographs. "The most convincing evidence was found in the many photographs showing deep, winding channels that may have once been fast-flowing streams. . . . We are forced to no other conclusion but that we are seeing the effects of water on Mars."

The *Mariner 9* findings were confirmed and augmented by the results of the *Viking 1* and *Viking 2* missions launched five years later; they examined Mars both from orbiters and from landers that descended to the planet's surface. They showed such features as evidence of several floodings by large quantities of water in an area designated Chryse Planitis; channels that once held and were formed by running water coming from the Vallis Marineris area; cyclical meltings of permafrost in the equatorial regions; rocks weathered and eroded by the force of water; and evidence of erstwhile lakes, ponds, and other "water basins."

Water vapor was found in the thin Martian atmosphere; Charles A. Barth, the principal scientist in charge of *Mariner 9*'s ultraviolet measurements, estimated that the evaporation amounted to the equivalent of 100,000 gallons of water daily. Norman Horowitz of Caltech reasoned that "large amounts of water in some form have in past eons been introduced to the surface and into the atmosphere of Mars," because that was required in order to have so much carbon dioxide (90 percent) in the Martian atmosphere. In a report published in 1977 by the American Geographical Union (*Journal of Geophysical Research*, September 30, 1977) on the scientific results of the Viking project, it was concluded that "a long time ago giant flash floods carved the Martian landscape in a number of places; a volume of water equal to Lake Erie poured . . . scouring great channels."

The *Viking 2* lander reported frost on the ground where it came to rest. The frost was found to consist of a combination of water, water ice, and frozen carbon dioxide (dry ice). The debate about whether the polar ice caps of Mars contain water ice or dry ice was resolved in January 1979 when JPL scientists reported at the 2nd International Colloquium on Mars, held at the California Institute of Technology (Caltech) in Pasadena, that "the north pole consists of water ice," though not so the south pole.

The final NASA report after the Viking missions (*Mars: The*

Viking Discoveries) concluded that "Mars once had enough water to form a layer several meters deep over the whole surface of the planet." This was possible, it is now believed, because Mars (like Earth) wobbles slightly as it spins about its axis. This action results in significant climatic changes every 50,000 years. When the planet was warmer it may have had lakes as large as Earth's Great Lakes in North America and as much as three miles deep. "This is an almost inescapable conclusion," stated Michael H. Carr and Jack McCauley of the U.S. Geological Survey in 1985. At two conferences on Mars held in Washington, D.C., in July 1986 under the auspices of NASA, Walter Sullivan reported in *The New York Times*, scientists expressed the belief that "there is enough water hidden in the crust of Mars to theoretically flood the entire planet to an average depth of at least 1,000 feet." Arizona State University scientists working for NASA advised Soviet scientists in charge of their country's Mars landing projects that some deep Martian canyons may still have flowing water in their depths, or at least just below the dry riverbeds.

What started out as a dry and barren planet has emerged, in the past decade, as a planet where water was once abundant—not just passively lying about but flowing and gushing and shaping the planet's features. Mars has joined Venus and Earth in corroborating the concept of the Sumerian texts of water "below the Firmament," on the inner planets.

The ancient assertion that the asteroid belt separated the waters that were below the Firmament from those that were above it implies that there was water on the celestial bodies that are located farther out. We have already reviewed the latest discoveries of *Voyager 2* that confirm the Sumerian description of Uranus and Neptune as "watery." What about the other two celestial bodies that are orbiting between those two outer planets and the asteroid belt, Saturn and Jupiter?

Saturn itself, a gaseous giant whose volume is more than eight hundred times greater than that of Earth, has not yet been penetrated down to its surface—assuming it has, somewhere below its vast atmosphere of hydrogen and helium, a solid or liquid core. But its various moons as well as its breathtaking rings (Fig. 18) are now known to be made, if not wholly then in large part, of water ice and perhaps even liquid water.

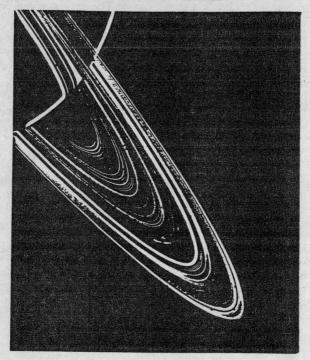

Figure 18

Originally, Earth-based observations of Saturn showed only seven rings; we now know from space probes that there are many more, with thinner rings and thousands of ringlets filling the spaces between the seven major rings; all together they create the effect of a disk that, like a phonograph record, is "grooved" with rings and ringlets. The unmanned spacecraft *Pioneer 11* established in 1979 that the rings and ringlets consist of icy material, believed at the time to be small pieces of ice a few inches in diameter or as small as snowflakes. What was originally described as "a carousel of bright icy particles" was revealed, however, by the data from *Voyager 1* and *Voyager 2* in 1980 and 1981 to consist of chunks of ice ranging from boulder size to that of "big houses." We are seeing "a sea of

sparkling ice,'' JPL's scientists said. The ice, at some primordial time, had been liquid water.

The several larger moons of Saturn at which the three spacecraft, especially *Voyager 2*, took a peek, appeared to have
much more water, and not only in the form of ice. *Pioneer 11*
reported in 1979 that the group of inner moons of Saturn—
Janus, Mimas, Enceladus, Tethys, Dione, and Rhea—appeared to be "icy bodies . . . consisting largely of ice." *Voyager 1* confirmed in 1980 that these inner satellites as well as
the newly discovered moonlets were "spheres of ice." On
Enceladus, which was examined more closely, the indications
were that its smooth plains resulted from the filling in of old
craters with liquid water that had oozed up to the surface and
then frozen.

Voyager 1 also revealed that Saturn's outer moons were ice
covered. The moon Iapetus, which puzzled astronomers because it showed dark and bright portions, was found to be
"coated with water ice" in the bright areas. *Voyager 2* confirmed in 1981 that Iapetus was "primarily a ball of ice with
some rock in its center." The data, Von R. Eshleman of Stanford University concluded, indicated that Iapetus was 55 percent water ice, 35 percent rock, and 10 percent frozen methane.
Saturn's largest moon, Titan—larger than the planet Mercury—was found to have an atmosphere and a surface rich in
hydrocarbons. But under them there is a mantle of frozen ice,
and some sixty miles farther down, as the internal heat of this
celestial body increases, there is a thick layer of water slush.
Farther down, it is now believed, there probably exists a layer
of bubbling hot water more than 100 miles deep. All in all,
the *Voyagers*' data suggested that Titan is 15 percent rock and
85 percent water and ice.

Is Saturn itself a larger version of Titan, its largest moon?
Future missions might provide the answer. For the time being
it is clear that wherever the modern instruments could reach—
moons, moonlets, and rings—there was water everywhere.
Saturn did not fail to confirm the ancient assertions.

Jupiter was investigated by *Pioneer 10* and *Pioneer 11* and
by the two *Voyagers*. The results were no different than at
Saturn. The giant gaseous planet was found to emit immense
amounts of radiation and heat and to be engulfed by a thick
atmosphere that is subject to violent storms. Yet even this

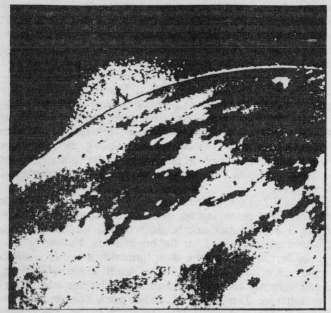

Figure 19

impenetrable envelope was found to be constituted primarily
of hydrogen, helium, methane, ammonia, *water vapor*, and
probably *droplets of water*; somewhere farther down inside the
thick atmosphere there is liquid water, the scientists have concluded.

As with Saturn, the moons of Jupiter proved more fascinating, revealing, and surprising than the planet itself. Of the
four Galilean moons, Io, the closest to Jupiter (Fig. 19), revealed totally unexpected volcanic activity. Although what the
volcanoes spew is mostly sulphur based, the erupted material
contains some water. The surface of Io shows vast plains with
troughs running through them, as if they had been carved by
running water. The consensus is that Io has ''some internal
sources of water.''

Europa, like Io, appears to be a rocky body, but its somewhat
lower density suggests that it may contain more internal water

than Io. Its surface shows a latticework of veinlike lines that suggested to the NASA teams shallow fissures in a sea of frozen ice. A close look at Europa by *Voyager 2* revealed a layer of mushy water ice under the cracked surface. At the December 1984 meeting of the American Geophysical Union in San Francisco, two scientists (David Reynolds and Steven Squyres) of NASA's Ames Research Center suggested that under Europa's ice sheet there might exist warmer oases of liquid water that could sustain living organisms. After a reexamination of *Voyager 2* photographs, NASA scientists tentatively concluded that the spacecraft witnessed volcanic eruptions of water and ammonia from the moon's interior. The belief now is that Europa has an ice covering several miles thick "overlaying an *ocean of liquid water* up to thirty miles deep, kept from freezing by radioactive decay and the friction of tidal forces."

Ganymede, the largest of Jupiter's moons, appears to be covered with water ice mixed with rock, suggesting it has undergone moonquakes that have cracked its crust of frozen ice. It is thought to be made almost entirely of water ice, with an inner ocean of liquid water near its core. The fourth Galilean moon, Callisto—about the size of the planet Mercury—also has an ice-rich crust; under it there are mush and liquid water surrounding a small, rocky core. Estimates are that Callisto is more than 50 percent water. A ring discovered around Jupiter is also made mostly, if not wholly, of ice particles.

Modern science has confirmed the ancient assertion to the fullest: there indeed have been "waters above the Firmament."

* * *

Jupiter is the Solar System's largest planet—as large as 1,300 Earths. It contains some 90 percent of the mass of the complete planetary system of the Sun. As stated earlier, the Sumerians called it KI.SHAR, "Foremost of the Firm Lands," of the planetary bodies. Saturn, though smaller than Jupiter, occupies a much larger portion of the heavens because of its rings, whose "disk" has a diameter of 670,000 miles. The Sumerians called it AN.SHAR, "Foremost of the Heavens."

Evidently they knew what they were talking about.

SEEING THE SUN

When we can see the Sun with the naked eye, as at dawn or at sunset, it is a perfect disk. Even when viewed with telescopes, it has the shape of a perfect globe. Yet the Sumerians depicted it as a disk with a triangular rays extending from its round surface, as seen on cylinder seal VA/243 (Plate B and Fig. 6a). Why?

In 1980 astronomers of the High Altitude Observatory of the University of Colorado took pictures of the Sun with a special camera during an eclipse observed in India. The pictures revealed that because of magnetic influences, the Sun's corona gives it the appearance of a disk with triangular rays extending from its surface—just as the Sumerians had depicted millennia earlier.

In January 1983, I brought the "enigmatic representation" on the Sumerian cylinder seal to the attention of the editor of *Scientific American*, a journal that reported the astronomers' discovery. In response, the editor, Dennis Flanagan, wrote to me on January 27, 1983:

"Thank you for your letter of January 25.

"What you have to say is most interesting, and we may well be able to publish it."

"In addition to the many puzzles posed by this depiction," I had written in my letter, "foremost of which is the source of the Sumerian knowledge, is now their apparent familiarity with the true shape of the Sun's corona."

Is it the need to acknowledge the source of Sumerian knowledge that is still holding up publication of what *Scientific American* has deemed "most interesting"?

4

THE MESSENGERS OF GENESIS

In 1986 Mankind was treated to a once-in-a-lifetime event: the appearance of a messenger from the past, a Messenger of Genesis. Its name was Halley's comet.

One of many comets and other small objects that roam the heavens, Halley's comet is unique in many ways; among them is the fact that its recorded appearances have been traced to millennia ago, as well as the fact that modern science was able, in 1986, to conduct for the first time a comprehensive, close-up examination of a comet and its core. The first fact underscores the excellence of ancient astronomy; because of the second, data was obtained that—once again—corroborated ancient knowledge and the tales of Genesis.

The chain of scientific developments that led Edmund Halley, who became British Astronomer Royal in 1720, to determine, during the years 1695–1705, that the comet he observed in 1682 and that came to bear his name was a periodic one, the same that had been observed in 1531 and 1607, involved the promulgation of the laws of gravitation and celestial motion by Sir Isaac Newton and Newton's consulting with Halley about his findings. Until then the theory regarding comets was that they crossed the heavens in straight lines, appearing at one end of the skies and disappearing in the other direction, never to be seen again. But based on Newtonian laws, Halley concluded that the curve described by comets is elliptical, eventually bringing these celestial bodies back to where they had been observed before. The "three" comets of 1531, 1607, and 1682 were unusual in that they were all orbiting in the "wrong" direction—clockwise rather than counterclockwise; had similar deviations from the general orbital plane of the planets around the Sun—being inclined about 17 to 18 degrees—and were

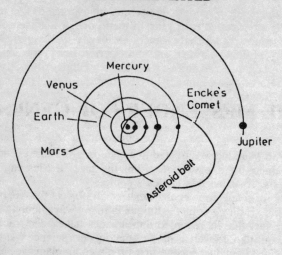

Figure 20

similar in appearance. Concluding they were one and the same comet, he plotted its course and calculated its period (the length of time between its appearances) to be about seventy-six years. He then predicted that it would reappear in 1758. He did not live long enough to see his prediction come true, but he was honored by having the comet named after him.

Like that of all celestial bodies, and especially because of a comet's small size, its orbit is easily perturbed by the gravitational pull of the planets it passes (this is especially true of Jupiter's effect). Each time a comet nears the Sun, its frozen material comes to life; the comet develops a head and a long tail and begins to lose some of its material as it turns to gas and vapor. All these phenomena affect the comet's orbit; therefore, although more precise measurements have somewhat narrowed the orbital range of Halley's comet from the seventy-four to seventy-nine years that he had calculated, the period of seventy-six years is only a practical average; the actual orbit and its period must be recalculated each time the comet makes an appearance.

With the aid of modern equipment, an average of five or six comets are reported each year; of them, one or two are comets on return trips, while the others are newly discovered. Most of the returning comets are short-period ones, the shortest known being that of Encke's comet, which nears the Sun and then returns to a region slightly beyond the asteroid belt (Fig. 20) in a little over three years. Most short-period comets average an orbital period of about seven years, which carries them to the environs of Jupiter. Typical of them is comet Giacobini-Zinner (named, like other comets, after its discoverers), which has a period of 6½ years; its latest passage within Earth's view was in 1985. On the other hand there are the very-long-period comets like comet Kohoutek, which was discovered in March 1973, was fully visible in December 1973 and January 1974, and then disappeared from view, perhaps to return in 75,000 years. By comparison, the cycle of 76 years for Halley's comet is short enough to remain in living memories, yet long enough to retain its magic as a once-in-a-lifetime celestial event.

When Halley's comet appeared on its next-to-last passage around the Sun, in 1910, its course and aspects had been well mapped out in advance (Fig. 21). Still, the Great Comet of

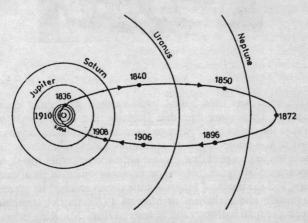

Figure 21

Figure 22

1910, as it was then hailed, was awaited with great appre-
hension. There was fear that Earth or life on it would not
survive the anticipated passage because Earth would be enveloped in the comet's tail of poisonous gases. There was also
alarm at the prospect that, as was believed in earlier times, the
appearance of the comet would be an ill omen of pestilence,
wars, and the death of kings. As the comet reached its greatest
magnitude and brilliance in May of 1910, its tail stretching
over more than half the vault of heaven (Fig. 22), King Edward
VII of Great Britain died. On the European continent, a series

of political upheavals culminated in the outbreak of World War
I in 1914.

The belief, or superstition, associating Halley's comet with
wars and upheavals was fed by much that was coming to light
about events that coincided with its previous appearances. The
Seminole Indians' revolt against the white settlers of Florida
in 1835, the Great Lisbon Earthquake of 1755, the outbreak
of the Thirty Years' War in 1618, the Turkish siege of Belgrade
in 1456, the outbreak of the Black Death (bubonic plague) in
1347—all were accompanied or preceded by the appearance
of a great comet, which was finally recognized as Halley's
Comet, thus establishing its role as the messenger of God's
wrath.

Figure 23

Whether divinely ordained or not, the coincidence of the
comet's appearance in conjunction with major historic events
seems to grow the more we go back in time. One of the most
celebrated appearances of a comet, definitely Halley's, is that
of 1066, during the Battle of Hastings in which the Saxons,
under King Harold, were defeated by William the Conqueror.
The comet was depicted (Fig. 23) on the famous Bayeux tapestry, which is thought to have been commissioned by Queen

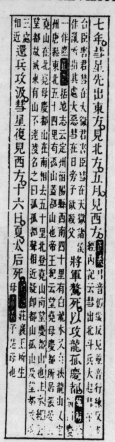

Figure 24

Matilda, wife of William the Conqueror, to illustrate his victory. The inscription next to the comet's tail, *Isti mirant stella*, means, "They are in awe of the star," and refers to the depiction of King Harold tottering on his throne.

The year A.D. 66 is considered by astronomers one in which Halley's comet made an appearance; they base their conclusion

sion on at least two contemporary Chinese observations. That was the year in which the Jews of Judea launched their Great Revolt against Rome. The Jewish historian Josephus (*Wars of the Jews*, Book VI) blamed the fall of Jerusalem and the destruction of its holy Temple on the misinterpretation by the Jews of the heavenly signs that preceded the revolt: ''a star resembling a sword which stood over the city, a comet that continued a whole year.''

Until recently the earliest certain record of the observation of a comet was found in the Chinese Chronological Tables of Shih-chi for the year 467 B.C., in which the pertinent entry reads, ''During the tenth year of Ch'in Li-kung a broom-star was seen.'' Some believe a Greek inscription refers to the same comet in that year. Modern astronomers are not sure that the 467 B.C. Shih-chi entry refers to Halley's comet; they are more confident regarding a Shih-chi entry for the year 240 B.C. (Fig. 24). In April 1985, F. R. Stephenson, K. K. C. Yau, and H. Hunger reported in *Nature* that a reexamination of Babylonian astronomical tablets that had been lying in the basement of the British Museum since their discovery in Mesopotamia more than a century ago, shows that the tablets recorded the appearance of extraordinary celestial bodies—probably comets, they said—in the years 164 B.C. and 87 B.C. The periodicity of seventy-seven years suggested to these scholars that the unusual celestial bodies were Halley's comet.

The year 164 B.C., as none of the scholars who have been preoccupied with Halley's comet have realized, was of great significance in Jewish and Near Eastern history. It was the very year in which the Jews of Judea, under the leadership of the Maccabees, revolted against Greek-Syrian domination, recaptured Jerusalem, and purified the defiled Temple. The Temple rededication ceremony is celebrated to this day by Jews as the festival of *Hanukkah* (''Rededication''). The 164 B.C. tablet (Fig. 25), numbered WA-41462 in the British Museum, is clearly dated to the relevant year in the reign of the Seleucid (Greek-Syrian) king Antiochus Epiphanes, the very evil King Antiochus of the Books of Maccabees. The unusual celestial object, which the three scholars believe was Halley's comet, is reported to have been seen in the Babylonian month of Kislimu, which is the Jewish month Kislev and, indeed, the one in which Hanukkah is celebrated.

Figure 25

In another instance, the comparison by Josephus of the comet to a celestial sword (as it seems to be depicted also in the Bayeux tapestry) has led some scholars to suggest that the Angel of the Lord that King David saw "standing between the earth and heaven, having a sword in his hand stretched out over Jerusalem" (I Chronicles 21:16) might have been in reality Halley's comet, sent by the Lord to punish the king for having conducted a prohibited census. The time of this incident, circa 1000 B.C., coincides with one of the years in which Halley's comet should have appeared.

In an article published in 1986, I pointed out that the Hebrew name for "comet" is *Kokhav shavit*, a "Scepter star." This has a direct bearing, I wrote, on the biblical tale of the seer Bilam. When the Israelites ended their wanderings in the desert after the Exodus and began the conquest of Canaan, the Moabite king summoned Bilam to curse the Israelites. But Bilam, realizing that the Israelite advance was divinely ordained, blessed them instead. He did so, he explained (Numbers 24:17), because he was shown a celestial vision:

> I see it, though not now;
> I behold it, though it is not near:
> A star of Jacob did course,
> A scepter of Israel did arise.

In *The Stairway to Heaven* I provided a chronology that fixed the date of the Exodus at 1433 B.C.; the Israelite entry into Canaan began forty years later, in 1393 B.C. Halley's comet, at an interval of 76 or 77 years, would have appeared circa 1390 B.C. Did Bilam consider that event as a divine signal that the Israelite advance could not and should not be stopped? If, in biblical times, the comet we call Halley's was considered the Scepter Star of Israel, it could explain why the Jewish revolts of 164 B.C. and A.D. 66 were timed to coincide with the comet's appearances. It is significant that in spite of the crushing defeat of the Judean revolt by the Romans in A.D. 66, the Jews took up arms again some seventy years later in a heroic effort to free Jerusalem and rebuild the Temple. The leader of that revolt, Shimeon Bar Kosiba, was renamed by the religious leaders *Bar Kokhba*, "Son of the Star," specifically because of the above-quoted verses in Numbers 24.

One can only guess whether the revolt the Romans put down after three years, in A.D. 135, was also intended as was the Maccabean one, to achieve the rededication of the Temple by the time of the return of Halley's comet, in A.D. 142. The realization that we, in 1986, have seen and experienced the return of a majestic celestial body that had great historic impact in the past, should send a shudder down some spines, mine among them.

How far back does this messenger of the past go? According

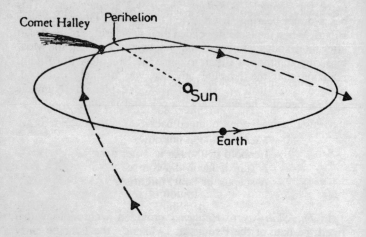

Figure 26

to the Sumerian creation epics, it goes all the way back to the time of the Celestial Battle. Halley's comet and its like are truly the Messengers of Genesis.

The Solar System, astronomers and physicists believe, was formed out of a primordial cloud of gaseous matter; like everything else in the universe, it was in constant motion—circling about its galaxy (the Milky Way) and rotating around its own center of gravity. Slowly the cloud spread as it cooled; slowly the center became a star (our Sun) and the planets coalesced out of the rotating disc of gaseous matter. Thenceforth, the motion of all parts of the Solar System retained the original direction of the primordial cloud, anticlockwise. The planets orbit the Sun in the same direction as did the original nebula; so do their satellites, or moons; so should also the debris that either did not coalesce or that resulted from the disintegration of bodies such as comets and asteroids. Everything must keep going anticlockwise. Everything must also remain within the plane of the original disk, which is called the Ecliptic.

Nibiru/Marduk did not conform to all that. Its orbit, as

previously reviewed, was retrograde—in the opposite direction, clockwise. Its effect on Pluto—which according to the Sumerian texts was GA.GA and was shifted by Nibiru to its present orbit, which is not within the ecliptic but inclined 17 degrees to it—suggests that Nibiru itself followed an inclined path. Sumerian instructions for its observation, fully discussed in *The 12th Planet*, indicate that relative to the ecliptic it arrived from the southeast, from *under* the ecliptic; formed an arc above the ecliptic; then plunged back below the ecliptic in its journey back to where it had come from.

Amazingly, Halley's comet shows the same characteristics, and except for the fact that its orbit is so much smaller than that of Nibiru (currently about 76 years compared with Nibiru's 3,600 Earth-years), an illustration of Haley's orbit (Fig. 26) could give us a good idea of Nibiru's inclined and retrograde path. Looking at Halley's comet, we see a miniature Nibiru! This orbital similarity is but one of the aspects that make this comet, and others too, messengers from the past—not only the historic past, but all the way back to Genesis.

Halley's comet is not alone in having an orbit markedly inclined to the ecliptic (a feature measured as an angle of Declination) and a retrograde direction. Nonperiodic comets—comets whose paths form not ellipses but parabolas or even hyperbolas and whose orbits are so vast and whose limits are so far away they cannot even be calculated—have marked declinations, and about half of them move in a retrograde direction. Of about 600 periodic comets (which are now given the letter "P" in front of their name) that have been classified and catalogued, about 500 have orbital periods longer than 200 years; they all have declinations more akin to that of Halley's than to the greater declinations of the nonperiodic comets, and more than half of them course in retrograde motion. Comets with medium orbital periods (between 200 and 20 years) and short periods (under 20 years) have a mean declination of 18 degrees, and some, like Halley's, have retained the retrograde motion in spite of the immense gravitational effects of Jupiter. It is noteworthy that of recently discovered comets, the one designated P/Hartley-IRAS (1983v) has an orbital period of 21 years, and its orbit is both retrograde and inclined to the ecliptic.

Where do comets come from, and what causes their odd orbits, of which the retrograde direction is the oddest in astronomers' eyes? In the 1820s the Marquis Pierre-Simon de Laplace believed that comets were made of ice and that their glowing head (''coma'') and tail that formed as they neared the Sun, were both made of vaporized ice. This concept was replaced after the discovery of the extent and nature of the asteroid belt, and theories developed that comets were ''flying sandbanks''—pieces of rock that might be the remains of a disintegrated planet. The thinking changed again in the 1950s mainly because of two hypotheses: Fred L. Whipple (then at Harvard) suggested that comets were ''dirty snowballs'' of ice (mainly water ice) mixed with darker specks of sandlike material; and Jan Oort, a Dutch astronomer, proposed that long-period comets come from a vast reservoir halfway between the Sun and the nearer stars. Because comets appear from all directions (traveling prograde, or anticlockwise; retrograde; and at different declinations), the reservoir of comets—billions of them—is not a belt or ring like the asteroid belt or the rings of Saturn but a sphere that surrounds the Solar System. This ''Oort Cloud,'' as the concept came to be named, settled at a mean distance, Oort calculated, of 100,000 astronomical units (AU) from the Sun, one AU being the average distance (93 million miles) of the Earth from the Sun. Because of perturbations and intercometal collisions, some of the cometary horde may have come closer, to only 50,000 AU from the Sun (which is still ten thousand times the distance of Jupiter from the Sun). Passing stars occasionally perturb these comets and send them flying toward the Sun. Some, under the gravitational influence of the planets, mainly Jupiter, become medium- or short-period comets; some, especially influenced by the mass of Jupiter, are forced into reversing their course (Fig. 27). This, briefly, is how the Oort Cloud concept is usually stated.

Since the 1950s the number of observed comets has increased by more than 50 percent, and computer technology has made possible the projection backward of cometary motions to determine their source. Such studies, as one by a team at the Harvard-Smithsonian Observatory under Brian G. Marsden, have shown that of 200 observed comets with periods of 250 years or more, no more than 10 percent could have entered the

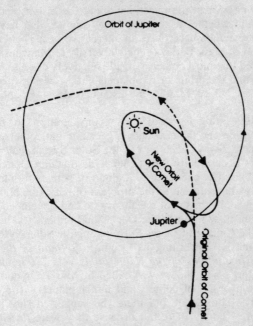

Figure 27

Solar System from outer space; 90 percent have always been bound to the Sun as the focus of their orbits. Studies of cometary velocities have shown, in the words of Fred L. Whipple in his book, *The Mystery of Comets*, that "if we are really seeing comets coming from the void, we should expect them to fly by much faster than just 0.8 kilometers per second," which they do not. His conclusion is that "with few exceptions, comets belong to the Sun's family and are gravitationally attached to it."

"During the past few years, astronomers have questioned the simple view of Oort's Cloud," stated Andrew Theokas of Boston University in the *New Scientist* (February 11, 1988); "astronomers still believe that the Oort Cloud exists, but the new results demand that they reconsider its size and shape.

They even reopen the questions about the origin of the Oort Cloud and whether it contains 'new' comets that have come from interstellar space.'' As an alternative idea Théokas mentions that of Mark Bailey of the University of Manchester, who suggested that most comets "reside relatively close to the Sun, just beyond the orbits of the planets.'' Is it perhaps, one may ask, where Nibiru/Marduk's "distant abode"—its aphelion— is?

The interesting aspect of the "reconsideration" of the Oort Cloud notion and the new data suggesting that comets, by and large, have always been part of the Solar System and not just outsiders occasionally thrust into it, is that Jan Oort himself had said so. The existence of a cloud of comets in interstellar space was his solution to the problem of parabolic and hyperbolic cometal orbits, not the theory he had developed. In the study that made him and the Oort Cloud famous ("The Structure of the Cloud of Comets Surrounding the Solar System and a Hypothesis Concerning its Origin," *Bulletin of the Astronomical Institutions of the Netherlands* vol. 11, January 13, 1950) Oort's new theory was called by him a "hypothesis of a common origin of comets and minor planets" (i.e., asteroids). The comets are out there, he suggested, not because they were "born" there but because they were *thrust out to there*. They were fragments of larger objects, "diffused away" by the perturbations of the planets and especially by Jupiter— just as more recently the Pioneer spacecraft were made to fly off into space by the "slingshot" effects of Jupiter's and Saturn's gravitation.

"The main process now," Oort wrote, "is the inverse one, that of a slow transfer of comets from a large cloud into short-period orbits. But at the epoch at which the minor planets (asteroids) were formed . . . the trend must have been the opposite, many more objects being transferred *from* the asteroid region *to* the comet cloud. . . . It appears far more probable that instead of having originated in the faraway regions, comets were born among the planets. It is natural to think in the first place of a relation with the minor planets (asteroids). There are indications that the two classes of objects"—comets and asteroids—"belong to the same 'species.' . . . *It seems reasonable to assume that the comets originated together with the minor planets.*" Summing up his study, Oort put it this way:

The existence of the huge cloud of comets finds a natural explanation if comets (and meteorites) are considered as minor planets escaped, at an early stage of the planetary system, from the ring of asteroids.

It all begins to sound like the *Enuma elish*. . . .

Placing the origin of the comets within the asteroid belt and considering both comets and asteroids as belonging to the same "species" of celestial objects—objects of a common birth—still leaves open the questions: How were these objects created? What gave "birth" to them? What "diffused" the comets? What gave comets their inclinations and retrograde motions?

A major and outspoken study on the subject was made public in 1978 by Thomas C. Van Flandern of the U.S. Naval Observatory, Washington, D.C. (*Icarus*, 36). He titled the study, "A Former Asteroidal Planet as the Origin of Comets," and openly subscribed to the nineteenth-century suggestions that the asteroids, and the comets, come from a former planet that had exploded. It is noteworthy that in the references to Oort's work, Van Flandern picked out its true essence: "Even the father of the modern 'cloud of comets' theory was led to conclude," Van Flandern wrote, "on the basis of evidence then available, that a solar system origin for these comets, perhaps in connection with 'the occurrence which gave birth to the belt of asteroids,' was still the least objectionable hypothesis." He also referred to studies, begun in 1972, by Michael W. Ovenden, a noted Canadian astronomer who introduced the concept of a "principle of least interaction action," a corollary of which was the suggestion that "there had existed, between Mars and Jupiter, a planet of a mass of about 90 times that of Earth, and that this planet had 'disappeared' in the relatively recent past, about 10^7 [10,000,000] years ago." This, Ovenden further explained in 1975 ("Bode's Law—Truth or Consequences?" vol. 18, *Vistas in Astronomy*), is the only way to meet the requirement that "the cosmogonic theory must be capable of producing *retrograde* as well as direct" celestial motions.

Summarizing his findings, Van Flandern said thus in 1978:

The principal conclusion of this paper is that the comets originated in a breakup event in the inner solar system.

In all probability it was the same event which gave rise to the asteroid belt and which produced most of the meteors visible today.

He said that it was less certain that the same "breakup event" may have also given birth to the satellites of Mars and the outer satellites of Jupiter, and he estimated that the "breakup event" occurred five million years ago. He had no doubt, however, that the "breakup event" took place "in the asteroid belt." Physical, chemical, and dynamic properties of the resulting celestial bodies, he stated emphatically, indicate "that a large planet did disintegrate" where the asteroid belt is today.

But what caused this large planet to disintegrate? "The most frequently asked question about this scenario," Van Flandern wrote, "is 'how can a planet blow up?' . . . There is presently," he conceded, "no satisfactory answer to this question."

No satisfactory answer, that is, except the Sumerian one: the tale of Tiamat and Nibiru/Marduk, the Celestial Battle, the breakup of half of Tiamat, the annihilation of its moons (except for "Kingu"), and the forcing of their remains into a retrograde orbit . . .

A key criticism of the destroyed-planet theory has been the problem of the whereabouts of the planet's matter; when astronomers estimate the total mass of the known asteroids and comets it adds up to only a fraction of the estimated mass of the broken-up planet. This is especially true if Ovenden's estimate of a planet with a mass ninety times that of Earth is used in the calculations. Ovenden's response to such criticism has been that the missing mass was probably swept up by Jupiter; his own calculations (*Monthly Notes of the Royal Astronomical Society*, 173, 1975) called for an increase in the mass of Jupiter by as much as 130 Earth-masses as a result of the capture of asteroids, including Jupiter's several retrograde moons. To allow for the discrepancy between the mass (ninety times that of Earth) of the broken-up planet and the accretion of 130 Earth-sized masses to Jupiter, Ovenden cited other studies that concluded that Jupiter's mass had decreased some time in its past.

Rather than to first inflate the size of Jupiter and then shrink it back, a better scenario would be to shrink the estimated size of the destroyed planet. That is what the Sumerian texts have put forth. If Earth is the remaining half of Tiamat, then Tiamat was roughly twice the size of Earth, not ninety times. Studies of the asteroid belt reveal not only capture by Jupiter but a dispersion of the asteroids from their assumed original site at about 2.8 AU to a zone so wide that it occupies the space between 1.8 AU and 4 AU. Some asteroids are found between Jupiter and Saturn; a recently discovered one (2060 Chiron) is located between Saturn and Uranus at 13.6 AU. The smashup of the destroyed planet must have been, therefore, extremely forceful—as in a catastrophic collision.

In addition to the voids between groups of asteroids, astronomers discern gaps within the clusters of asteroids (Fig. 28). The latest theories hold that there had been asteroids in the gaps but they were ejected, all the way to outer space except for those that may have been captured on the way by the gravitational forces of the outer planets; also, the asteroids that used to be in the "gaps" were probably destroyed "by catastrophic collisions"! (*McGraw-Hill Encyclopedia of Astronomy*, 1983). In the absence of valid explanations for such ejections and catastrophic collisions, the only plausible theory is that offered by the Sumerian texts, which describe the orbit of Nibiru/Marduk as a vast, elliptical path that brings it periodically (every 3,600 Earth years, by my calculations) back into the asteroid belt. As Figures 10 and 11 show, the conclusion drawn from the ancient texts was that Nibiru/Marduk

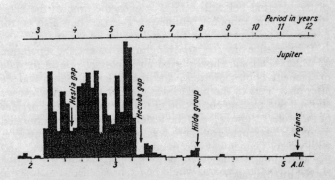

Figure 28

passed by Tiamat on her outer, or Jupiter, side; repeated returns to that celestial zone can account for the size of the "gap" there. It is the periodic return of Nibiru/Marduk that causes the "ejecting" and "sweeping."

By the acknowledgment of the existence of Nibiru and its periodic return to the Place of the Battle, the puzzle of the "missing matter" finds a solution. It also addresses the theories that place the accretions of mass by Jupiter at a relatively recent time (millions, not billions, of years ago). Depending on where Jupiter was at the times of Nibiru's perihelion, the accretions might have occurred during various passages of Nibiru and not necessarily as a one-and-only event at the time of the catastrophic breakup of Tiamat. Indeed, spectrographic studies of asteroids reveal that some of them "were heated within the first few hundred million years after the origin of the solar system" by heat so intense as to melt them; "iron sank to their centers, forming strong stony-iron cores, while basaltic lavas floated to their surface, producing minor planets like Vesta" (*McGraw-Hill Encyclopedia of Astronomy*). The suggested time of the catastrophe is the very time indicated in *The 12th Planet*—some 500 million years after the formation of the Solar System.

Recent scientific advances in astronomy and astrophysics go beyond corroborating the Sumerian cosmogony in regard to the celestial collision as the common origin of the comets and the asteroids, the site of that collision (where the remains of the asteroid belt still orbit), or even the time of the catastrophic event (about 4 billion years ago). They also corroborate the ancient texts in the vital matter of *water*.

The presence of water, the mingling of waters, the separation of waters—all somehow played an important role in the tale of Tiamat, Nibiru/Marduk, and the Celestial Battle and its aftermath. Part of the puzzle was already answered when we showed that the ancient notion of the asteroid belt as a divider of the waters "above" and the water "below" is corroborated by modern science. But there was more to this preoccupation with water. Tiamat was described as a "watery monster," and the Mesopotamian texts speak of the handling of her waters by Nibiru/Marduk:

Half of her he stretched as a ceiling to be Sky,
As a bar at the Place of Crossing he posted it to guard;
Not to allow her waters to escape was its command.

The concept of an asteroid belt not only as a divider between the waters of the planets above and below it but also as a "guardian" of Tiamat's own waters is echoed in the biblical verses of Genesis, where the explanation is given that the "Hammered-out bracelet" was also called *Shama'im*, the place "where the waters were." References to the waters where the Celestial Battle and the creation of the Earth and the Shama'im took place are frequent in the Old Testament, indicating millennia-old familiarity with Sumerian cosmogony even at the time of the Prophets and Judean kings. An example is found in Psalm 104, which depicts the Creator as the Lord

Who has stretched out the Shama'im as a curtain,
Who in the waters for His ascents put a ceiling.

These verses are almost a word-for-word copy of the verses in *Enuma elish*; in both instances, the placing of the asteroid belt "where the waters were" followed the earlier acts of the splitting up of Tiamat and having the invader's "wind" thrust the half that became Earth into a new orbit. The waters of Earth would explain the whereabouts of some or most of Tiamat's waters. But what about the remains of her other part and of her satellites? If the asteroids and comets are those remains, should they not also contain water?

What would have been a preposterous suggestion when these objects were deemed "chunks of debris" and "flying sandbanks" has turned out, as the result of recent discoveries, to be not so preposterous: the asteroids are celestial objects in which water—yes, water—is a major component.

Most asteroids belong to two classes. About 15 percent belong to the *S* type, which have reddish surfaces made up of silicates and metallic iron. About 75 percent are of the C type: they are carbonaceous (containing carbon), and it is these that have been found to contain water. The water discovered in such asteroids (through spectrographic studies) is not in liquid form; since asteroids have no atmospheres, any water on their surface would quickly dissipate. But the presence of water molecules in the surface materials indicates that the minerals that make up the asteroid have captured water and combined with it. Direct confirmation of this finding was observed in August 1982, when a small asteroid that came too close to Earth plunged into the Earth's atmosphere and disintegrated; it was seen as "a rainbow with a long tail going across the sky." A rainbow appears when sunlight falls on a collection of water drops, such as rain, fog, or spray.

When the asteroid is more like what its name originally implied, "minor planet," actual water in liquid form could well be present. Examination of the infrared spectrum of the largest and first-to-be-discovered asteroid Ceres shows an extra dip in the spectral readings that is the result of free water rather than water bound to minerals. Since free water even on Ceres will quickly evaporate, the astronomers surmise that Ceres must have a constant source of water welling up from its interior. "If that source has been there throughout the career of Ceres," wrote the British astronomer Jack Meadows (*Space Garbage—Comets, Meteors and Other Solar-System Debris*), "then it must have started life as a very wet lump of rock." He pointed out that carbonaceous meteorites also "show signs of having been extensively affected by water in times past."

The celestial body designated 2060 Chiron, interesting in many ways, also confirms the presence of water in the remnants of the Celestial Battle. When Charles Kowal of the Hale Observatories on Mount Palomar, California, discovered it in November 1977, he was not certain what it was. He simply referred to it as a planetoid, named it temporarily "O-K" for "Object Kowal," and opined that it might be a wayward satellite of either Saturn or Uranus. Several weeks of follow-up studies revealed an orbit much more elliptical than that of planets or planetoids, one closer to that of comets. By 1981 the object was determined to be an asteroid, perhaps one of others to be found reaching as far out as Uranus, Neptune or beyond, and was given the designation 2060 Chiron. However, by 1989, further observations by astronomers at Kitt Peak National Observatory (Arizona) detected an extended atmosphere of carbon dioxide and dust around Chiron, suggesting that it is more cometlike. The latest observations have also established that Chiron "is essentially a dirty snowball composed of water, dust and carbon-dioxide ice."

If Chiron proves to be more a comet than an asteroid, it will only serve as further evidence that both classes of these remnants of the Genesis event contain water.

When a comet is far away from the Sun, it is a dark and invisible object. As it nears the Sun, the Sun's radiation brings the comet's nucleus to life. It develops a gaseous head (the coma) and then a tail made up of gases and dust ejected by the nucleus as it heats up. It is the observation of these emissions that has by and large confirmed Whipple's view of comets as "dirty snowballs," first by determining that the onset of activity in comets as the nucleus begins to heat up is consistent with the thermodynamic properties of water ice, and then by spectroscopic analysis of the gaseous emissions, which have invariably shown the presence of the compound H_2O (i.e., water).

The presence of water in comets has been definitely established in recent years through enhanced examination of arriving comets. Comet Kohoutek (1974) was studied not only from Earth but also with rockets, from orbiting manned spacecraft (Skylab), and from the *Mariner 10* spacecraft that was on its way to Venus and Mercury. The findings, it was reported at the time, provided "the first direct proof of water" in a comet. "The water finding, as well as that of two complex molecules in the comet's tail, are the most significant to date," stated Stephen P. Moran, who directed the scientific project for NASA. And all scientists concurred with the evaluation by astrophysicists at the Max Planck Institute for Physics and Astrophysics in Munich that was seen were "the oldest and essentially unchanged specimens of the material from the birth of the Solar System."

Subsequent cometary observations confirmed these findings. However, none of those studies, accomplished with a variety of instruments, match the intensity with which Halley's comet was probed in 1986. The Halley findings established unequivocally that the comet was a watery celestial body.

Apart from several only partly successful efforts by the United States to examine the comet from a distance, Halley's comet was met by a virtual international welcoming flotilla of

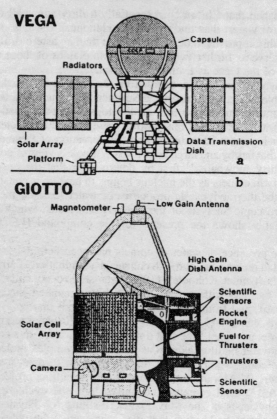

Figure 29

five spacecraft, all unmanned. The Soviets directed to a Comet Halley rendevouz *Vega 1* and *Vega 2* (Fig. 29a), the Japanese sent the spacecraft *Sakigake* and *Suisei*, and the European Space Agency launched *Giotto* (Fig. 29b)—so named in honor of the Florentine master painter Giotto di Bondone (fourteenth century), who was so enchanted by Halley's comet when it appeared in his time that he included it, streaking across the

sky, in his famous fresco *Adoration of the Magi*, suggesting
that this comet was the Star of Bethlehem in the tale of the
birth of Christ (Fig. 30).

As intensive observations began when Halley's comet developed its coma and tail in November 1985, astronomers at
the Kitt Peak Observatory tracking the comet with telescopes
reported it was certain "that the comet's dominant constituent
is water ice, and that much of the tenuous 360,000-mile-wide
cloud surrounding it consisted of water vapor." A statement
by Susan Wyckoff of Arizona State University claimed that

Figure 30

"this was the first strong evidence that water ice was prevalent." These telescopic observations were augmented in January 1986 by infrared observations from high-altitude aircraft, whereupon a team made up of NASA scientists and astronomers from several American universities announced "direct confirmation that water was a major constituent of Halley's comet."

By January 1986, Halley's comet had developed an immense tail and a halo of hydrogen gas that measured 12.5 million miles across—fifteen times bigger than the diameter of the Sun. It was then that NASA's engineers commanded the spacecraft *Pioneer-Venus* (which was orbiting Venus) to turn its instruments toward the nearing comet (at its perihelion Halley's passed between Venus and Mercury). The spacecraft's spectrometer, which "sees" the atoms of its subject, revealed that "the comet was losing 12 tons of water per second." As it neared perihelion on March 6, 1986, Ian Stewart, the director of NASA's Halley's project at the Ames Research Center, reported that the rate of water loss "increased enormously," first to 30 tons a second and then to 70 tons a second; he assured the press, however, that even at this rate Halley's comet had "enough water ice to last thousands of more orbits."

The close encounters with Halley's comet began on March 6, 1986, when *Vega 1* plunged through Halley's radiant atmosphere and, from a distance of less than 6,000 miles, sent the first-ever pictures of its icy core. The press dutifully noted that what Mankind was seeing was the nucleus of a celestial body that had evolved when the Solar System began. On March 9, *Vega 2* flew within 5,200 miles of Halley's nucleus and confirmed the findings of *Vega 1*. The spacecraft also revealed that the comet's "dust" contained chunks of solid matter, some boulder size, and that this heavier crust or layer enveloped a nucleus where the temperature—almost 90 million miles from the Sun—was a hot 85 degrees Fahrenheit.

The two Japanese spacecraft, designed to study the effect of the solar wind on the comet's tail and the comet's huge hydrogen cloud, were targeted to pass at substantial distances from Halley's. But *Giotto*'s mission was to meet the comet virtually head-on, swooping at an immense encounter speed within 300 miles from the comet's core. On March 14 (European time), *Giotto* streaked past the heart of Halley's comet and revealed a "mysterious nucleus," its color blacker than coal, its size bigger than had been thought (about half the size of Manhattan Island). The shape of the nucleus was rough and irregular (Fig. 31), some describing it as "two peas in a pod" and some as an irregularly shaped "potato." From the nucleus five main jets were emitting streams of dust and 80 percent water vapor, indicating that within the carbonaceous crust the comet contained "melted ice"—*liquid water*.

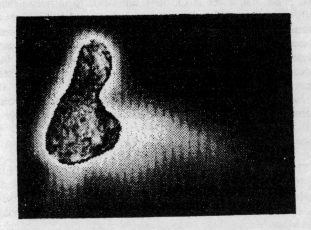

Figure 31

The first comprehensive review of the results of all these close-up observations was published in *Nature*'s special supplement of 15–21 May, 1986. In the series of very detailed reports, the Soviet team confirmed the first findings that water (H_2O) is the comet's major component, followed by carbon and hydrogen compounds. The *Giotto* report stated repeatedly that "H_2O is the dominant parent molecule in Halley's coma," and that "water vapor accounts for about 80% of the volume of gases escaping from the comet." These preliminary conclusions were reaffirmed in October 1986, at an international conference in Heidelberg, West Germany. And in December 1986, scientists at the John Hopkins University announced that evaluation of data collected in March 1986 by the small Earth-orbiting satellite IUE (*International Ultraviolet Explorer*) revealed an explosion on Halley's Comet that blew 100 cubic feet of ice out of the comet's nucleus.

There was water everywhere on these Messengers of Genesis!

Studies have shown that comets coming in from the cold "come to life" as they reach a distance of between 3 to 2.5 AU, and that water is the first substance to unfreeze there. Little significance has been given to the fact that this distance from the Sun is the zone of the asteroid belt, and one must wonder whether it is there that comets come to life because it is where they were born—whether water comes to life there because there is where it had been, on Tiamat and her watery host. . . .

In the discoveries concerning the comets and the asteroids, something else came to life: the ancient knowledge of Sumer.

CELESTIAL "SEEING EYES"

When the Anunnaki's Mission Earth reached its full complement, there were six hundred of them on Earth, while three hundred remained in orbit, servicing the shuttle craft. The Sumerian term for the latter was *IGI.GI*, literally "Those who observe and see."

Archaeologists have found in Mesopotamia many objects they call "eye idols" (a), as well as shrines dedicated to these "gods" (b). Texts refer to devices used by the Anunnaki to "scan the Earth from end to end." These texts and depictions imply the use by the Anunnaki of Earth-orbiting, celestial "seeing eyes"—satellites that "observe and see."

Perhaps it is no coincidence that some of the Earth-scanning, and especially fixed-position communications satellites launched in our own modern times, such as *Intelsat-IV* and *Intelsat IV-A* (c, d), look so much like these millennia-old depictions.

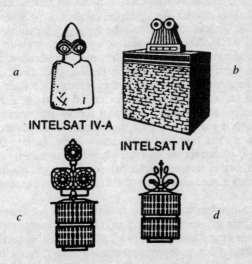

a

INTELSAT IV-A

b

INTELSAT IV

c

d

5

GAIA: THE CLEAVED PLANET

Why do we call our planet "Earth"?

In German it is *Erde*, from *Erda* in Old High German; *Jördh* in Icelandic, *Jord* in Danish. *Erthe* in Middle English, *Airtha* in Gothic; and going eastward geographically and backward in time, *Ereds* or *Aratha* in Aramaic, *Erd* or *Ertz* in Kurdish, *Eretz* in Hebrew. The sea we nowadays call the Arabian Sea, the body of water that leads to the Persian Gulf, was called in antiquity the Sea of *Erythrea*; and to this day, *ordu* means an encampment or settlement in Persian. Why?

The answer lies in the Sumerian texts that relate the arrival of the first group of Anunnaki/Nefilim on Earth. There were fifty of them, under the leadership of E.A ("Whose Home is Water"), a great scientist and the Firstborn son of the ruler of Nibiru, ANU. They splashed down in the Arabian Sea and waded ashore to the edge of the marshlands that, after the climate warmed up, became the Persian Gulf (Fig. 32). And at the head of the marshlands they established their first settlement on a new planet; it was called by them E.RI.DU—"Home In the Faraway"—a most appropriate name.

And so it was that in time the whole settled planet came to be called after that first settlement—Erde, Erthe, Earth. To this day, whenever we call our planet by its name, we invoke the memory of that first settlement on Earth; unknowingly, we remember *Eridu* and honor the first group of Anunnaki who established it.

The Sumerian scientific or technical term for Earth's globe and its firm surface was KI. Pictographically it was represented as a somewhat flattened orb (Fig. 33a) crossed by vertical lines not unlike modern depictions of meridians (Fig. 33b). Since Earth does indeed bulge somewhat at its equator, the Sumerian

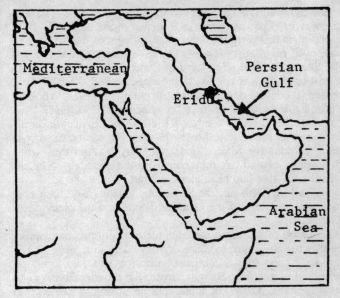

Figure 32

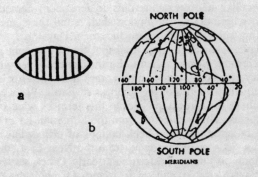

Figure 33

representation is more correct scientifically than the usual modern way of depicting Earth as a perfect globe. . . .

After Ea had completed the establishment of the first five of the seven original settlements of the Anunnaki, he was given the title/epithet EN.KI, "Lord of Earth." But the term KI, as a root or verb, was applied to the planet called "Earth" for a reason. It conveyed the meaning "to cut off, to sever, to hollow out." Its derivatives illustrate the concept: KI.LA meant "excavation," KI.MAH "tomb," KI.IN.DAR "crevice, fissure." In Sumerian astronomical texts the term KI was prefixed with the determinative MUL ("celestial body"). And thus when they spoke of *mul*.KI, they conveyed the meaning, "the celestial body that had been cleaved apart."

By calling Earth KI, the Sumerians thus invoked their cosmogony—the tale of the Celestial Battle and the cleaving of Tiamat.

Unaware of its origin we continue to apply this descriptive epithet to our planet to this very day. The intriguing fact is that over time (the Sumerian civilization was two thousand years old by the time Babylon arose) the pronunciation of the term *ki* changed to *gi*, or sometimes *ge*. It was so carried into the Akkadian and its linguistic branches (Babylonian, Assyrian, Hebrew), at all times retaining its geographic or topographic connotation as a cleavage, a ravine, a deep valley. Thus the biblical term that through Greek translations of the Bible is read *Gehenna* stems from the Hebrew *Gai-Hinnom*, the crevicelike narrow ravine outside Jerusalem named after Hinnom, where divine retribution shall befall the sinners via an erupting subterranean fire on Judgment Day.

We have been taught in school that the component *geo* in all the scientific terms applied to Earth sciences—*geo*-graphy, *geo*-metry, *geo*-logy, and so on—comes from the Greek *Gaia* (or *Gaea*), their name for the goddess of Earth. We were not taught where the Greeks picked up this term or what its real meaning was. The answer is, from the Sumerian KI or GI.

Scholars agree that the Greek notions of primordial events and of the gods were borrowed from the Near East, through Asia Minor (at whose western edge early Greek settlements like Troy were located) and via the island of Crete in the eastern Mediterranean. According to Greek tradition Zeus, who was

Hebrew name	CANAANITE-PHOENICIAN	EARLY GREEK	LATER GREEK	Greek name	LATIN
Aleph				Alpha	A
Beth				Beta	B
Gimel				Gamma	C G
Daleth				Delta	D
He				E(psilon)	E
Vau				Vau	F V
Zayin				Zeta	
Heth (1)				(H)eta	H
Teth				Theta	
Yod				Iota	I
Khaph				Kappa	
Lamed				Lambda	L
Mem				Mu	M
Nun				Nu	N
Samekh				Xi	X
Ayin				O(nicron)	O
Pe				Pi	P
Şade (2)				San	
Koph				Koppa	Q
Resh				Rho	R
Shin				Sigma	S
Tav				Tau	T

Figure 34

the chief god of the twelve Olympians, arrived on the Greek mainland via Crete, whence he had fled after abducting the beautiful Europa, daughter of the Phoenician king of Tyre. Aphrodite arrived from the Near East via the island of Cyprus. Poseidon (whom the Romans called Neptune) came on horseback via Asia Minor, and Athena brought the olive to Greece from the lands of the Bible. There is no doubt that the Greek alphabet developed from a Near Eastern one (Fig. 34). Cyrus

H. Gordon (*Forgotten Scripts: Evidence for the Minoan Language* and other works) deciphered the enigmatic Cretan script known as Linear A by showing that it represented a Semitic, Near Eastern language. With the Near Eastern gods and the terminology came also the "myths" and legends.

The earliest Greek writings concerning antiquity and the affairs of gods and men were the *Iliad*, by Homer; the *Odes* of Pindar of Thebes; and above all the *Theogony* ("*Divine Genealogy*") by Hesiod, who composed this work and another *(Works and Days)*. In the eighth century B.C., Hesiod began the divine tale of events that ultimately led to the supremacy of Zeus—a story of passions, rivalries, and struggles covered in *The Wars of Gods and Men*, third book of my series The Earth Chronicles—and the creation of the celestial gods, of Heaven and Earth out of Chaos, a tale not unlike the biblical Beginning:

> Verily, at first Chaos came to be,
> and next the wide-bosomed Gaia—
> she who created all the immortal ones
> who hold the peaks of snowy Olympus:
> Dim Tartarus, wide-pathed in the depths,
> and Eros, fairest among the divine immortals. . . .
> From Chaos came forth Erebus and black Nyx;
> And of Nyx were born Aether and Hemera.

At this point in the process of the formation of the "divine immortals"—the celestial gods—"Heaven" does not yet exist, just as the Mesopotamian sources recounted. Accordingly, the "Gaia" of these verses is the equivalent of Tiamat, "she who bore them all" according to the *Enuma elish*. Hesoid lists the celestial gods who followed "Chaos" and "Gaia" in three pairs (Tartarus and Eros, Erebus and Nyx, Aether and Hemera). The parallel with the creation of the three pairs in Sumerian cosmogony (nowadays named Venus and Mars, Saturn and Jupiter, Uranus and Neptune) should be obvious (though this comparability seems to have gone unnoticed).

Only after the creation of the principal planets that made up the Solar System when Nibiru appeared to invade it does the tale by Hesiod—as in the Mesopotamian and biblical texts—speak of the creation of Ouranos, "Heaven." As explained in the Book of Genesis, this *Shama'im* was the Hammered-Out-Bracelet, the asteroid belt. As related in the *Enuma elish*, this was the half of Tiamat that was smashed to pieces, while the other, intact half became Earth. All this is echoed in the ensuing verses of Hesiod's *Theogony*:

> And Gaia then bare starry Ouranos
> —equal to herself—
> to envelop her on every side,
> to be an everlasting abode place for the gods.

Equally split up, Gaia ceased to be Tiamat. Severed from the smashed-up half that became the Firmament, everlasting abode of the asteroids and comets, the intact half (thrust into another orbit) became Gaia, the Earth. And so did this planet, first as Tiamat and then as Earth, live up to its epithets: *Gaia*, *Gi*, *Ki*—the Cleaved One.

How did the Cleaved Planet look in the aftermath of the Celestial Battle, now orbiting as Gaia/Earth? On one side there were the firm lands that had formed the crust of Tiamat; on the other side there was a hollow, an immense cleft into which the waters of the erstwhile Tiamat must have poured. As Hesiod put it, Gaia (now the half equivalent to Heaven) on one side "brought forth long hills, graceful haunts of the goddess-Nymphs"; and on the other side "she bare Pontus, the fruitless deep with its raging swell."

This is the same picture of the cleaved planet provided by the Book of Genesis:

> And Elohim said,
> "Let the waters under the heaven
> be gathered together into one place,
> and let the dry land appear."
> And it was so.
> And Elohim called the dry land "Earth,"
> and the gathered-together water He called "Seas."

Earth, the new Gaia, was taking shape.

Three thousand years separated Hesiod from the time when the Sumerian civilization had blossomed out; and it is clear that throughout those millennia ancient peoples, including the authors or compilers of the Book of Genesis, accepted the Sumerian cosmogony. Called nowadays "myth," "legend," or "religious beliefs," in those previous millennia it was science—knowledge, the Sumerians asserted, bestowed by the Anunnaki.

According to that ancient knowledge, Earth was not an original member of the Solar System. It was the cleaved-off half of a planet then called Tiamat, "she who bore them all." The Celestial Battle that led to the creation of Earth occurred several hundred million years after the Solar System with its planets had been created. Earth, as a part of Tiamat, retained much of the water that Tiamat, "the watery monster," was known for. As Earth evolved into an independent planet and attained the shape of a globe dictated by the forces of gravity, the waters were gathered into the immense cavity on the torn-off side, and dry land appeared on the other side of the planet.

This, in summary, is what the ancient peoples firmly believed. What does modern science have to say?

The theories concerning planetary formation hold that they started as balls congealing from the gaseous disk extending from the Sun. As they cooled, heavier matter—iron, in Earth's case—sank into their centers, forming a solid inner core. A less solid, plastic, or even fluid outer core surrounded the inner one; in Earth's case, it is believed to consist of molten iron. The two cores and their motions act as a dynamo, producing the planet's magnetic field. Surrounding the solid and fluid cores is a mantle made of rocks and minerals; on Earth it is estimated to be some 1,800 miles thick. While the fluidity and heat generated at the planet's core (some 12,000 degrees Fahrenheit in the Earth's center) affect the mantle and what is on top of it, it is the uppermost 400 miles or so of the mantle (on Earth) that mostly account for what we see on the surface of the planet—its cooled crust.

The processes that produce, over billions of years, a spherical orb—the uniform force of gravity and the planet's rotation around its axis—should also result in an orderly layering. The solid inner core, the flexible or fluid outer core, the thick lower mantle of silicates, the upper mantle of rocks, and the uppermost crust should encompass one another in ordered layers,

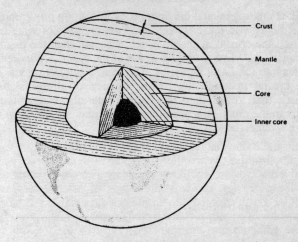

Figure 35

like the skin of an onion. This holds true for the orb called Earth (Fig. 35)—but only up to a point; the main abnormalities concern Earth's uppermost layer, the crust.

Ever since the extensive probes of the Moon and Mars in the 1960s and 1970s, geophysicists have been puzzled by the paucity of the Earth's crust. The crusts of the Moon and of Mars comprise 10 percent of their masses, but the Earth's crust comprises less than one half of 1 percent of the Earth's landmass. In 1988, geophysicists from Caltech and the University of Illinois at Urbana, led by Don Anderson, reported to the American Geological Society meeting in Denver, Colorado, that they had found the "missing crust." By analyzing shock waves from earthquakes, they concluded that material that belongs in the crust has sunk down and lies some 250 miles below the Earth's surface. There is enough crustal material there, these scientists estimated, to increase the thickness of the Earth's crust tenfold. But even so, it would have given Earth a crust comprising no more than about 4 percent of its landmass—still only about half of what seems to be the norm (judging by the Moon and Mars); half of the Earth's crust will still be missing even if the findings by this group prove correct. The theory also leaves unanswered the question of what force caused the crustal material, which is lighter than the mantle's material, to "dive"—in the words of the report—hundreds of miles into the Earth's interior. The team's suggestion was that the crustal material down there consists of "huge slabs of crust" that "dived into the Earth's interior" where fissures exist in the crust. But what force had broken up the crust into such "huge slabs"?

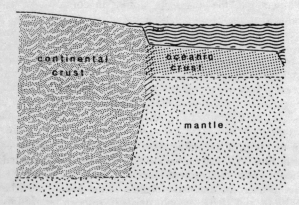

Figure 36

Another abnormality of the Earth's crust is that it is not uniform. In the parts we call "continents," its thickness varies from about 12 miles to almost 45 miles; but in the parts taken up by the oceans the crust is only 3.5 to five miles thick. While the average elevation of the continents is about 2,300 feet, the average depth of the oceans is more than 12,500 feet. The combined result of these factors is that the much thicker continental crust reaches much farther down into the mantle, whereas the oceanic crust is just a thin layer of solidified material and sediments (Fig. 36).

There are other differences between the Earth's crust where the continents are and where the oceans are. The composition of the continental crust, consisting in large part of rocks resembling granite, is relatively light in comparison with the composition of the mantle: the average continental density is 2.7–2.8 grams per cubic centimeter, while that of the mantle is 3.3 grams per cubic centimeter. The oceanic crust is heavier and denser than the continental crust, averaging a density of 3.0 to 3.1 grams per cubic centimeter; it is thus more akin to the mantle, with its composition of basaltic and other dense rocks, than to the continental crust. It is noteworthy that the "missing crust" the scientific team mentioned above suggested had dived into the mantle is similar in composition to the oceanic crust, not to the continental crust.

This leads to one more important difference between the Earth's continental and oceanic crusts. The continental part of the crust is not only lighter and thicker, it is also much older than the oceanic part of the crust. By the end of the 1970s the consensus among scientists was that the greater part of today's continental surface was formed some 2.8 billion years ago. Evidence of a continental crust from that time that was about as thick as today's is found in all the continents in what geologists term Archean Shield areas; but within those areas, crustal rocks were discovered that turned out to be 3.8 billion years old. In 1983, however, geologists of the Australian National University found, in western Australia, rock remains of a continental crust whose age was established to be 4.1 to 4.2 billion years old. In 1989, tests with new, sophisticated methods on rock samples collected a few years earlier in northern Canada (by researchers from Washington University in St. Louis and from the Geological Survey of Canada) determined the rocks' age to be 3.96 billion years; Samuel Bowering of Washington University reported evidence that nearby rocks in the area were as much as 4.1 billion years old.

Scientists are still hard put to explain the gap of about 500 million years between the age of the Earth (which meteor fragments, such as those found at Meteor Crater in Arizona, show to be 4.6 billion years) and the age of the oldest rocks thus far found; but no matter what the explanation, the fact that Earth had its continental crust at least 4 *billion* years ago is by now undisputed. On the other hand, no part of the oceanic crust has been found to be more than 200 *million* years old.

This is a tremendous difference that no amount of speculation about rising and sinking continents, forming and vanishing seas can explain. Someone has compared the Earth's crust to the skin of an apple. Where the oceans are, the "skin" is fresh—relatively speaking, born yesterday. Where the oceans began in primordial times, the "skin," and a good part of the "apple" itself, appear to have been shorn off.

The differences between the continental and oceanic crusts must have been even greater in earlier times, because the continental crust is constantly eroded by the forces of nature, and a good deal of the eroded solids are carried into the oceanic basins, increasing the thickness of the oceanic crust. Furthermore, the oceanic crust is constantly enhanced by the upwelling of molten basaltic rocks and silicates that flow up from the mantle through faults in the sea floor. This process, which puts down ever-new layers of oceanic crust, has been going on for 200 million years, giving the oceanic crust its present form. What was there at the bottom of the seas before then? Was there no crust at all, just a gaping "wound" in the Earth's surface? And is the ongoing oceanic crust formation akin to the process of blood clotting, where the skin is pierced and wounded?

Is Gaia—a living planet—trying to heal her wounds?

The most obvious place on the surface of the Earth where it was so "wounded" is the Pacific Ocean. While the average plunge in the crust's surface in its oceanic parts is about 2.5 miles, in the Pacific the crust has been gouged out to a present depth reaching at some points 7 miles. If we could remove from the Pacific's floor the crust built up there over the last 200 million years, we would arrive at depths reaching 12 miles below the water's surface and between some 20 to nearly 60 miles below the continental surface. This is quite a cavity. . . . How deep was it before the crustal buildup over the past 200 million years—how large was the "wound" 500 million years ago, a billion years ago, 4 billion years ago? No one can even guess, except to say that it was substantially deeper.

What can be said with certainty is that the extent of the gouging was more extensive, affecting a vastly greater part of the planet's surface. The Pacific Ocean at present occupies about a third of Earth's surface; but (as far as can be ascertained for the past 200 million years) it has been shrinking. The reason for the shrinkage is that the continents flanking it—the Americas on the east, Asia and Australia on the west—are moving closer to each other, squeezing out the Pacific slowly but relentlessly, reducing its size inch by inch year by year.

The science and explanations dealing with this process have come to be known as the Theory of Plate Tectonics. Its origin lies, as in the study of the Solar System, in the discarding of notions of a uniform, stable, permanent condition of the planets in favor of the recognition of catastrophism, change, and even evolution—concerning not only flora and fauna but the globes on which they evolved as "living" entities that can grow and shrink, prosper and suffer, even be born and die.

The new science of plate tectonics, it is now generally recognized, owes its beginning to Alfred Wegener, a German meteorologist, and his book *Die Entstehung der Kontinente und Ozeane*, published in 1915. As it was for others before him, his starting point was the obvious "fit" between the contours of the continents on both sides of the southern Atlantic. But before Wegener's ideas, the solution had been to postulate the disappearance, by sinking, of continents or land bridges: the belief that the continents have been where they are from time immemorial, but that a midsection sank below sea level, giving the appearance of continental separation. Augmenting available data on flora and fauna with considerable geological "matches" between the two sides of the Atlantic, Wegener came up with the notion of *Pangaea*—a supercontinent, a single huge landmass into which he could fit all the present continental masses like pieces in a jigsaw puzzle. Pangaea, which covered about one half of the globe, Wegener suggested, was surrounded by the primeval Pacific Ocean. Floating in the midst of the waters like an ice floe, the single landmass underwent a series of riftings and healings until a definite and final breakup in the Mesozoic Era, the geological period that lasted from 225 to 65 million years ago. Gradually the pieces began to drift apart. Antarctica, Australia, India, and Africa began to break away and separate (Fig. 37a). Subsequently, Africa and South America split apart (Fig. 37b) as North America began to move away from Europe and India was thrust toward Asia (Fig. 37c); and so the continents continued to drift until they rearranged themselves in the pattern we know today (Fig. 37d).

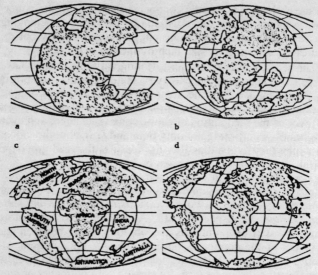

Figure 37

The split-up of Pangaea into several separate continents was accompanied by the opening up and closing down of bodies of water between the separating pieces of the landmass. In time the single "Panocean" (if I may be allowed to coin a term) also separated into a series of connecting oceans or enclosed seas (such as the Mediterranean, Black, and Caspian seas), and such major bodies of water as the Atlantic and the Indian oceans took shape. But all these bodies of water were "pieces" of the original "Panocean," of which the Pacific Ocean still remains.

Wegener's view of the continents as "pieces of a cracked ice floe" shifting atop an impermanent surface of the Earth was mostly received with disdain, even ridicule, by the geologists and paleontologists of the time. It took half a century for the idea of Continental Drift to be accepted into the halls of science. What helped bring about the changed attitude were surveys of the ocean floors begun in the 1960s that revealed such features as the Mid-Atlantic Ridge that, it was surmised, was formed by the rise of molten rock (called "magma") from the Earth's interior. Welling up, in the case of the Atlantic, through a fissure in the ocean floor that runs almost the whole ocean's length, the magma cooled and formed a ridge of basaltic rock. But then as one welling up followed another, the old sides of the ridge were pushed to either side to make way for the new magma flow. A major advance in these studies of the ocean floors took place with the aid of *Seasat*, an oceanographic satellite launched in June 1978 that orbited the Earth for three months; its data were used to map the sea floors, giving us an entirely new understanding of our oceans, with their ridges, rifts, seamounts, underwater volcanoes, and fracture zones. The discovery that as each upwelling of magma cooled and solidified it retained the magnetic direction of its position at that time was followed by the determination that a series of such magnetic lines, almost parallel to one another, provided a time scale as well as a directional map for the ongoing expansion of the ocean's floor. This expansion of the sea floor in the Atlantic was a major factor in pushing apart Africa and South America and in the creation of the Atlantic Ocean (and its continuing widening).

Other forces, such as the gravitational pull of the Moon, the Earth's rotation, and even movements of the underlying mantle, also are believed to act to split up the continental crust and shift the continents about. These forces also exert their influence, naturally, in the Pacific region. The Pacific Ocean revealed even more midocean ridges, fissures, underwater volcanoes, and other features like those that have worked to expand the Atlantic Ocean. Why, then, as all the evidence shows, have the landmasses flanking the Pacific not moved apart (as the continents flanking the Atlantic have done) but rather keep moving closer, slowly but surely, constantly *reducing* the size of the Pacific Ocean?

The explanation is found in a companion theory of continental drift, the Theory of Plate Tectonics. The continents, it has been postulated, rest upon giant movable ''plates'' of the Earth's crust, and so do the oceans. When the continents drift, when oceans expand (as the Atlantic) or contract (as the Pacific), the underlying cause is the movement of the plates on which they ride. At present scientists recognize six major plates (some of which are further subdivided): the Pacific, American, Eurasian, African, Indo-Australian, and Antarctic (Fig. 38).

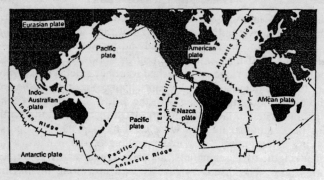

Figure 38

The spreading seafloor of the Atlantic Ocean is still distancing the Americas from Europe and Africa, inch by inch. The concomitant shrinking of the Pacific Ocean is now recognized to be accommodated by the dipping, or "subduction," of the Pacific plate under the American plate. This is the primary cause of the crustal shifts and earthquakes all along the Pacific rim, as well as of the rise of the major mountain chains along that rim. The collision of the Indian plate with the Eurasian one created the Himalayas and fused the Indian subcontinent to Asia. In 1985, Cornell University scientists discovered the "geological suture" where a part of the western African plate remained attached to the American plate when the two broke apart some fifty million years ago, "donating" Florida and southern Georgia to North America.

With some modifications, almost all scientists today accept Wegener's hypothesis of an Earth initially consisting of a single landmass surrounded by an all-embracing ocean. Notwithstanding (geologically) the young age (200 million years) of the present seafloor, scholars recognize that there had been a primeval ocean on Earth whose traces can be found not in the newly covered depths of the oceans but on the continents. The Archean Shield zones, where the youngest rocks are 2.8 billion years old, contain belts of two kinds: one of greenstone, another of granite-gneiss. Writing in *Scientific American* of March, 1977, Stephen Moorbath ("The Oldest Rocks and the Growth of Continents") reported that geologists "believe that the greenstone belt rocks were deposited in a primitive oceanic environment and in effect represent ancient oceans, and that the granite-gneiss terrains may be remnants of ancient oceans.'' Extensive rock records in virtually all the continents indicate that they were contiguous to oceans of water for more than three billion years; in some places, such as Zimbabwe in southern Africa, sedimentary rocks show that they accreted within large bodies of water some 3.5 billion years ago. And recent advances in scientific dating have extended the age of the Archean belts—those that include rocks that had been deposited in primeval oceans—back to 3.8 billion years (*Scientific American*, September, 1983; special issue: ''The Dynamic Earth'').

How long has continental drift been going on? Was there a Pangaea?

Stephen Moorbath, in the above-mentioned study, offered the conclusion that the process of continental breakup began some 600 million years ago: ''Before that there may have been just the one immense supercontinent known as Pangaea, or possibly two supercontinents: Laurasia to the north and Gondwanaland to the south.'' Other scientists, using computer simulations, suggest that 550 million years ago the landmasses that eventually formed Pangaea or its two connected parts were no less separate than they are today, that plate-tectonic processes of one kind or another have been going on since at least about four billion years ago. But whether the mass of dry land was first a single supercontinent or separate landmasses that then joined, whether a superocean surrounded a single mass of dry land or bodies of water first stretched between several dry lands, is, in the words of Moorbath, like the chicken-and-the-egg argument: ''Which came first, the continents or the oceans?''

Modern science thus confirms the scientific notions that were expressed in the ancient texts, but it cannot see far enough back to resolve the landmass/ocean sequence. If every modern scientific discovery seems to have corroborated this or that aspect of ancient knowledge, why not also accept the ancient answer in this instance: that the waters covered the face of the Earth and—on the third ''day,'' or phase—were ''gathered into'' one side of the Earth to reveal the dry land. Was the

uncovered dry land made up of isolated continents or one
supercontinent, a Pangaea? Although it really matters not as
far as the corroboration of ancient knowledge is concerned, it
is interesting to note that Greek notions of Earth, although they
led to a belief that the Earth was disklike rather than a globe,
envisioned it as a landmass with a solid foundation surrounded
by waters. This notion must have drawn on earlier and more
accurate knowledge, as most of Greek science did. We find
that the Old Testament repeatedly referred to the "foundations" of Earth and expressed knowledge of the earlier times
regarding the shape of Earth in the following verses praising
the Creator:

> The Lord's is the Earth and its entirety,
> the world and all that dwells therein.
> For He hath founded it upon the seas
> and established it upon the waters.
>
> (Psalm 24:1–2)

In addition to the term *Eretz* which means both planet
"Earth" and "earth, ground," the narrative in Genesis em-
ploys the term *Yabashah*—literally, "the dried-out landmass"—when it states that the waters "were gathered together
into one place" to let the Yabashah appear. But throughout
the Old Testament another term, *Tebel*, is frequently used to
denote that part of Earth that is habitable, arable, and useful
to Mankind (including being a source of ores). The term *Tebel*—usually translated as either "the earth" or "the world"—
is mostly employed to indicate the part of Earth distinct from
its watery portions; the "foundations" of this *Tebel* were in
juxtaposition to the sea basins. This was best expressed in the
Song of David (2 Samuel 22:16 and Psalm 18:16):

> The Lord thundered from the heavens,
> the Most High his sounds uttered.
> He loosed his arrows, sped them far and wide;
> a shaft of lightning, and disconcerted them.
> The channels of the seabed were revealed,
> the foundation of *Tebel* were laid bare.

With what we know today about the "foundations of the
Earth," the word *Tebel* clearly conveys the concept of conti-

nents whose foundations—tectonic plates—are laid in the midst of the waters. What a thrill to discover the latest geophysical theories echoed in a 3,000-year-old psalm!

The Genesis narrative states clearly that the waters were "gathered together" to one side of the Earth so that the dry land could emerge; this implies the existence of a cavity into which the waters could be gathered. Such a cavity, somewhat over half the Earth's surface, is still there, shrunken and reduced, in the shape of the Pacific Ocean.

Why is the crustal evidence that can be found not older than about 4 billion years, rather than the 4.6 billion years that is the presumed age of the Earth and of the Solar System? The first Conference on the Origins of Life, held in Princeton, New Jersey, in 1967, under the sponsorship of NASA and the Smithsonian Institution, dwelt at length on this problem. The only hypothesis the learned participants could come up with was that, at the time the oldest rock specimens that have been found were formed, Earth was subjected to a "cataclysm." In the discussion of the origins of Earth's atmosphere, the consensus was that it did not result from a "continuous outgassing" through volcanic activity but was (in the words of Raymond Siever of Harvard University) the result of "a rather early and rather large outgassing episode . . . a great big belch of the gases that are now characteristic of the Earth's atmosphere and sediments." This "big belch" was also dated to the same time as the catastrophe recorded by the rocks.

It thus becomes evident that in its specifics—the breakup of the Earth's crust, the process of plate tectonics, the differences between the continental and the oceanic crusts, the emergence of a Pangaea from under the waters, the primordial encircling ocean—the findings of modern science have corroborated the ancient knowledge. They have also led scientists from all disciplines to conclude that the only explanation of the way in which Earth's landmasses, oceans, and atmosphere have evolved is to assume a cataclysm occurring about four billion years ago—about half a billion years after the initial formation of Earth as part of the Solar System.

What was that cataclysm? Mankind has possessed the Sumerian answer for six thousand years: the Celestial Battle between Nibiru/Marduk and Tiamat.

In that Sumerian cosmogony, the members of the Solar System were depicted as celestial gods, male and female, whose creation was compared to birth, whose existence was that of living creatures. In the *Enuma elish* text, Tiamat in particular was described as a female, a mother who gave birth to a host of eleven satellites, her "horde," led by Kingu "whom she elevated." As Nibiru/Marduk and his horde neared her, "in fury Tiamat cried out aloud, her legs shook to their roots . . . against her attacker she repeatedly cast a spell." When the "Lord spread his net to enmesh her" and "the Evil Wind, which followed behind, he let loose in her face, Tiamat opened her mouth to consume it"; but then other "winds" of Nibiru/Marduk "charged her belly" and "distended her body." Indeed, "go and cut off the life of Tiamat" was the order given by the outer planets to the Invader; he accomplished that by "cutting through her insides, splitting her heart. . . . Having thus subdued her, he extinguished her life."

For a long time this view of the planets, and especially of Tiamat, as living entities that could be born and could die has been dismissed as primitive paganism. But the exploration of the planetary system in recent decades has, in fact, revealed worlds for which the word "alive" has been repeatedly used. That Earth itself is a living planet was forcefully put forth as the Gaia Hypothesis by James E. Lovelock in the 1970s (*Gaia—A New Look at Life on Earth*) and was most recently reinforced by him in *The Ages of Gaia: A Biography of Our Living Earth*. It is a hypothesis that views the Earth and the life that has evolved upon it as a single organism; Earth is not just an inanimate globe upon which there is life; it is a coherent if complex body that is itself alive through its mass and land surface, its oceans and atmosphere, and through the flora and fauna which it sustains and which in turn sustain Earth. "The largest living creature on Earth," Lovelock wrote, "is the Earth itself." And in that, he admitted, he was revisiting the ancient "concept of Mother Earth, or as the Greeks called her long ago, Gaia."

But in fact he had gone back to Sumerian times, to their ancient knowledge of the planet that was cleaved apart.

6

WITNESS TO GENESIS

Perhaps as an overreaction to Creationism, scientists have considered the biblical tale of Genesis as a subject of faith, not fact. Yet when one of the rocks brought back from the Moon by Apollo astronauts turned out to be almost 4.1 billion years old, it was nicknamed "the Genesis rock." When a tiny piece of green glass shaped like a lima bean turned up in lunar soil samples gathered by the Apollo 14 astronauts, the scientists dubbed it "the Genesis bean." It thus appears that in spite of all the objections and reservations, even the scientific community cannot escape the age-old faith, belief, gut feelings, or perhaps some genetic memory of the species called Mankind, that a primordial truth underlies the narrative of the Book of Genesis.

However the Moon became a constant companion of Earth—the various theories will soon be examined—it, like Earth, belonged to the same Solar System, and the histories of both go back to its creation. On Earth, erosion caused by the forces of nature as well as by the life that has evolved on it has obliterated much of the evidence bearing on that creation, to say nothing of the cataclysmic event that changed and revamped the planet. But the Moon, so it was assumed, had remained in its pristine condition. With neither winds, atmosphere, nor waters, there were no forces of erosion. A look at the Moon was tantamount to a peek at Genesis.

Man has peered at the Moon for eons, first with the naked eye, then with Earth-based instruments. The space age made it possible to probe the Moon more closely. Between 1959 and 1969, a number of Soviet and American unmanned spacecraft photographed and otherwise examined the Moon either by orbiting it or by landing on it. Then Man finally set foot on the

Plate D

Moon when the landing module of *Apollo 11* touched down on the Moon's surface on July 20, 1969, and Neil Armstrong announced, for all the world to hear: "Houston! Tranquility Base here. The *Eagle* has landed!"

In all, six *Apollo* spacecraft set down a total of twelve astronauts on the Moon; the last manned mission was that of *Apollo 17*, in December 1972. The first one was admittedly intended primarily to "beat the Russians to the Moon"; but the missions became increasingly scientific as the Apollo program progressed. The equipment for the tests and experiments became more sophisticated, the choice of landing sites was more scientifically oriented, the areas covered increased with the aid of surface vehicles, and the length of stay increased from hours to days. Even the crew makeup changed, to include in the last mission a trained geologist, Harrison Schmitt; his expertise was invaluable in the on-the-spot selection of rocks and soil to be taken back to Earth, in the description and evaluation of dust and other lunar materials left behind, and in the choice and description of topographic features—hills, valleys, small canyons, escarpments, and giant boulders (Plate D)—without which the true face of the Moon would have remained inscrutable. Instruments were left on the Moon to measure and record its phenomena over long periods; deeper soil samples were obtained by drilling into the face of the Moon; but most scientifically precious and rewarding were the 838 pounds of lunar soil and Moon rocks brought back to Earth. Their examination, analysis, and study were still in progress as the twentieth anniversary of the first landing was being celebrated.

The notion of "Genesis rocks" to be found on the Moon was proposed to NASA by the Nobel laureate Harold Urey. The so-called Genesis rock that was one of the very first to be picked up on the Moon proved, as the Apollo program progressed, not to be the oldest one. It was "only" some 4.1 billion years old, whereas the rocks later found on the Moon ranged from 3.3 billion-year-old "youngsters" to 4.5 billion-year "old-timers." Barring a future discovery of somewhat older rocks, the oldest rocks found on the Moon have thus brought its age to within 100 million years of the estimated age of the Solar System—of 4.6 billion years—which until then was surmised only from the age of meteorites that struck the Earth.

The Moon, the lunar landings established, was a Witness to Genesis.

Establishing the age of the Moon, the time of its creation, intensified the debate concerning the question of *how* the Moon was created.

"The hope of establishing the Moon's origin was a primary scientific rationale for the manned landings of the Apollo project in the 1960s," James Gleick wrote in June 1986 for *The New York Times* Science Service. It was, however, "the great question that Apollo failed to answer."

How could modern science read an uneroded "Rosetta stone" of the Solar System, so close by, so much studied, landed upon six times—and not come up with an answer to the basic question? The answer to the puzzle seems to be that the findings were applied to a set of preconceived notions; and because none of these notions is correct, the findings appear to leave the question unanswered.

One of the earliest scientific theories regarding the Moon's origin was published in 1879 by Sir George H. Darwin, second son of Charles Darwin. Whereas his father put forth the theory regarding the origin of species on Earth, Sir George was the first to develop a theory of origins for the Sun-Earth-Moon system based on mathematical analysis and geophysical theory. His specialty was the study of tides; he therefore conceived of the Moon as having been formed from matter pulled off Earth by solar tides. The Pacific basin was later postulated to be the scar that remained after this "pinching off" of part of Earth's body to form the Moon.

Although, as the *Encyclopaedia Britannica* puts it so mildly, it is "a hypothesis now considered unlikely to be true," the idea reappeared in the twentieth century as one of three contenders for being proved or disproved by the lunar findings. Given a high-tech name, the *Fission Theory*, it was revived with a difference. In the reconstructed theory, the simplistic idea of the tidal pull of the Sun was dropped; instead it was proposed that the Earth divided into two bodies while spinning very rapidly during its formation. The spinning was so rapid that a chunk of the material of which the Earth was forming was thrown off, coalesced at some distance from the bulk of the Earthly matter, and eventually remained orbiting its bigger twin brother as its permanent satellite (Fig. 39).

The "thrown-off chunk" theory, whether in its earlier or renewed form, has been conclusively rejected by scientists from various disciplines. Studies presented at the third Conference on the Origins of Life (held in Pacific Palisades, California, in 1970) established that tidal forces as the cause of the fission could not account for the origin of the Moon beyond a distance of five Earth radii, whereas the Moon is some 60 Earth radii away from the Earth. Also, scientists consider a study by Kurt S. Hansen in 1982 (*Review of Geophysics and Space Physics*, vol. 20) as showing conclusively that the Moon could never have been closer to Earth than 140,000 miles; this would rule out any theory that the Moon was once part of Earth (the Moon is now an average distance of about 240,000 miles from Earth, but this distance has not been constant).

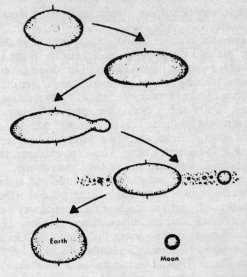

Figure 39

Proponents of the Fission Theory have offered various variants thereof in order to overcome the distance problem, which is further constrained by a concept termed the *Roche limit* (the distance within which the tidal forces overcome the gravitational force). But all variants of the fission theory have been rejected because they violate the laws of the preservation of energy. The theory requires much more angular momentum than has been preserved in the energy that exists to spin the Earth and the Moon around their axes and to orbit around the Sun. Writing in the book *Origin of the Moon* (1986), John A. Wood of the Harvard-Smithsonian Center for Astrophysics ("A Review of Hypotheses of Formation of Earth's Moon") summed up this constraint thus: "The fission model has very severe dynamic problems: In order to fission, the Earth had to have about four times as much angular momentum as the Earth-Moon system now has. There is no good explanation why the Earth had such an excess of angular momentum in the first place, or where the surplus angular momentum went after fission occurred.''

The knowledge about the Moon acquired from the Apollo program has added geologists and chemists to the lineup of scientists rejecting the fission theory. The Moon's composition is in many respects similar to that of Earth, yet different in key respects. There is sufficient "kinship" to indicate they are very close relatives, but there are enough differences to show they are not twin brothers. This is especially true of the Earth's crust and mantle, from which the Moon had to be formed, according to the fission theory. Thus, for example, the Moon has too little of the elements called "siderophile," such as tungsten, phosphorus, cobalt, molybendum, and nickel, compared with the amount of these substances present in the Earth's mantle and crust; and too much of the "refractory" elements such as aluminum, calcium, titanium, and uranium. In a highly technical summary of the various findings ("The Origin of the Moon," *American Scientist*, September–October 1975), Stuart R. Taylor stated: "For all these reasons, it is difficult to match the composition of the bulk of the Moon to that of the terrestrial mantle.''

The book *Origin of the Moon*, apart from its introductions and summaries (such as the above-mentioned article by J. A. Wood), is a collection of papers presented by sixty-two scientists at the Conference on the Origin of the Moon held at Kona, Hawaii, in October 1984—the most comprehensive since the conference twenty years earlier that had mapped out the scientific goals of the unmanned and manned Moon probes. In their papers, the contributing scientists, approaching the problem from various disciplines, invariably reached conclusions against the fission theory. Comparisons of the composition of the upper mantle of the Earth with that of the Moon, Michael J. Drake of the University of Arizona stated, "rigorously exclude" the Rotational Fission hypothesis.

The laws of angular momentum plus the comparisons of the composition of the Moon with that of Earth's mantle also ruled out, after the landings on the Moon, the second favored theory, that of *Capture*. According to this theory, the Moon was formed not near the Earth but among the outer planets or even beyond them. Somehow thrown off into a vast elliptical orbit around the Sun, it passed too closely to the Earth, was caught by the Earth's gravitational force, and became Earth's satellite.

This theory, it was pointed out after numerous computer studies, required an extremely slow approach by the Moon toward the Earth. This capture process not unlike that of the satellites we have sent to be captured and remain in orbit around Mars or Venus, fails to take into account the relative sizes of Earth and Moon. Relative to the Earth, the Moon (about one-eightieth the mass of Earth) is much too large to have been snared from a vast elliptical orbit unless it was moving very slowly; but then, all the calculations have shown, the result would be not a capture but a collision. This theory was further laid to rest by comparisons of the compositions of the two celestial bodies: the Moon was too similar to Earth and too dissimilar to the outer bodies to have been born so far away from Earth.

Extensive studies of the Capture Theory suggested that the Moon would have remained intact only if it had neared Earth, not from way out, but from the very same part of the heavens where Earth itself was formed. This conclusion was accepted even by S. Fred Singer of George Mason University—a proponent of the capture hypothesis—in his paper ("Origin of the Moon by Capture") presented at the above-mentioned Conference on the Origin of the Moon. "Capture from an eccentric heliocentric orbit is neither feasible nor necessary," he stated; the oddities in the Moon's composition "can be explained in terms of a Moon formed in an Earthlike orbit": the Moon was "captured" while forming near Earth.

These admissions by proponents of the fission and the capture theories lent support to the third main theory that was previously current, that of *Coaccretion*, a common birth. This theory has its roots in the hypothesis proposed at the end of the eighteenth century by Pierre-Simon de Laplace, who said that the Solar System was born of a nebular gas cloud that coalesced in time to form the Sun and the planets—a hypothesis that has been retained by modern science. Showing that lunar accelerations are dependent on eccentricities in the Earth's orbit, Laplace concluded that the two bodies were formed side by side, first the Earth and then the Moon. The Earth and the Moon, he suggested, were sister planets, partners in a binary, or two-planet, system, in which they orbit the Sun together while one "dances" around the other.

That natural satellites, or moons, coalesce from the remainder of the same primordial matter of which their parent planet was formed is now the generally accepted theory of how planets acquired moons and should also apply to Earth and the Moon. As has been found by the Pioneer and Voyager spacecraft, the moons of the outer planets—that had to be formed, by and large, out of the same primordial material as their "parents"— are both sufficiently akin to their parent planets and at the same time reveal individual characteristics as "children" do; this might well be true also for the basic similarities and sufficient dissimilarities between the Earth and the Moon.

What nevertheless makes scientists reject this theory when it is applied to the Earth and the Moon is their relative sizes. The Moon is simply too large relative to the Earth—not only about one-eightieth of its mass but about one quarter of its diameter. This relationship is out of all proportion to what has been found elsewhere in the Solar System. When the mass of all the moons of each planet (excluding Pluto) is given as a ratio of the planet's mass, the result is as follows:

Mercury	0.0 (no moons)
Venus	0.0 (no moons)
EARTH	0.0122
Mars	0.00000002 (2 asteroids)
Jupiter	0.00021
Saturn	0.00025
Uranus	0.00017
Neptune	0.00130

A comparison of the relative sizes of the largest moon of each of the other planets with the size of the Moon relative to Earth (Fig. 40) also clearly shows the anomaly. One result of this disproportion is that there is too much angular momentum in the combined Earth-Moon system to support the Binary Planets hypothesis.

With all three basic theories unable to meet some of the required criteria, one may end up wondering how Earth ended up with its satellite at all . . . Such a conclusion, in fact, does

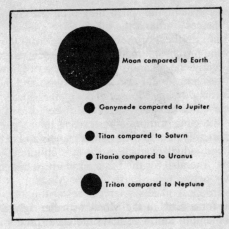

Figure 40

not bother some; they point to the fact that none of the terrestrial planets (other than Earth) have satellites: the two tiny bodies that orbit Mars are, all are agreed, captured asteroids. If conditions in the Solar System were such that none of the planets formed between the Sun and Mars (inclusive) obtained satellites in any one of the considered methods—Fission, Capture, Coaccretion—should not Earth, too, being within this moonless zone, have been without a moon? But the fact remains that Earth as we know it and *where we know it* does have a moon, and an extremely large one (in proportion) to boot. So how to account for that?

Another finding of the Apollo program also stands in the way of accepting the coaccretion theory. The Moon's surface as well as its mineral content suggest a "magma ocean" created by partial melting of the Moon's interior. For that, a source of heat great enough to melt the magma is called for. Such heat can result only from cataclysmic or catastrophic event; in the coaccretion scenario no such heat is produced. How then explain the magma ocean and other evidence on the Moon of a cataclysmic heating?

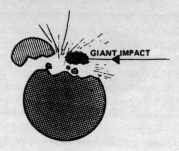

Figure 41

The need for a birth of the Moon with the right amount of angular momentum and a cataclysmic, heat-producing event led to a post-Apollo program hypothesis that has been dubbed the *Big Whack Theory*. It developed from the suggestion by William Hartmann, a geochemist at the Planetary Science Institute in Tucson, Arizona, and his colleague Donald R. Davis in 1975 that collisions and impacts played a role in the creation of the Moon ("Satellite-sized Planetesimals and Lunar Origin," *Icarus*, vol. 24). According to their calculations, the rate at which planets were bombarded by small and large asteroids during the late stages of the planets' formation was much higher than at present; some of the asteroids were big enough to deliver a blow that could chip off parts of the planet they hit; in Earth's case, the blown-off chunk became the Moon.

The idea was taken up by two astrophysicists, Alastair G. W. Cameron of Harvard and William R. Ward of Caltech. Their study, "The Origin of the Moon" (*Lunar Science*, vol. 7, 1976) envisioned a planet-sized body—*at least* as large as the planet Mars—racing toward the Earth at 24,500 miles per hour; coming from the outer reaches of the Solar System, its path arced toward the Sun—but the Earth, in its formative orbit, stood in the way. The "glancing blow" that resulted (Fig. 41) slightly tilted the Earth, giving it its ecliptic obliquity (currently about 23.5 degrees); it also melted the outer layers of both bodies, sending a plume of vaporized rock into orbit around the Earth. More than twice as much material as was needed to form the Moon was shot up, with the force of the expanding vapor acting to distance the debris from Earth. Some of the ejected material fell back to Earth, but enough remained far enough away to eventually coalesce and become the Moon.

This *Collision-Ejection* theory was further perfected by its authors as various problems raised by it were pointed out; it was also modified as other scientific teams tested it through computer simulations (the leading teams were those of A. C. Thompson and D. Stevenson at Caltech, H. J. Melosh and M. Kipp at Sandia National Laboratories, and W. Benz and W. L. Slattery at Los Alamos National Laboratory).

Under this scenario (Fig. 42 shows a simulated sequence,

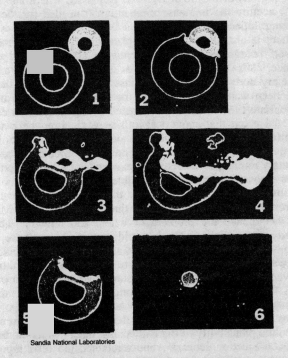

Sandia National Laboratories

Figure 42

lasting about eighteen minutes in all), the impact resulted in immense heat (perhaps 12,000 degrees Fahrenheit) that caused a melting of both bodies. The bulk of the impactor sank to the center of the molten Earth; portions of both bodies were vaporized and thrust out. On cooling, the Earth re-formed with the iron-rich bulk of the impactor at its core. Some of the ejected material fell back to Earth; the rest, mostly from the impactor, cooled and coalesced at a distance—resulting in the Moon that now orbits the Earth.

Another major departure from the original Big Whack hypothesis was the realization that in order to resolve chemical composition constraints, the impactor had to come from the same place in the heavens as Earth itself did—not from the outer regions of the Solar System. But if so, where and how did it acquire the immense momentum it needed for the vaporizing impact?

There is also the question of plausibility, which Cameron himself recognized in his presentation at the Hawaii conference. "Is it plausible," he asked, "that an extra-planetary body with about the mass of Mars or more should have been wandering around in the inner solar system at an appropriate time to have participated in our postulated collision?" He felt that about 100 million years after the planets were formed, there were indeed enough planetary instabilities in the newborn Solar System and enough "proto-planetary remnants" to make the existence of a large impactor and the postulated collision plausible.

Subsequent calculations showed that in order to achieve the end results, the impactor had to be three times the size of Mars. This heightened the problem of where and how in Earth's vicinity such a celestial body could accrete. In response, astronomer George Wetherill of the Carnegie Institute calculated backward and found that the terrestrial planets could have evolved from a roaming band of some five hundred planetesimals. Repeatedly colliding among themselves, the small moonlets acted as the building blocks of the planets and of the bodies that continued to bombard them. The calculations supported the plausibility of the Big Whack theory in its modified Collision-Ejection scenario, but it retained the resulting immense heat. "The heat of such an impact," Wetherill concluded, "would have melted both bodies." This, it seemed, could explain a) how the Earth got its iron core and b) how the Moon got its molten magma oceans.

Although this latest version left many other constraints unmet, many of the participants in the 1984 Conference on the Origin of the Moon were ready, by the time the conference ended, to treat the collision-ejection hypothesis as the leading contender—not so much out of conviction of its correctness as out of exasperation. "This happened," Wood wrote in his summary, "mainly because several independent investigators showed that coaccretion, the model that had been most widely accepted by lunar scientists (at least at a subconscious level), could not account for the angular momentum content of the Earth-Moon system." In fact, some of the participants at the conference, including Wood himself, saw vexing problems inherent in the new theory. Iron, Wood pointed out, "is actually quite volatile and would have suffered much the same fate as the other volatiles, like sodium and water"; in other words, it would not have sunk intact into the Earth's core as the theory postulates. The abundance of water on Earth, to say nothing of the abundance of iron in the Earth's mantle, would not have been possible if Earth had melted down.

Since each variant of the Big Whack hypothesis involved a total meltdown of the Earth, it was necessary that other evidence of such a meltdown be found. But as was overwhelmingly reported at the 1988 Origin of the Earth Conference at Berkeley, California, no such evidence exists. If Earth had melted and resolidified, various elements in its rocks would have crystallized differently from the way they actually are found, and they would have reappeared in certain ratios, but this is not the case. Another result should have been the distortion of the chondrite material—the most primordial matter on Earth that is also found in the most primitive meteorites— but no such distortion has been found. One investigator, A. E. Ringwood of the Australian National University, extended these tests to more than a dozen elements whose relative abundance should have been altered had the first crust of Earth been formed after an Earth meltdown; but there was no such alteration to any significant extent. In a review of these findings in *Science* (March 17, 1989) it was pointed out that at the 1988 conference the geochemists "contended that a giant impact and its inevitable melting of Earth do not jibe with what they know of geochemistry. In particular, the composition of the upper few hundred kilometers of the mantle implies it has not been totally molten at any time." "Geochemistry," the authors of the article in *Science* concluded, "would thus seem to be a potential stumbling block for the giant-impact origin of the moon." In "Science and Technology," (*The Economist*, July 22, 1989) it was likewise reported that numerous studies have led geochemists "to be skeptical about the impact story."

Like the previous theories, the Big Whack also ended up meeting some constraints but failing others. Still, one should ask whether, while this theory of impact-meltdown ran into problems when applied to Earth, did it not at least solve the problem of the melting that is evident on the Moon?

As it turned out, not exactly so. Thermal studies did, indeed, indicate the Moon had experienced a great meltdown. "The indications are that the Moon was largely or totally molten early in lunar history," Alan B. Binder of NASA's Johnson Space Center said at the 1984 Conference on the Origin of the Moon. "Early," but not "initial," countered other scientists. This crucial difference was based on studies of stresses in the Moon's crust (by Sean C. Solomon of the Massachusetts Institute of Technology), as well of isotope ratios (when atomic nuclei of the same element have different masses because they have different numbers of neutrons) studied by D. L. Turcotte and L. H. Kellog of Cornell University. These studies, the 1984 conference was told, "support a relatively cool origin for the Moon."

What, then, of the evidence of meltings on the Moon? There is no doubt that they have occurred: the giant craters, some a hundred or more miles in diameter, are silent witnesses visible to all. There are the maria ("seas"), that, it is now known, were not bodies of water but areas of the Moon's surface flattened by immense impacts. There are the magma oceans. There are glass and glassy material embedded in the rocks and grains of the Moon's surface that resulted from shock melting of the surface caused by high-velocity impacts (as distinct from heated lava as a source). At the third Conference on the Origins of Life, a whole day was devoted to the subject of "Glass on the Moon,'' so important was this clue held to be. Eugene Shoemaker of NASA and Caltech reported that such evidence of ''shock vitrified'' glasses and other types of melted rock were found in abundance on the Moon; the presence of nickel in the glassy spheres and beads suggested to him that the impactor had a composition different from that of the Moon, since the Moon's own rocks lack nickel.

When did all these impacts that caused the surface melting take place? Not, the findings showed, when the Moon was created but some 500 million years afterward. It was then, NASA scientists reported at a 1972 press conference and subsequently, that ''the Moon had undergone a convulsive evolution.'' ''The most cataclysmic period came 4 billion years ago, when celestial bodies the size of large cities and small countries came crashing into the Moon and formed its huge basins and towering mountains. The huge amounts of radioactive minerals left by the collisions began heating the rock beneath the surface, melting massive amounts of it and forcing seas of lava through cracks in the surface. . . . Apollo 15 found rockslides in the crater Tsiolovsky six times greater than any rockslide on Earth. Apollo 16 discovered that the collision that created the Sea of Nectar deposited debris as much as 1,000 miles away. Apollo 17 landed near a scarp eight times higher than any on Earth.''

The oldest rocks on the Moon were judged to be 4.25 billion years old; soil particles gave a date of 4.6 billion years. The age of the Moon, all 1,500 or so scientists who have studied the rocks and soil brought back agree, dates back to the time the Solar System first took shape. But then something happened about 4 billion years ago. Writing in *Scientific American* (January 1977), William Hartmann, in his article ''Cratering in the Solar System,'' reported that ''various Apollo analysts have found that the age of many samples of lunar rocks cuts off rather sharply at four billion years; few older rocks have survived.'' The rocks and soil samples that contained the glasses formed by the intense impacts were as old as 3.9 billion years. ''We know that a widespread cataclysmic episode of intense bombardment destroyed older rocks and surfaces of the planets,'' Gerald J. Wasserburg of Caltech stated on the eve of the last Apollo mission; the remaining question, then, was "what happened between the origin of the Moon about 4.6 billion years ago and 4 billion years ago," when the catastrophe occurred.

So the rock found by astronaut David Scott that was nick-named "the Genesis Rock" was not formed at the time the Moon was formed, it was actually formed as a result of that catastrophic event some 600 million years later. Even so, it was appropriately named; for the tale in Genesis is not that of the primordial forming of the Solar System 4.6 billion years ago, but of the Celestial Battle of Nibiru/Marduk with Tiamat some 4 billion years ago.

Unhappy with all the theories that have so far been offered for the origin of the Moon, some have attempted to select the best one by grading the theories according to certain constraints and criteria. A "Truth Table" prepared by Michael J. Drake of the University of Arizona Lunar and Planetary Laboratory had the Coaccretion theory far ahead of all others. In John A. Wood's analysis it met all the criteria except that of the Earth-Moon angular momentum and the melting on the Moon; otherwise it bettered all others. The consensus has now focused again on the Coaccretion theory, with some elements borrowed from the Giant Impact and Fission theories. According to the theory offered at the 1984 Conference by A. P. Boss of the Carnegie Institute and S. J. Peale of the University of California, the Moon is indeed seen as coaccreting with Earth from the same primoridal matter, but the gas cloud within which the coaccretion took place was subjected to bombardments by planetesimals, which sometimes disintegrated the forming Moon and sometimes added foreign material to its mass (Fig. 43). The net result was an ever-larger Moon attracting and absorbing other moonlets that were forming within the circumterrestrial ring—a Moon both akin to and somewhat different from the Earth.

Having swung from theory to theory, modern science now embraces as a theory for the origin of our Moon the same process that gave the outer planets their multimoon systems. The hurdle still to be overcome is the need to explain why, instead of a swarm of smaller moons, a too-small Earth has ended up with a single, too-large Moon.

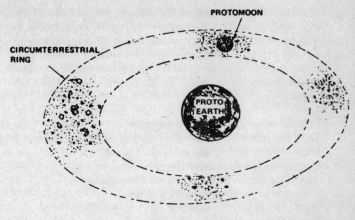

Figure 43

For the answer, we have to go back to Sumerian cosmogony. The first help it offers modern science is its assertion that the Moon originated not as a satellite of Earth but of the much larger Tiamat. Then—millennia before Western civilization had discovered the swarms of moons encircling Jupiter, Saturn, Uranus, and Neptune—the Sumerians ascribed to Tiamat a swarm of satellites, "eleven in all." They placed Tiamat beyond Mars, which would qualify her as an outer planet; and the "celestial horde" was acquired by her no differently than by the other outer planets.

When we compare the latest scientific theories with Sumerian cosmogony, we find not only that modern scientists have come around to accepting the same ideas found in the Sumerian body of knowledge but are even using terminology that mimics the Sumerian texts. . . .

Just as the latest modern theories do, the Sumerian cosmogony also describes the scene as that of an early, unstable Solar System where planetesimals and emerging gravitational forces disturb the planetary balance and, sometimes, cause moons to grow disproportionately. In *The 12th Planet*, I described the celestial conditions thus: "With the end of the

majestic drama of the birth of the planets, the authors of the
Creation Epic now raise the curtain on Act II, on a drama of
celestial turmoil. The newly created family of planets was far
from being stable. The planets were gravitating toward each
other; they were converging on Tiamat, disturbing and endan-
gering the primordial bodies.'' In the poetic words of the *Enuma elish*,

> The divine brothers banded together;
> They disturbed Tiamat as they surged back and forth.
> They were troubling the belly of Tiamat
> by their antics in the dwellings of heaven.
> Apsu [the Sun] could not lessen their clamor;
> Tiamat was speechless at their ways.
> Their doings were loathsome . . .
> Troublesome were their ways;
> they were overbearing.

''We have here obvious references to erratic orbits,'' I wrote
in *The 12th Planet*. The new planets ''surged back and forth'';
they got too close to each other (''banded together''); they
interfered with Tiamat's orbit; they got too close to her
''belly''; their ''ways''—orbits—''were troublesome''; their
gravitational pull was ''overbearing''—excessive, disregard-
ing the others' orbits.

Abandoning earlier concepts of a Solar System slowly cooling and gradually freezing into its present shape out of the hot
primordial cloud, scientific opinion has now swung in the opposite direction. ''As faster computers allow celestial me-
chanicians longer looks at the behavior of the planets,'' Richard
A. Kerr wrote in *Science* (''Research News,'' April 14, 1989),
''chaos is turning up everywhere.'' He quoted such studies as
that by Gerald J. Sussman and Jack Wisdom of the Massachusetts Institute of Technology in which they went back by
computer simulations and discovered that ''many orbits that
lie between Uranus and Neptune become chaotic,'' and that
''the orbital behavior of Pluto is chaotic and unpredictable.''
J. Laskar of the Bureau des Longitudes in Paris found original
chaos throughout the Solar System, ''but especially among the
inner planets, including Earth.''

George Wetherill, updating his calculations of multicollisions by some five hundred planetesimals (*Science*, May 17, 1985), described the process in the zone of the terrestrial planets as the accretion of "lots of brothers and sisters" that collided to form "trial planets." The process of accretion—crashing into one another, breaking up, capturing the material of others, until some grew larger and eventually became the terrestrial planets—he said, was nothing short of a "battle royal" that lasted most of the first 100 million years of the Solar System.

The eminent scientist's words are astoundingly similar to those of the *Enuma elish*. He speaks of "lots of brothers and sisters" moving about, colliding with each other, affecting each other's orbits and very existence. The ancient text speaks of "divine brothers" who "disturbed," "troubled," "surged back and forth" in the heavens in the very zone where Tiamat was, near her "belly." He uses the expression "battle royal" to describe the conflict between these "brothers and sisters." The Sumerian narrative uses the very same word—"battle"—to describe what happened, and recorded for all time the events of Genesis as the Celestial Battle.

We read in the ancient texts that as the celestial disturbances increased, Tiamat brought forth her own "host" with which "to do battle" with the celestial "brothers" who were encroaching on her:

> She has set up an Assembly
> and is furious with rage. . . .
> Withall, eleven of this kind she brought forth. . . .

> They thronged and marched at the side of Tiamat;
> Enraged, they plot ceaselessly day and night.
> They are set for combat, fuming and raging;
> They have assembled, prepared for conflict.

Just as modern astronomers are troubled by the disproportionately large size of the Moon, so were the authors of the *Enuma elish*. Putting words in the mouths of the other planets, they point to the expanding size and disturbing mass of "Kingu" as their chief complaint:

From among the gods who formed her host
her first-born, Kingu, she elevated;
In their midst she made him great.
To be head of her ranks, to command her host,
to raise weapons for the encounter,
to be in the lead for combat,
in the battle to be the commander—
these to the hand of Kingu she entrusted.
As she caused him to be in her host,
"I have cast a spell for thee," she said to him;
"I have made thee great in the assembly of the gods;
Dominion over the gods I have given unto thee.
Verily, thou art supreme!"

According to this ancient cosmogony, one of the eleven
moons of Tiamat did grow to an unusual size because of the
ongoing perturbations and chaotic conditions in the newly
formed Solar System. How the creation of this monstrous moon
affected these conditions is regrettably not clear from the ancient text; the enigmatic verses, with some of the original words
subject to different readings and translations, seem to say that
making Kingu "exalted" resulted in "making the fire subside"
(per E. A. Speiser), or "quieting the fire-god" (per A. Heidel)
and humbling /vanquishing the "Power-weapon which is so
potent in its sweep"—a possible reference to the disturbing
pull of gravitation.

Whatever quieting effect the enlargement of "Kingu" may
have had on Tiamat and her host, it proved increasingly dis-
ruptive to the other planets. Especially disturbing to them was
the elevation of Kingu to the status of a full-fledged planet:

She gave him a Tablet of Destinies,
fastened it on his breast. . . .
Kingu was elevated,
had received a heavenly rank.

It was this "sin" of Tiamat, her giving Kingu his own orbital
"destiny," that enraged the other planets to the point of "calling in" Nibiru/Marduk to put an end to Tiamat and her out-
of-line consort. In the ensuing Celestial Battle, as described

earlier, Tiamat was split in two: one half was shattered; the other half, accompanied by Kingu, was thrust into a new orbit to become the Earth and its Moon.

We have here a sequence that conforms with the best points of the various modern theories regarding the origin, evolution, and final fate of the Moon. Though the nature of the "power-weapon . . . so potent in its sweep" or that of "the fire-god" that caused Kingu to grow disproportionately large remain unclear, the fact of the disproportionate size of the Moon (even relative to the larger Tiamat) is recorded in all its disturbing details. All is there—except that it is not Sumerian cosmogony that corroborates modern science, but modern science that catches up with ancient knowledge.

Could the Moon have indeed been a planet-in-the-making, as the Sumerians said? As reviewed in earlier chapters, this was quite conceivable. Did it in fact assume planetary aspects? Contrary to long-held views that the Moon was always an inert object, it was found, in the 1970s and 1980s, to possess virtually all the attributes of a planet except its own independent orbit around the Sun. Its surface has regions of rugged and tangled mountains; it has plains and "seas" that, if not formed by water, were probably formed by molten lava. To the scientists' surprise the Moon was found to be layered, as the Earth is. In spite of the depletion of its iron by the catastrophic event discussed earlier, it appears to have retained an iron core. Scientists debate whether the core is still molten, for to their astonishment the Moon was found to have once possessed a magnetic field, which is caused by the rotation of a molten iron core, as is true of the Earth and other planets. Significantly, as studies by Keith Runcorn of Britain's University of New-castle-upon-Tyne indicate, the magnetism "dwindled away circa four billion years ago"—the time of the Celestial Battle.

Instruments installed on the Moon by Apollo astronauts relayed data that revealed "unexpectedly high heat flows from beneath the lunar surface," indicating ongoing activity inside the "lifeless orb." Vapor—*water* vapor—was detected by Rice University scientists, who reported (in October 1971) seeing "geysers of water vapor erupting through cracks in the lunar surface." Other unexpected findings reported at the Third Lunar Science Conference in Houston in 1972 disclosed ongoing volcanism on the Moon, which "would imply the simultaneous existence near the lunar surface of significant quantities of heat *and water*."

In 1973, "bright flashes" sighted on the Moon were found to be emissions of gas from the Moon's interior. Reporting this, Walter Sullivan, science editor of *The New York Times*, observed that it appeared that the Moon, even if not a "living celestial body . . . is at least a breathing one." Such puffs of gas and darkish mists have been observed in several of the Moon's deep craters from the very first Apollo mission and at least through 1980.

The indications that lunar volcanism may still be going on have led scientists to assume that the Moon once had a full-fledged atmosphere whose volatile elements and compounds included hydrogen, helium, argon, sulfur, carbon compounds, *and water*. The possibility that there may still be water below the Moon's surface has raised the intriguing question of whether water once flowed on the face of the Moon—water that, as a very volatile compound, evaporated and was dissipated into space.

Were it not for budgetary constraints, NASA would have been willing to adopt the recommendations of a panel of scientists to explore the Moon with a view to begin mining its mineral resources. Thirty geologists, chemists, and physicists who met in August 1977 at the University of California in San Diego pointed out that research on the Moon—both from orbit and on its surface—had been limited to its equatorial regions; they urged the launching of a lunar *polar* orbiter, not only because such an orbiter could collect data from the entire Moon, but also with a view to discovering if there is now water on the Moon. "One target of the orbiter's observations," according to James Arnold of the University of California, "would be small areas near each pole where the Sun never shines. It has been theorized by scientists that as much as 100 billion tons of water in the form of ice are likely to be found in those places. . . . If you're going to have large-scale activities in space, like mining and manufacturing, it's going to involve a lot of water; the Moon's polar regions could be a good source."

Whether the Moon still has water, after all the cataclysmic

events it has undergone, is still to be ascertained. But the increasing evidence that it may still have water in its interior and may have had water on its surface should not be surprising. After all, the Moon—alias Kingu—was the leading satellite of the "watery monster" Tiamat.

On the occasion of the last Apollo mission to the Moon, *The Economist* (Science and Technology, December 11, 1972) summed up the program's discoveries thus: "Perhaps the most important of all, exploration of the moon has shown that it is not a simple, uncomplicated sphere but a true planetary body."

"A true planetary body." Just as the Sumerians described millennia ago. And just as they stated millennia ago, the planet-to-be was not to become a planet with its own orbit around the Sun because it was deprived of that status as a result of the Celestial Battle. Here is what Nibiru/Marduk did to "Kingu":

> And Kingu, who had become chief among them,
> he made shrink, as a DUG.GA.E god he counted him.
> He took from him the Tablet of Destinies
> which was not rightfully his;
> He sealed on it his own seal
> and fastened it to his own breast.

Deprived of its orbital momentum, Kingu was reduced to the status of a mere satellite—our Moon.

The Sumerian observation that Nibiru/Marduk made Kingu "shrink" has been taken to refer to its reduction in rank and importance. But as recent findings indicate, the Moon has been depleted of the bulk of its iron by a cataclysmic event, resulting in a marked decrease in its density. "There are two planetary bodies within the Solar System whose peculiar mean density implies that they are unique and probably the products of unusual circumstances," Alastair Cameron wrote in *Icarus* (vol. 64, 1985); "these are the Moon and Mercury. The former has a low mean density and is greatly depleted in iron." In other words, Kingu has indeed shrunk!

There is other evidence that the Moon became more compact as a result of heavy impacts. On the side facing away from Earth—its far side—the surface has highlands and a thick

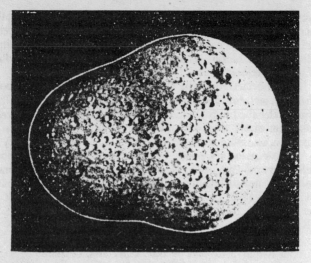

Figure 44

crust, while the near side—the side facing Earth—shows large, flat plains, as though the elevated features had been wiped off. Inside the Moon, gravitational variations reveal the existence of compacted, heavier masses in several concentrations, especially where the surface had been flattened out. Though outwardly the Moon (as do all celestial bodies larger than a minimal size) has a spherical shape, the mass in its core appears to have the shape of a gourd, as a computer study shows (Fig. 44). It is a shape that bears the mark of the "big whack" that compressed the Moon and thrust it into its new place in the heavens, just as the Sumerians had related.

The Sumerian assertion that Kingu was turned into a DUG.GA.E is equally intriguing. The term, I wrote in *The 12th Planet*, literally means "pot of lead." At the time I took it to be merely a figurative description of the Moon as "a mass of lifeless clay." But the Apollo discoveries suggest that the Sumerian term was not just figurative but was literally and scientifically correct. One of the initial puzzles encountered on the Moon was so-called "parentless lead." The Apollo program revealed that the top few miles of the Moon's crust are unusually rich in radioactive elements such as uranium. There was also evidence of the existence of extinct radon. These elements decay and become lead at either final or intermediary stages of the radioactive-decay process.

How the Moon became so enriched in radioactive elements remains an unresolved puzzle, but that these elements had mostly decayed into lead is now evident. Thus, the Sumerian assertion that Kingu was turned into a "pot of lead" is an accurate scientific statement.

The Moon was not only a Witness to Genesis. It is also a witness to the veracity of the biblical *Genesis*—to the accuracy of ancient knowledge.

IN THE ASTRONAUTS' OWN WORDS

Feeling changes of "almost a spiritual nature" in their views of themselves, of other humans, and of the possibility of intelligent life existing beyond Earth have been reported by almost all the American astronauts.

Gordon Cooper, who piloted *Mercury 9* in 1963 and co-piloted *Gemini 5* in 1965, returned with the belief that "intelligent, extraterrestrial life has visited Earth in ages past" and became interested in archaeology. Edward G. Gibson, a scientist aboard *Skylab 3* (1974), said that orbiting the Earth for days "makes you speculate a little more about life existing elsewhere in the universe."

Especially moved were the astronauts of the Apollo missions to the Moon. "Something happens to you out there," stated *Apollo 14* astronaut Ed Mitchell. Jim Irwin *(Apollo 15)* was "deeply moved . . . and felt the presence of God." His comrade on the mission, Al Worden, speaking on the twentieth anniversary of the first landing on the Moon on a TV program ("The Other Side of the Moon" produced by Michael G. Lemle) compared the lunar module that was used to land on and take off vertically from the Moon to the spaceship described in Ezekiel's vision.

"In my mind," said Al Worden, "the universe has to be cyclic; in one galaxy there is a planet becoming unlivable and in another part or a different galaxy there is a planet that is perfect for habitation, and I see some intelligent being, like us, skipping around from planet to planet, as South Pacific Indians do on islands, to continue the species. I think that's what the space program is all about. . . . I think we may be a combination of creatures that were living here on Earth some time in the past, and had a visitation by beings from somewhere else in the universe; and those two species getting together and having progeny. . . . In fact, a very small group of explorers could land on a planet and create successors to themselves who would eventually take up the pursuit of inhabiting the rest of the universe."

And Buzz Aldrin *(Apollo 11)* expressed the belief that "one of these days, through telescopes that may be in orbit, like the Hubble telescope, or other technical breakthroughs, we may learn that indeed we are not alone in this marvelous universe."

7

THE SEED OF LIFE

Of all the mysteries confronting Mankind's quest for knowledge, the greatest is the mystery called "life."

Evolution theory explains how life on Earth *evolved*, all the way from the earliest, one-celled creatures to *Homo sapiens*; it does not explain how life on Earth *began*. Beyond the question Are we alone? lies the more fundamental question: Is life on Earth unique, unmatched in our Solar System, our galaxy, the whole universe?

According to the Sumerians, life was brought into the Solar System by Nibiru; it was Nibiru that imparted the "seed of life" to Earth during the Celestial Battle with Tiamat. Modern science has come a long way toward the same conclusion.

In order to figure out how life might have begun on the primitive Earth, the scientists had to determine, or at least assume, what the conditions were on the newly born Earth. Did it have water? Did it have an atmosphere? What of life's main building blocks—molecular combinations of hydrogen, carbon, oxygen, nitrogen, sulfur, and phosphorus? Were they available on the young Earth to initiate the precursors of living organisms? At present the Earth's dry air is made up of 79 percent nitrogen (N_2), 20 percent oxygen (O_2) and 1 percent argon (Ar), plus traces of other elements (the atmosphere contains water vapor in addition to the dry air). This does not reflect the relative abundance of elements in the universe, where hydrogen (87 percent) and helium (12 percent) make up 99 percent of all abundant elements. It is therefore believed (among other reasons) that the present earthly atmosphere is not Earth's original one. Both hydrogen and helium are highly volatile, and their diminished presence in Earth's atmosphere, as well as its deficiency of "noble" gases such as neon, argon, krypton, and xenon (relative to their cosmic abundance), suggest to scientists that the Earth experienced a "thermal episode" sometime before 3.8 billion years ago—an occurrence with which my readers are familiar by now. . . .

By and large the scientists now believe that Earth's atmosphere was reconstituted initially from the gases spewed out by the volcanic convulsions of a wounded Earth. As clouds thrown up by these eruptions shielded the Earth and it began to cool, the vaporized water condensed and came down in torrential rains. Oxidation of rocks and minerals provided the first reservoir of higher levels of oxygen on Earth; eventually, plant life added both oxygen and carbon dioxide (CO_2) to the atmosphere and started the nitrogen cycle (with the aid of bacteria).

It is noteworthy that even in this respect the ancient texts stand up to the scrutiny of modern science. The fifth tablet of *Enuma elish*, though badly damaged, describes the gushing lava as Tiamat's "spittle" and places the volcanic activity earlier than the formation of the atmosphere, the oceans, and the continents. The spittle, the text states, was "laying in layers" as it poured forth. The phase of "making the cold" and the "assembling of the water clouds" are described; after that the "foundations" of Earth were raised and the oceans were gathered—just as the verses in Genesis have reiterated. It was only thereafter that life appeared on Earth: green herbage upon the continents and "swarms" in the waters.

But living cells, even the simplest ones, are made up of complex molecules of various organic compounds, not just of separate chemical elements. How did these molecules come about? Because many of these compounds have been found elsewhere in the Solar System, it has been assumed that they form naturally, given enough time. In 1953 two scientists at the University of Chicago, Harold Urey and Stanley Miller, conducted what has since been called "a most striking experiment." In a pressure vessel they mixed simple organic molecules of methane, ammonia, hydrogen, and water vapor, dissolved the mixture in water to simulate the primordial watery "soup," and subjected the mixture to electrical sparks to emulate primordial lightning bolts. The experiment produced several amino and hydroxy acids—the building blocks of proteins, which are essential to living matter. Other researchers later subjected similar mixtures to ultraviolet light, ionizing radiation, or heat to simulate the effects of the Sun's rays as well as various other types of radiation on the Earth's primitive atmosphere and murky waters. The results were the same.

But it was one thing to show that nature itself could, under certain conditions, come up with life's building blocks—not just simple but even complex organic compounds; it was another thing to breathe life into the resulting compounds, which remained inert and lifeless in the compression chambers. "Life" is defined as the ability to absorb nutrients (of any kind) and to replicate, not just to exist. Even the biblical tale of Creation recognizes that when the most complex being on Earth, Man, was shaped out of "clay," divine intervention was needed to "breathe the spirit/breath of life" into him. Without that, no matter how ingeniously created, he was not yet animate, not yet living.

As astronomy has done in the celestial realm, so, in the 1970s and 1980s, did biochemistry unlock many of the secrets of terrestrial life. The innermost reaches of living cells have been pried open, the genetic code that governs replication has been understood, and many of the complex components that make the tiniest one-celled being or the cells of the most advanced creatures have been synthesized. Pursuing the research, Stanley Miller, now at the University of California at San Diego, has commented that "we have learned how to make organic compounds from inorganic elements; the next step is to learn how they organize themselves into a replicating cell."

The murky-waters, or "primordial-soup," hypothesis for the origin of life on Earth envisions a multitude of those earliest organic molecules in the ocean, bumping into each other as the result of waves, currents, or temperature changes, and eventually sticking to one another through natural cell attractions to form cell groupings from which polymers—long-chained molecules that lie at the core of body formation—eventually developed. But what gave these cells the genetic memory to know, not just how to combine, but how to replicate, to make the ultimate bodies grow? The need to involve the genetic code in the transition from inanimate organic matter to an animate state has led to a "Made-of-Clay" hypothesis.

The launching of this theory is attributed to an announcement in April 1985 by researchers at the Ames Research Center, a NASA facility at Mountainview, California; but in fact the idea that clay on the shores of ancient seas played an important role in the origin of life on Earth was made public at the October 1977 Pacific Conference on Chemistry. There James A. Lawless, who headed a team of researchers at NASA's Ames facility, reported on experiments in which simple amino acids (the chemical building blocks of proteins) and nucleotides (the chemical building blocks of genes)—assuming they had already developed in the murky "primordial soup" in the sea—began to form into chains when deposited on clays that contained traces of metals such as nickel or zinc, and allowed to dry.

What the researchers found to be significant was that the traces of nickel selectively held on only to the twenty kinds of amino acids that are common to all living things on Earth, while the traces of zinc in the clay helped link together the nucleotides, which resulted in a compound analogous to a crucial enzyme (called DNA-polymerase) that links pieces of genetic material in all living cells.

In 1985 the scientists of the Ames Research Center reported substantial advances in understanding the role of clay in the processes that had led to life on Earth. Clay, they discovered, has two basic properties essential to life: the capacity to store and the ability to transfer energy. In the primordial conditions such energy might have come from radioactive decay, among other possible sources. Using the stored energy, clays might have acted as chemical laboratories where inorganic raw materials were processed into more complex molecules. There was more: one scientist, Armin Weiss of the University of Munich, reported experiments in which clay crystals seemed to reproduce themselves from a "parent crystal"—a primitive replication phenomenon; and Graham Cairns-Smith of the University of Glasgow held that the inorganic "proto-organisms" in the clay were involved in "directing" or actually acting as a "template" from which the living organisms eventually evolved.

Explaining these tantalizing properties of clay—even common clay—Lelia Coyne, who headed one research team, said that the ability of the clays to trap and transmit energy was due to "mistakes" in the formation of clay crystals; these defects in the clays' microstructure acted as the sites where energy was stored and from which the chemical directions for the formation of the proto-organisms emanated.

"If the theory can be confirmed," *The New York Times* commented in its report of the announcements, "it would seem that an accumulation of chemical mistakes led to life on Earth." So the "life-from-clay" theory, in spite of the advances it offered, depended, as the "murky-soup" theory did, on random occurrences—microstructural mistakes here, occasional lightning strikes and collisions of molecules there—to explain the transition from chemical elements to simple organic molecules to complex organic molecules and from inanimate to animate matter.

The improved theory seemed to do another thing, which did not escape notice. "The theory," *The New York Times* continued, "is also evocative of the biblical account of the Creation. In Genesis it is written, 'And the Lord God formed man of dust of the ground,' and in common usage the primordial dust is called clay." This news story, and the biblical parallel implicit in it, merited an editorial in the venerable newspaper. Under the headline "Uncommon Clay," the editorial said:

> Ordinary clay, it seems, has two basic properties essential to life. It can store energy and also transmit it. So, the scientists reason, clay could have acted as a "chemical factory" for turning inorganic raw materials into more complex molecules. Out of those complex molecules arose life—and, one day, us.
>
> That the Bible's been saying so all along, clay being what Genesis meant by the "dust of the ground" that formed man, is obvious. What is not so obvious is how often we have been saying it to one another, and without knowing it.

The combined murky-soup and life-from-clay theories, few have realized, have gone even further in substantiating the ancient accounts. Further experiments by Lelia Coyne together with Noam Lahab of the Hebrew University, Israel, have shown that to act as catalysts in the formation of short strings of amino acids, the clays must undergo cycles of wetting and drying. This process calls for an environment where water can alternate with dryness, either on dry land that is subjected to on-and-off rains or where seas slosh back and forth as a result of tides. The conclusion, which appeared to gain support from experiments aimed at searching for "protocells" that were conducted at the Institute for Molecular and Cellular Evolution at the University of Miami, pointed to primitive algae as the first one-celled living creatures on Earth. Still found in ponds and in damp places, algae appear little changed in spite of the passage of billions of years.

Because until a few decades ago no evidence for land life older than about 500 million years had been found, it was assumed that the life that evolved from algae was limited to the oceans. "There were algae in the oceans but the land was yet devoid of life," textbooks used to state. But in 1977 a scientific team led by Elso S. Barghoorn of Harvard discovered in sedimentary rocks in South Africa (at a site in Swaziland called Figtree) the remains of microscopic, one-celled creatures that were 3.1 (and perhaps as much as 3.4) billion years old; they were similar to today's blue-green algae and pushed back by almost a billion years the time when this precursor of more complex forms of life evolved on Earth.

Until then evolutionary progression was believed to have occurred primarily in the oceans, with land creatures evolving from maritime forms, with amphibian life forms as an intermediary. But the presence of *green* algae in sedimentary rocks of such a great age required revised theories. Though there is no unanimity regarding the classification of algae as either plant or nonplant, since it has backward affinities with bacteria and forward affinities with the earliest fauna, either green or blue-green algae is undoubtedly the precursor of chlorophyllic plants—the plants that use sunlight to convert their nutrients to organic compounds, emitting oxygen in the process. Green algae, though without roots, stems, or leaves, began the plant family whose descendants now cover the Earth.

It is important to follow the scientific theories of the ensuing evolution of life on Earth in order to grasp the accuracy of the biblical record. For more complex life forms to evolve, oxygen was needed. This oxygen became available only *after* algae or proto-algae began to spread upon the dry land. For these green plantlike forms to utilize and process oxygen, they needed an environment of rocks containing iron with which to "bind" the oxygen (otherwise they would have been destroyed by oxidation; free oxygen was still a poison to these life forms). Scientists believe that as such "banded-iron formations" sank into ocean bottoms as sediments, the single-celled organisms evolved into multicelled ones in the water. In other words, the covering of the lands with green algae had to *precede* the emergence of maritime life.

The Bible, indeed, says as much: Green herbage, it states, was created on Day Three, but maritime life not until Day Five. It was on the third "day," or phase, of creation that Elohim said:

> Let the Earth bring forth green herbage,
> and grasses that yield seeds, and fruit trees
> that bear fruit of all kinds
> in accordance with the seeds thereof.

The presence of fruits and seeds as the green growth advanced from grasses to trees also illustrates the evolution from asexual reproduction to sexual reproduction. In this, too, the Bible includes in its scientific account of evolution a step that modern science believes took place, in algae, some two billion years ago. That is when the "green herbage" began to increase the air's oxygen.

At that point, according to Genesis, there were no "creatures" on our planet—neither in the waters, nor in the air, nor on dry land. To make the eventual appearance of vertebrate (inner-skeleton) "creatures" possible, Earth had to set the pattern of the biological clocks that underlie the life cycles of all living forms on Earth. The Earth had to settle into its orbital and rotational patterns and be subjected to the effects of the Sun and the Moon, which were primarily manifested in the cycles of light and darkness. The Book of Genesis assigns the fourth "day" to this organization and to the resulting year,

Figure 45

month, day, and night repetitious periods. Only then, with all celestial relationships and cycles and their effects firmly established, did the creatures of the sea, air, and land make their appearance.

Modern science not only agrees with this biblical scenario but may also provide a clue to the reason the ancient authors of the scientific summary called *Genesis* inserted a celestial "chapter" ("day four") between the evolutionary record of "day three"—time of the earliest appearance of life forms—and "day five," when the "creatures" appeared. In modern science, too, there is an unfilled gap of about 1.5 billion years—from about 2 billion years to about 570 million years ago—about which little is known because of the paucity of geological and fossil data. Modern science calls this era "Precambrian"; lacking the data, the ancient savants used this gap to describe the establishment of celestial relationships and biological cycles.

Although modern science regards the ensuing Cambrian period (so named after the region in Wales where the first geologic data for it were obtained) as the first phase of the Paleozoic ("Old Life") era, it was not yet the time of vertebrates—the life forms with an inner skeleton that the Bible calls "creatures." The first maritime vertebrates appeared about 500 million years ago, and land vertebrates followed about 100 million years later, during periods that are regarded by scientists as the transition from the Lower Paleozoic era to the Upper Paleozoic era. When that era ended, about 225 million years ago, (Fig. 45) there were fish in the waters as well as sea plants, and amphibians had made the transition from water to dry land and the plants upon the dry lands attracted the amphibians to evolve into reptiles; today's crocodiles are a remnant of that evolutionary phase.

The following era, named the Mesozoic ("Middle Life"), embraces the period from about 225 million to 65 million years ago and has often been nicknamed the "Age of the Dinosaurs." Alongside a variety of amphibians and marine lizards there evolved, away from the oceans and their teeming marine life, two main lines of egg-laying reptilians: those who took to flying and evolved into birds; and those who, in great variety, roamed and dominated the Earth as dinosaurs ("terrible lizards") (Fig. 46).

It is impossible to read the biblical verses with an open mind without realizing that the creational events of the fifth "day" of Genesis describe the above-listed developments:

And Elohim said:
"Let the waters swarm with living creatures,
and let aves fly above the earth, under the dome of the sky."
And Elohim created the large reptilians,
and all the living creatures that crawl

and that swarmed in the waters,
all in accordance with their kinds,
and all the winged aves by their kinds.
And Elohim blessed them, saying:
"Be fruitful and multiply and fill the waters of the seas,
and let the aves multiply upon the earth."

The tantalizing reference in these verses of Genesis to the "large reptilians" as a recognition of the dinosaurs cannot be dismissed. The Hebrew term used here, *Taninim* (plural of *Tanin*) has been variously translated as "sea serpent," "sea monsters," and "crocodile." To quote the *Encyclopaedia Britannica*, "the crocodiles are the last living link with the dinosaur-like reptiles of prehistoric times; they are, at the same

Figure 46

Figure 47

time, the nearest living relatives of the birds.'' The conclusion that by ''large *Taninim*'' the Bible meant not simply large reptilians but dinosaurs seems plausible—not because the Sumerians had seen dinosaurs, but because Anunnaki scientists had surely figured out the course of evolution on Earth at least as well as twentieth-century scientists have done.

No less intriguing is the order in which the ancient text lists the three branches of vertebrates. For a long time scientists held that birds evolved from dinosaurs, when these reptiles began to develop a gliding mechanism to ease their jumping from tree branches in search of food or, another theory holds, when ground-bound heavy dinosaurs attained greater running speed by reducing their weight through the development of hollow bones. A fossil confirmation of the origin of birds from the latter, gaining further speed for soaring by evolving two-leggedness, appeared to have been found in the remains of *Deinonychus* (''terrible-clawed'' reptile), a fast runner whose tail skeleton assumed a featherlike shape (Fig. 47). The discovery of fossilized remains of a creature now called *Archaeopteryx* (''old feather''—Fig. 48a) was deemed to have provided the ''missing link'' between dinosaurs and birds and gave rise to the theory that the two—dinosaurs and birds—had an early common land ancestor at the beginning of the Triassic period. But even this antedating of the appearance of birds has come into question since additional fossils of *Archaeopteryx*

a

b

Figure 48

were discovered in Germany; they indicate that this creature was by and large a fully developed bird (Fig. 48b) that had not evolved from the dinosaurs but rather directly from a much earlier ancestor who had come from the seas.

The biblical sources appear to have known all that. Not only does the Bible not list the dinosaurs ahead of birds (as scientists did for awhile); it actually lists birds ahead of the dinosaurs. With so much of the fossil record still incomplete, paleontologists may still find evidence that will indeed show that early birds had more in common with sea life than with desert lizards.

About 65 million years ago the era of the dinosaurs came to an abrupt end; theories regarding the causes range from climatic changes to viral epidemics to destruction by a "Death Star." Whatever the cause, there was an unmistakable end of one evolutionary period and the beginning of another. In the words of Genesis, it was the dawn of the sixth "day." Modern science calls it the Cenozoic ("current life") era, when mammals spread across the Earth. This is how the Bible put it:

And Elohim said:
"Let the Earth bring forth living animals
according to their kind:
bovines, and those that creep,
and beasts of the land,
all according to their kind;"
And it was so.
Thus did Elohim make all the animals of the land
according to their kinds,
and all the bovines according to their kinds,
and all those that creep upon the earth by their kinds.

There is full agreement here between Bible and Science. The conflict between Creationists and Evolutionists reaches its crux in the interpretation of what happened next—the appearance of Man on Earth. It is a subject that will be dealt with in the next chapter. Here it is important to point out that although one might expect that a primitive or unknowing society, seeing how Man is superior to all other animals, would assume Man to be the oldest creature on Earth and thus the most developed, the wisest. But the Book of Genesis does not say so at all. On the contrary, it asserts that Man was a latecomer to Earth. We are not the oldest story of evolution but only its last few pages. Modern science agrees.

That is exactly what the Sumerians had taught in their schools. As we read in the Bible, it was only after all the "days" of creation had run their course, after "all the fishes of the sea and all the fowl that fly the skies and all the animals that fill the earth and all the creeping things that crawl upon the earth" that "Elohim created the Adam."

On the sixth "day" of creation, God's work on Earth was done.

"This," the Book of Genesis states, "is the way the Heaven and the Earth have come to be."

Up to the point of Man's creation, then, modern science and ancient knowledge parallel each other. But by charting the course of evolution, modern science has left behind the initial question about the *origin* of life as distinct from its development and evolution.

The murky-soup and life-from-clay theories only suggest that, given the right materials and conditions, life could arise spontaneously. This notion, that life's elemental building blocks, such as ammonia and methane (the simplest stable compounds of nitrogen and hydrogen and of carbon and hydrogen, respectively) could have formed by themselves as part of nature's processes, seemed fortified by the discovery in recent decades that these compounds are present and even plentiful on other planets. But how did chemical compounds become animate?

That the feat is possible is obvious; the evidence is that life *did* appear on Earth. The speculation that life, in one form or another, may also exist elsewhere in our Solar System, and probably in other star systems, presupposes the feasibility of the transition from inanimate to animate matter. So, the question is not *can* it happen but *how did* it happen here on Earth?

For life as we see it on Earth to happen, two basic molecules are necessary: proteins, which perform all the complex metabolic functions of living cells; and nucleic acids, which carry the genetic code and issue the instructions for the cell's processes. The two kinds of molecules, as the definition itself suggests, function within a unit called a cell—quite a complex organism in itself, which is capable of triggering the replication not only of itself but of the whole animal of which the single cell is but a minuscule component. In order to become proteins, amino acids must form long and complex chains. In the cell they perform the task according to instructions stored in one nucleic acid (DNA—deoxyribonucleic acid) and transmitted by another nucleic acid (RNA—ribonucelic acid). Could random conditions prevailing on the primordial Earth have caused amino acids to combine into chains? In spite of varied attempts and theories (notable experiments were conducted by Clifford Matthews of the University of Illinois), the pathways sought by the scientists all required more ''compressive energy'' than would have been available.

Did DNA and RNA, then, precede amino acids on Earth? Advances in genetics and the unraveling of the mysteries of the living cell have increased, rather than diminished, the problems. The discovery in 1953 by James D. Watson and Francis H. Crick of the ''double-helix'' structure of DNA opened up vistas of immense complexity regarding these two chemicals of life. The relatively giant molecules of DNA are in the form of two long, twisted strings connected by ''rungs'' made of four very complex organic compounds (marked on genetic charts by the initials of the names of the compounds, A-G-C-T). These four nucleotides can combine in pairs in sequences of limitless variety and are bound into place (Fig. 49) by sugar compounds alternating with phosphates. The nucleic acid RNA, no less complex and built of four nucleotides whose initials are A-G-C-U, may contain thousands of combinations.

How much time did evolution take on Earth to develop these complex compounds, without which life as we know it would have never evolved?

The fossil remains of algae found in 1977 in South Africa were dated to 3.1 to 3.4 billion years ago. But while that discovery was of microscopic, single-celled organisms, other discoveries in 1980 in western Australia deepened the wonderment. The team, led by J. William Schopf of the University of California at Los Angeles, found fossil remains of organisms that not only were much older—3.5 billion years—but that

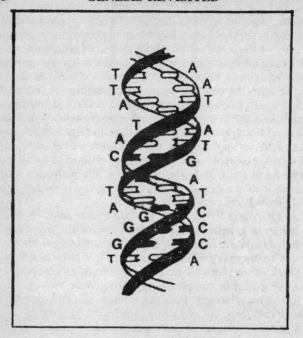

Figure 49

were multicelled and looked under the microscope like chain-like filaments (Fig. 50). These organisms already possessed both amino acids and complex nucleic acids, the replicating genetic compounds, 3.5 billion years ago; they therefore had to represent, not the beginning of the chain of life on Earth, but an already advanced stage of it.

What these finds had set in motion can be termed the search for the first gene. Increasingly, scientists believe that before algae there were bacteria. "We are actually looking at cells which are the direct morphological remains of the bugs themselves," stated Malcolm R. Walter, an Australian member of the team. "They look like modern bacteria," he added. In fact, they looked like five different types of bacteria whose structures, amazingly, "were almost identical to serveral modern-day bacteria."

Figure 50

The notion that self-replication on Earth began with bacteria that preceded algae seemed to make sense, since advances in genetics showed that all life on Earth, from the simplest to the most complex, has the same genetic "ingredients" and the same twenty or so basic amino acids. Indeed, much of the early genetic research and development of techniques in genetic engineering were done on the lowly bacterium *Escherichia coli* (*E. coli*, for short), which can cause diarrhea in humans and cattle. But even this minuscule, single-celled bacterium that reproduces not sexually but simply by dividing, has almost 4,000 different genes!

That bacteria have played a role in the evolutionary process is apparent, not only from the fact that so many marine, plant and animal higher organisms depend on bacteria for many vital processes, but also from discoveries, first in the Pacific Ocean and then in other seas, that bacteria did and still make possible life forms that do not depend on photosynthesis but metabolize sulfur compounds in the oceans' depths. Calling such early bacteria "archaeo-bacteria," a team led by Carl R. Woese of the University of Illinois dated them to a time between 3.5 and 4 billion years ago. Such an age was corroborated in 1984 by finds in an Austrian lake by Hans Fricke of the Max Planck Institute and Karl Stetter of the University of Regensburg (both in West Germany).

Sediments found off Greenland, on the other hand, bear chemical traces that indicate the existence of photosynthesis as early as 3.8 billion years ago. All these finds have thus shown that, within a few hundred million years of the impenetrable limit of 4 billion years, there were prolific bacteria and archaeo-bacteria of a marked variety on Earth. In more recent studies (*Nature*, November 9, 1989), an august team of scientists led by Norman H. Sleep of Stanford University concluded that the "window of time" when life on Earth began was just the 200 million years between 4 and 3.8 billion years ago. "Everything alive today," they stated, "evolved from organisms that originated within that Window of Time." They did not attempt, however, to establish *how* life originated at such a time.

Based on varied evidence, including the very reliable isotopic ratios of carbon, scientists have concluded that no matter how life on Earth began, it did so about 4 billion years ago. Why then only and not sooner, when the planets were formed some 4.6 billion years ago? All scientific research, conducted on Earth as well as on the Moon, keeps bumping against the 4-billion-year date, and all that modern science can offer in explanation is some "catastrophic event." To know more, read the Sumerian texts. . . .

Since the fossil and other data have shown that celled and replicating organisms (be they bacteria or archaeo-bacteria) already existed on Earth a mere 200 million years after the "Window of Time" first opened, scientists began to search for the "essence" of life rather than for its resulting organisms: for traces of DNA and RNA themselves. Viruses, which are pieces of nucleic acids looking for cells in which to replicate, are prevalent not only on land but also in water, and that has made some believe that viruses may have preceded bacteria. But what gave them their nucleic acids?

An avenue of research was opened a few years ago by Leslie Orgel of the Salk Institute in La Jolla, California, when he proposed that the simpler RNA might have preceded the much more complex DNA. Although RNA only transmits the genetic messages contained in the DNA blueprint, other researchers, among them Thomas R. Cech and co-workers at the University of Colorado and Sidney Altman of Yale University concluded that a certain type of RNA could catalyze itself under certain conditions. All this led to computerized studies of a type of RNA called transfer-RNA undertaken by Manfred Eigen, a Nobel-prize winner. In a paper published in *Science* (May 12, 1989) he and his colleagues from Germany's Max Planck Institute reported that by sequencing transfer-RNA backward on the Tree of Life, they found that the genetic code on Earth cannot be older than 3.8 billion years, plus or minus 600 million years. At that time, Manfred Eigen said, a primordial gene might have appeared "whose message was the biblical injunction 'Go out into the world, be fruitful and multiply'." If the leeway, as it appears, had to be on the plus side—i.e., older than 3.8 billion years—"this would be possible only in the case of *extraterrestrial origin*," the authors of the learned paper added.

In her summation of the fourth Conference on the Origin of Life, Lynn Margulis had predicted this astounding conclusion. "We now recognize that if the origin of our self-replicating system occurred on the early Earth, it must have occurred quite quickly—millions, not billions of years," she stated. And she added:

> The central problem inspiring these conferences, perhaps slightly better defined, is as unsolved as ever. *Did our organic matter originate in interstellar space?* The infant science of radioastronomy has produced evidence that some of the smaller organic molecules are there.

Writing in 1908, Svante Arrhenius (*Worlds in the Making*) proposed that life-bearing spores were driven to Earth by the pressure of light waves from the star of another planetary system where life had evolved long before it did on Earth. The notion came to be known as "the theory of Panspermia"; it languished on the fringes of accepted science because, at the time, one fossil discovery after another seemed to corroborate the theory of evolution as an unchallenged explanation for the origin of life on Earth.

These fossil discoveries, however, raised their own questions and doubts; so much so that in 1973 the Nobel laureate (now Sir) Francis Crick together with Leslie Orgel, in a paper titled "Directed Panspermia" (*Icarus*, vol. 19), revived the notion of the seeding of Earth with the first organisms or spores *from an extraterrestrial source*—not, however, by chance but as "the deliberate activity of an extraterrestrial society." Whereas our Solar System was formed only some 4.6 billion years ago, other solar systems in the universe may have formed as much as 10 billion years earlier; while the interval between the formation of Earth and the appearance of life on Earth is much too short, there has been as much as six billion years available for the process on other planetary systems. "The time available makes it possible, therefore, that technological societies existed elsewhere in the galaxy *even before the formation of the Earth*," according to Crick and Orgel. Their suggestion was therefore that the scientific community "consider a new 'infective' theory, namely that a primitive form of life was deliberately planted on Earth by a technologically advanced society on another planet." Anticipating criticism—which indeed followed—that no living spores could survive the rigors of space, they suggested that the microorganisms were not sent to just drift in space but were placed in a specially designed spaceship with due protection and a life-sustaining environment.

In spite of the unquestionable scientific credentials of Crick and Orgel, their theory of Directed Panspermia met with disbelief and even ridicule. However, more recent scientific advances changed these attitudes; not only because of the narrowing of the Window of Time to a mere couple of hundred million years, almost ruling out the possibility that the essential genetic matter had enough time to evolve here on Earth. The change in opinion was also due to the discovery that of the myriad of amino acids that exist, it is only the same twenty or so that are part of all living organisms on Earth, no matter what these organisms are and when they evolved; and that the same DNA, made up of the same four nucleotides—that and no other—is present in all living things on Earth.

It was therefor that the participants of the landmark eighth Conference on the Origins of Life, held at Berkeley, California, in 1986, could no longer accept the random formation of life inherent in the murky-soup or life-from-clay hypotheses, for according to these theories, a variety of life forms and genetic codes should have arisen. Instead, the consensus was that "all life on Earth, from bacteria to sequoia trees to humans, evolved from a single ancestral cell."

But where did this single ancestral cell come from? The 285 scientists from 22 countries did not endorse the cautious suggestions that, as some put it, fully formed cells were planted on Earth from space. Many were, however, willing to consider that "the supply of organic precursors to life was augmented from space." When all was said and done, the assembled scientists were left with only one avenue that, they hoped, might provide the answer to the puzzle of the origin of life on Earth: space exploration. The research should shift from Earth to Mars, to the Moon, to Saturn's satellite Titan, it was suggested, because their more pristine environments might have better preserved the traces of the beginnings of life.

Such a course of research reflects the acceptance, it must be obvious, of the premise that life is not unique to Earth. The first reason for such a premise is the extensive evidence that organic compounds permeate the Solar System and outer space. The data from interplanetary probes have been reviewed in an earlier chapter; the data indicating life-related elements and compounds in outer space are so voluminous that only a few instances must suffice here. In 1977, for example, an international team of astronomers at the Max Planck Institute discovered water molecules outside our own galaxy. The density of the water vapor was the same as in Earth's galaxy, and Otto Hachenberg of the Bonn Institute for Radio Astronomy considered that finding as support for the conclusion that "conditions exist at some other place which, like those on Earth, are suitable for life." In 1984 scientists at the Goddard Space Center found "a bewildering array of molecules, including the beginning of organic chemistry" in interstellar space. They had discovered "complex molecules composed of the same atoms that make up living tissue," according to Patrick Thaddeus of the Center's Institute for Space Studies, and it was "reasonable to assume that these compounds were deposited on Earth at the time of its forming and that life ultimately came from them." In 1987, to give one more instance, NASA instruments discovered that exploding stars (supernovas) produced most of the ninety-odd elements, including carbon, that are contained in living organisms on Earth.

How did such life-essential compounds, in forms that enabled life to sprout on Earth, arrive on Earth from space, near or distant? Invariably, the celestial emissaries under consideration are comets, meteors, meteorites, and impacting asteroids. Of particular interest to scientists are meteorites containing carbonaceous chondrites, believed to represent the most primordial planetary matter in the Solar System. One, which fell near Murchison in Victoria, Australia, in 1969, revealed an array of organic compounds, including amino acids and nitrogenous bases that embraced all the compounds involved in DNA. According to Ron Brown of Monash University in Melbourne, researchers have even found "formations in the meteorite reminiscent of a very primitive form of cell structure."

Until then, carbonaceous chondrite meteorites, first collected in France in 1806, were dismissed as unreliable evidence because their life-related compounds were explained away as terrestrial contamination. But in 1977 two meteorites of this type were discovered buried in the icy wilderness of Antarctica, where no contamination was possible. These, and meteorite fragments collected elsewhere in Antarctica by Japanese scientists, were found to be rich in amino acids and to contain at least three of the nucleotides (the A, G, and U of the genetic "alphabet") that make up DNA and/or RNA. Writing in *Scientific American* (August 1983), Roy S. Lewis and Edward Anders concluded that "carbonaceous chondrites, the most primitive meteorites, incorporate material originating outside the Solar System, including matter expelled by supernovas and other stars." Radiocarbon dating has given these meteorites an age of 4.5 to 4.7 billion years; it makes them not only as old as but even older than Earth and establishes their extraterrestrial origin.

Reviving, in a way, the old beliefs that comets cause plagues on Earth, two noted British astronomers, Sir Fred Hoyle and Chandra Wickramasinghe, suggested in a study in the *New Scientist* (November 17, 1977) that "life on Earth began when stray comets bearing the building blocks of life crashed into the primitive Earth.'' In spite of criticism by other scientists, the two have persisted in pressing this theory forward at scientific conferences, in books (*Lifecloud* and others) and in scholarly publications, offering each time more supportive arguments for the thesis that ''about four billion years ago life arrived in a comet.''

Recent close studies of comets, such as Halley's, have shown that the comets, as do the other messengers from far out in space, contain water and other life-building compounds. These findings have led other astronomers and biophysicists to concede the possibility that cometary impacts had played a role in giving rise to life on Earth. In the words of Armand Delsemme of the University of Toledo, ''A large number of comets hitting Earth contributed a veneer of chemicals needed for the formation of amino acids; the molecules in our bodies were likely in comets at one time.''

As scientific advances made more sophisticated studies of meteorites, comets, and other celestial objects possible, the results included an even greater array of the compounds essential to life. The new breed of scientists, given the name ''Exobiologists,'' have even found isotopes and other elements in these celestial bodies that indicate an origin preceding the formation of the Solar System. An extrasolar origin for the life that eventually evolved on Earth has thus become a more acceptable proposition. The argument between the Hoyle-Wickramasinghe team and others has by now shifted its focus to whether the two are right in suggesting that ''spores''—actual microorganisms—rather than the antecedent life-forming compounds were delivered to Earth by the cometary/meteoritic impacts.

Could ''spores'' survive in the radiation and cold of outer space? Skepticism regarding this possibility was greatly dispelled by experiments conducted at Leiden University, Holland, in 1985. Reporting in *Nature* (vol. 316) astrophysicist J. Mayo Greenberg and his associate Peter Weber found that this was possible if the ''spores'' journeyed inside an envelope of molecules of water, methane, ammonia, and carbon monoxide—all readily available on other celestial bodies. Panspermia, they concluded, was possible.

How about *directed* panspermia, the deliberate seeding of Earth by another civilization, as suggested earlier by Crick and Orgel? In their view, the "envelope" protecting the spores was not made up just of the required compounds, but was a spaceship in which the microorganisms were kept immersed in nutrients. As much as their proposal smacks of science fiction, the two held fast to their "theorem." "Even though it sounds a bit cranky," Sir Francis Crick wrote in *The New York Times* (October 26, 1981), "all the steps in the argument are scientifically plausible." Foreseeing that Mankind might one day send its "seeds of life" to other worlds, why could it not be that a higher civilization elsewhere had done it to Earth in the distant past?

Lynn Margulis, a pioneer of the Origin of Life conferences and now a member of the U.S. National Academy of Sciences, held in her writings and interviews that many organisms, when faced with harsh conditions, "release tough little packages"— she named them "Propagules"—"that can carry genetic material into more hospitable surroundings" (*Newsweek*, October 2, 1989). It is a natural "strategy for survival" that has accounted for "space age spores"; it will happen in the future because it has happened in the past.

In a detailed report concerning all these developments, headlined "NASA to Probe Heavens for Clues to Life's Origins on Earth" in *The New York Times* (September 6, 1988), Sandra Blakeslee summed up the latest scientific thinking thus:

Driving the new search for clues to life's beginnings is the recent discovery that comets, meteors and interstellar dust carry vast amounts of complex organic chemicals as well as the elements crucial to living cells.

Scientists believe that Earth and other planets have been seeded from space with these potential building blocks of life.

"*Seeded from space*"—the very words written down millennia ago by the Sumerians!

It is noteworthy that in his presentations, Chandra Wickramasinghe has frequently invoked the writings of the Greek philosopher Anaxagoras who, about 500 B.C., believed that the "seeds of life" swarm through the universe, ready to sprout and create life wherever a proper environment is found. Coming as he did from Asia Minor, his sources, as was true for so much of early Greek knowledge, were the Mesopotamian writings and traditions.

After a detour of 6,000 years, modern science has come back to the Sumerian scenario of an invader from outer space that brings the seed of life into the Solar System and imparts it to "Gaia" during the Celestial Battle.

The Anunnaki, capable of space travel about half a million years before us, discovered this phenomenon long before us; in this respect, modern science is just catching up with ancient knowledge.

8

THE ADAM: A SLAVE MADE TO ORDER

The biblical tale of Man's creation is, of course, the crux of the debate—at times bitter—between Creationists and Evolutionists and of the ongoing confrontation between them—at times in courts, always on school boards. As previously stated, both sides had better read the Bible again (and in its Hebrew original); the conflict would evaporate once Evolutionists recognized the scientific basis of *Genesis* and Creationists realized what its text really says.

Apart from the naive assertion by some that in the account of Creation the "days" of the Book of Genesis are literally twenty-four-hour periods and not eras or phases, the sequence in the Bible is, as previous chapters should have made clear, a description of Evolution that is in accord with modern science. The insurmountable problem arises when Creationists insist that we, Mankind, *Homo sapiens sapiens*, were created instantaneously and without evolutionary predecessors by "God." "And the Lord God formed Man of the dust of the ground, and breathed into his nostrils the breath of life, and Man became a living soul." This is the tale of Man's creation as told in chapter 2, verse 7 of the Book of Genesis—according to the King James English version; and this is what the Creationist zealots firmly believe.

Were they to learn the Hebrew text—which is, after all, the original—they would discover that, first of all, the creative act is attributed to certain *Elohim*—a plural term that at the least should be translated as "gods," not "God." And second, they would become aware that the quoted verse also explains why "The Adam" was created: "For there was no Adam to till the land." These are two important—and unsettling—hints to who had created Man and why.

Then, of course, there exists the other problem, that of another (and prior) version of the creation of Man, in Genesis 1:26–27. First, according to the King James version, "God said, Let us make men in our image, after our likeness"; then the suggestion was carried out: "And God created man in his own image, in the image of God created He him; male and female created He them." The biblical account is further complicated by the ensuing tale in Chapter 2, according to which "The Adam" was alone until God provided him with a female counterpart, created of Adam's rib.

While Creationists might be hard put to decide which particular version is the *sine qua non* tenet, there exists the problem of pluralism. The suggestion for Man's creation comes from a plural entity who addresses a plural audience, saying, "Let *us* make an Adam in *our* image and after *our* likeness." What, those who believe in the Bible must ask, is going on here?

As both Orientalists and Bible scholars now know, what went on was the editing and summarizing by the compilers of the Book of Genesis of much earlier and considerably more detailed texts first written down in Sumer. Those texts, reviewed and extensively quoted in *The 12th Planet* with all sources listed, relegate the creation of Man to the Anunnaki. It happened, we learn from such long texts as *Atra Hasis*, when the rank-and-file astronauts who had come to Earth for its gold mutinied. The backbreaking work in the gold mines, in southeast Africa, had become unbearable. *Enlil*, their commander-in-chief, summoned the ruler of Nibiru, his father Anu, to an Assembly of the Great Anunnaki and demanded harsh punishment of his rebellious crew. But Anu was more understanding. "What are we accusing them of?" he asked as he heard the complaints of the mutineers. "Their work was heavy, their distress was much!" Was there no other way to obtain the gold, he wondered out loud.

Yes, said his other son Enki (Enlil's half brother and rival), the brilliant chief scientist of the Anunnaki. It is possible to relieve the Anunnaki of the unbearable toil by having someone else take over the difficult work: Let a Primitive Worker be created!

The idea appealed to the assembled Anunnaki. The more they discussed it, the more clear their clamor grew for such a

Primitive Worker, an *Adamu*, to take over the work load. But, they wondered, how can you create a being intelligent enough to use tools and to follow orders? How was the creation or "bringing forth," of the Primitive Worker to be achieved? Was it, indeed, a feasible undertaking?

A Sumerian text has immortalized the answer given by Enki to the incredulous assembled Anunnaki, who saw in the creation of an *Adamu* the solution to their unbearable toil:

> The creature whose name you uttered—
> IT EXISTS!

All you have to do, he added, is to

> Bind upon it the image of the gods.

In these words likes the key to the puzzle of Man's creation, the magical wand that removes the conflict between Evolution and Creationism. The Anunnaki, the *Elohim* of the biblical verses, did not create Man from nothing. The being was already there, on Earth, the *product of evolution*. All that was needed to *upgrade it* to the required level of ability and intelligence was to "bind upon it the image of the gods," the image of the *Elohim* themselves.

For the sake of simplicity let us call the "creature" that already existed then Apeman/Apewoman. The process envisioned by Enki was to "bind" upon the existing creature the "image"—the inner, genetic makeup—of the Anunnaki; in other words, to upgrade the existing Apeman/Apewoman through genetic manipulation and, by thus jumping the gun on evolution, bring "Man"—Homo sapiens—into being.

The term *Adamu*, which is clearly the inspiration for the biblical name "Adam," and the use of the term "image" in the Sumerian text, which is repeated intact in the biblical text, are not the only clues to the Sumerian/Mesopotamian origin of the Genesis creation of Man story. The biblical use of the plural pronoun and the depiction of a group of *Elohim* reaching a consensus and following it up with the necessary action also lose their enigmatic aspects when the Mesopotamian sources are taken into account.

In them we read that the assembled Anunnaki resolved to proceed with the project, and on Enki's suggestion assigned the task to Ninti, their chief medical officer:

> They summoned and asked the goddess,
> the midwife of the gods, the wise birthgiver,
> [saying:]
> "To a creature give life, create workers!
> Create a Primitive Worker,
> that he may bear the yoke!
> Let him bear the yoke assigned by Enlil,
> Let The Worker carry the toil of the gods!"

One cannot say for certain whether it was from the *Atra Hasis* text, from which the above lines are quoted, or from much earlier Sumerian texts that the editors of *Genesis* got their abbreviated version. But we have here the background of events that led to the need for a Primitive Worker, the assembly of the gods and the suggestion and decision to go ahead and have one created. Only by realizing what the biblical sources were can we understand the biblical tale of the Elohim—the Lofty Ones, the "gods"—saying: "Let us make the Adam in our image, after our likeness," so as to remedy the situation that "there was no Adam to till the land."

In *The 12th Planet* it was stressed that until the Bible begins to relate the genealogy and history of Adam, a specific person, the Book of Genesis refers to the newly created being as "*The* Adam," a generic term. Not a person called Adam, but, literally, "the Earthling," for that is what "Adam" means, coming as it does from the same root as *Adamah*, "Earth." But the term is also a play on words, specifically *dam*, which means "blood" and reflects, as we shall soon see, the manner in which The Adam was "manufactured."

The Sumerian term that means "Man" is LU. But its root meaning is not "human being"; it is rather "worker, servant," and as a component of animal names implied "domesticated." The Akkadian language in which the *Atra Hasis* text was written (and from which all Semitic languages have stemmed) applied to the newly created being the term *lulu*, which means, as in the Sumerian, "Man" but which conveys the notion of mixing. The word *lulu* in a more profound sense thus meant "the mixed one." This also reflected the manner in which The Adam—"Earthling" as well as "He of the blood"—was created.

Numerous texts in varying states of preservation or fragmentation have been found inscribed on Mesopotamian clay tablets. In sequels to *The 12th Planet* the creation "myths" of other peoples, from both the Old and New Worlds, have been reviewed; they all record a process involving the mixing of a godly element with an earthly one. As often as not, the godly element is described as an "essence" derived from a god's blood, and the earthly element as "clay" or "mud." There can be no doubt that they all attempt to tell the same tale, for they all speak of a First Couple. There is no doubt that their origin is Sumerian, in whose texts we find the most elaborate descriptions and the greatest amount of detail concerning the wonderful deed: the mixing of the "divine" genes of the Anunnaki with the "earthly" genes of Apeman by fertilizing the egg of an Apewoman.

It was fertilization in vitro—in glass tubes, as depicted in this rendering on a cylinder seal (Fig. 51). And, as I have been saying since modern science and medicine achieved the feat of in vitro fertilization, *Adam was the first test-tube baby*. . . .

* * *

Figure 51

There is reason to believe that when Enki made the surprising suggestion to create a Primitive Worker through genetic manipulation, he had already concluded that the feat was possible. His suggestion to call in Ninti for the task was also not a spur-of-the-moment idea.

Laying the groundwork for ensuing events, the *Atra Hasis* text begins the story of Man on Earth with the assignment of tasks among the leading Anunnaki. When the rivalry between the two half brothers, Enlil and Enki, reached dangerous levels, Anu made them draw lots. As a result, Enlil was given mastery over the old settlements and operations in the E.DIN (the biblical Eden) and Enki was sent to Africa, to supervise the AB.ZU, the land of mines. Great scientist that he was, Enki was bound to have spent some of his time studying the flora and fauna of his surroundings as well as the fossils that, some 300,000 years later, the Leakeys and other paleontologists have been uncovering in southeastern Africa. As scientists do today, Enki, too, must have contemplated the course of evolution on Earth. As reflected in the Sumerian texts, he came to the conclusion that the same "seed of life" that Nibiru had brought with it from its previous celestial abode had given rise to life on both planets; much earlier on Nibiru, and later on Earth, once the latter had been seeded by the collision.

The being that surely fascinated him most was Apeman—a step above the the other primates, a hominid already walking erect and using sharpened stones as tools, a proto-Man—but not yet a fully evolved human. And Enki must have toyed with the intriguing challenge of "playing God" and conducting experiments in genetic manipulation.

To aid his experiments he asked Ninti to come to Africa and be by his side. The official reason was plausible. She was the chief medical officer; her name meant "Lady Life" (later on she was nicknamed *Mammi*, the source of the universal *Mamma/Mother*). There was certainly a need for medical services, considering the harsh conditions under which the miners toiled. But there was more to it: from the very beginning, Enlil and Enki vied for her sexual favors, for both needed a male heir by a half sister, which she was. The three of them were children of Anu, the ruler of Nibiru, but not of the same mother; and according to the succession rules of the Anunnaki (later adopted by the Sumerians and reflected in the biblical tales of the Patriarchs), it was not necessarily the Firstborn son but a son born by a half sister from the same royal line who became the Legal Heir. Sumerian texts describe torrid lovemaking between Enki and Ninti (with unsuccessful results, though: the offspring were all females); there was thus more than an interest in science that led to Enki's suggestion to call in Ninti and assign the task to her.

Knowing all this, we should not be surprised to read in the creation texts that, first, Ninti said she could not do it alone, that she had to have the advice and help of Enki; and second, that she had to attempt the task in the Abzu, where the right materials and facilities were available. Indeed, the two must have conducted experiments together there long before the suggestion was made at the assembly of the Anunnaki to "let us make an Adamu in our image." Some ancient depictions show "Bull-Men" accompanied by naked Ape-men (Fig. 52) or Bird-Men (Fig. 53). Sphinxes (bulls or lions with human heads) that adorned many ancient temples may have been more than imaginary representations; and when Berossus, the Babylonian priest, wrote down Sumerian cosmogony and tales of creation for the Greeks, he described a prehuman period when

Figure 52

Figure 53

"men appeared with two wings," or "one body and two heads," or with mixed male and female organs, or "some with the legs and horns of goats" or other hominid-animal mixtures.

That these creatures were not freaks of nature but the result of deliberate experiments by Enki and Ninti is obvious from the Sumerian texts. The texts describe how the two came up with a being who had neither male nor female organs, a man who could not hold back his urine, a woman incapable of bearing children, and creatures with numerous other defects. Finally, with a touch of mischief in her challenging announcement, Ninti is recorded to have said:

> How good or bad is man's body?
> As my heart prompts me,
> I can make its fate good or bad.

Having reached this stage, where genetic manipulation was sufficiently perfected to enable the determination of the resulting body's good or bad aspects, the two felt they could master the final challenge: to mix the genes of hominids, Apemen, not with those of other Earth creatures but with the genes of the Anunnaki themselves. Using all the knowledge they had amassed, the two Elohim set out to manipulate and speed up the process of Evolution. Modern Man would have undoubtedly eventually evolved on Earth in any case, just as he had done on Nibiru, both having come from the same "seed of life." But there was still a long way and a long time to go from the stage hominids were at 300,000 years ago to the level of development the Anunnaki had reached at that time. If, in the course of 4 billion years, the evolutionary process had been earlier on Nibiru just 1 percent of that time, Evolution would have been forty million years ahead on Nibiru compared with the course of evolution on Earth. Did the Anunnaki jump the gun on evolution on our planet by a million or two million years? No one can say for sure how long it would have taken *Homo sapiens* to evolve naturally on Earth from the earlier hominids, but surely forty million years would have been more than enough time.

Called upon to perform the task of "fashioning servants for the gods"—"to bring to pass a great work of wisdom," in the words of the ancient texts—Enki gave Ninti the following instructions:

> Mix to a core the clay
> from the Basement of the Earth,
> just above the Abzu,
> and shape it into the form of a core.
> I shall provide good, knowing young Anunnaki
> who will bring the clay to the right condition.

In *The 12th Planet*, I analyzed the etymology of the Sumerian and Akkadian terms that are usually translated "clay" or "mud" and showed that they evolved from the Sumerian TI.IT, literally, "that which is with life," and then assumed the derivative meanings of "clay" and "mud," as well as "egg." The earthly element in the procedure for "binding upon" a being who already existed "the image of the gods" was thus to be the female egg of that being—of an Apewoman.

All the texts dealing with this event make it clear that Ninti relied on Enki to provide the earthly element, this egg of a female Apewoman, from the Abzu, from southeast Africa. Indeed, the specific location is given in the above quote: not exactly the same site as the mines (an area identified in *The 12th Planet* as Southern Rhodesia, now Zimbabwe) but a place "above" it, farther north. This area was, indeed, as recent finds have shown, where *Homo sapiens* emerged. . . .

The task of obtaining the "divine" elements was Ninti's. Two extracts were needed from one of the Anunnaki, and a young "god" was carefully selected for the purpose. Enki's instructions to Ninti were to obtain the god's blood and *shiru*, and through immersions in a "purifying bath" obtain their "essences." What had to be obtained from the blood was termed TE.E.MA, at best translated "personality," a term that expresses the sense of the word: that which makes a person what he is and different from any other person. But the translation "personality" does not convey the scientific precision of the term, which in the original Sumerian meant "That which houses that which binds the memory." Nowadays we call it a "gene."

The other element for which the young Anunnaki was selected, *shiru*, is commonly translated "flesh." In time, the word did acquire the meaning "flesh" among its various connotations. But in the earlier Sumerian it referred to the sex or reproductive organs; its root had the basic meaning "to bind," "that which binds." The extract from the *shiru* was referred to in other texts dealing with non-Anunnaki offspring of the "gods" as *kisru*; coming from the male's member, it meant "semen," the male's sperm.

These two divine extracts were to be mixed well by Ninti in a purifying bath, and it is certain that the epithet *lulu* ("The mixed one") for the resulting Primitive Worker stemmed from this mixing process. In modern terms we would call him a hybrid.

All these procedures had to be performed under strict sanitary conditions. One text even mentions how Ninti first washed her hands before she touched the "clay." The place where these procedures were carried out was a special structure called in Akkadian *Bit Shimti*, which, coming from the Sumerian SHI.IM.TI literally meant "house where the wind of life is breathed in"—the source, no doubt, of the biblical assertion that after having fashioned the Adam from the clay, *Elohim* "blew in his nostrils the breath of life." The biblical term, sometimes translated "soul" rather than "breath of life," is *Nephesh*. The identical term appears in the Akkadian account of what took place in the "house where the wind of life is breathed in" after the purifying and extracting procedures were completed:

> The god who purifies the *napishtu*, Enki,
> spoke up.
> Seated before her [Ninti] he was prompting her.
> After she had recited her incantation,
> she put her hand to the clay.

A depiction on a cylinder seal (Fig. 54) may well have illustrated the ancient text. It shows Enki seated, "prompting" Ninti (who is identified by her symbol, the umbilical cord), with the "test-tube" flasks behind her.

The mixing of the "clay" with all the component extracts and "essences" was not yet the end of the procedure. The egg of the Apewoman, fertilized in the "purifying baths" with the sperm and genes of the young Anunnaki "god," was then deposited in a "mold," where the "binding" was to be completed. Since this part of the process is described again later in connection with the determining of the sex of the engineered being, one may surmise that was the purpose of the "binding" phase.

The length of time the fertilized egg thus processed stayed

Figure 54

in the "mold" is not stated, but what was to be done with it was quite clear. The fertilized and "molded" egg was to be reimplanted in a female womb—but not in that of its original Apewoman. Rather, it was to be implanted in the womb of a "goddess," an Anunnaki female! Only thus, it becomes clear, was the end result achievable.

Could the experimenters, Enki and Ninti, now be sure that, after all their trial-and-error attempts to create hybrids, they would then obtain a perfect lulu by implanting the fertilized and processed egg in one of their own females—that what she would give birth to would not be a monster and that her own life would not be at risk?

Evidently they could not be absolutely sure; and as often happens with scientists who use themselves as guinea pigs for a dangerous first experiment calling for a human volunteer, Enki announced to the gathered Anunnaki that his own spouse, Ninki ("Lady of the Earth") had volunteered for the task. "Ninki, my goddess-spouse," he announced, "will be the one for labor"; she was to be the one to determine the fate of the new being:

> The newborn's fate thou shalt pronounce;
> Ninki would fix upon it the image of the gods;
> And what it will be is "Man."

The female Anunnaki chosen to serve as Birth Goddesses if the experiment succeeded, Enki said, should stay and observe what was happening. It was not, the texts reveal, a simple and smooth birth-giving process:

> The birth goddesses were kept together.
> Ninti sat, counting the months.
> The fateful tenth month was approaching,
> The tenth month arrived—
> the period of opening the womb had elapsed.

The drama of Man's creation, it appears, was compounded by a late birth; medical intervention was called for. Realizing what had to be done, Ninti "covered her head" and, with an instrument whose description was damaged on the clay tablet,

"made an opening." This done, "that which was in the womb
came forth." Grabbing the newborn baby, she was overcome
with joy. Lifting it up for all to see (as depicted in Fig. 51),
she shouted triumphantly:

> I have created!
> My hands have made it!

The first Adam was brought forth.

The successful birth of The Adam—by himself, as the first
biblical version states—confirmed the validity of the process
and opened the way for the continuation of the endeavor. Now,
enough "mixed clay" was prepared to start pregnancies in
fourteen birth goddesses at a time:

> Ninti nipped off fourteen pieces of clay,
> Seven she deposited on the right,
> Seven she deposited on the left;
> Between them she placed the mold.

Now the procedures were genetically engineered to come
up with seven males and seven females at a time. We read on
another tablet that Enki and Ninti,

> The wise and learned,
> Double-seven birth-goddesses had assembled.
> Seven brought forth males,
> Seven brought forth females;
> The birth-goddesses brought forth
> the Wind of the Breath of Life.

There is thus no conflict among the Bible's various versions
of Man's creation. First, The Adam was created by himself;
but then, in the next phase, the Elohim indeed created the first
humans "male and female."

How many times the "mass production" of Primitive Workers was repeated is not stated in the creation texts. We read
elsewhere that the Anunnaki kept clamoring for more, and that
eventually Anunnaki from the Edin—Mesopotamia—came to
the Abzu in Africa and forcefully captured a large number of

Primitive Workers to take over the manual work back in Mesopotamia. We also learn that in time, tiring of the constant need for Birth Goddesses, Enki engaged in a second genetic manipulation to enable the hybrid people to procreate on their own; but the story of that development belongs in the next chapter.

Bearing in mind that these ancient texts come to us across a bridge of time extending back for millennia, one must admire the ancient scribes who recorded, copied, and translated the earliest texts—as often as not, probably, without really knowing what this or that expression or technical term originally meant but always adhering tenaciously to the traditions that required a most meticulous and precise rendition of the copied texts.

Fortunately, as we enter the last decade of the twentieth century of the Common Era, we have the benefit of modern science on our side. The "mechanics" of cell replication and human reproduction, the function and code of the genes, the cause of many inherited defects and illnesses—all these and so many more biological processes are now understood; perhaps not yet completely but enough to allow us to evaluate the ancient tale and its data.

With all this modern knowledge at our disposal, what is the verdict on that ancient information? Is it an impossible fantasy, or are the procedures and processes, described with such attention to terminology, corroborated by modern science?

The answer is yes, it is all the way we would do it today—the way we have been following, indeed, in recent years.

We know today that to have someone or something "brought forth" in the "image" and "after the likeness" of an existing being (be it a tree, a mouse, a man) the new being must have the genes of its creator; otherwise, a totally different being would emerge. Until a few decades ago all that science was aware of was that there are sets of chromosomes lurking within every living cell that impart both the physical and mental/emotional characteristics to offspring. But now we know that the chromosomes are just stems on which long strands of DNA are positioned. With only four nucleotides at its disposal, the DNA can be sequenced in endless combinations, in short or long stretches interspersed with chemical signals that can mean "stop" or "go" instructions (or, it seems, to do nothing at all anymore). Enzymes are produced and act as chemical busybodies, launching chemical processes, sending off RNAs to do their job, creating proteins to build body and muscles, produce the myriad differentiated cells of a living creature, trigger the immune system, and, of course, help the being procreate by bringing forth offspring in its own image and after its likeness.

The beginnings of genetics are now credited to Gregor Johann Mendel, an Austrian monk who, experimenting with plant hybridization, described the hereditary traits of common peas in a study published in 1866. A kind of genetic engineering has of course been practiced in horticulture (the cultivation of flowers, vegetables, and fruits) through the procedure called grafting, where the part of the plant whose qualities are desired to be added to those of another plant is added via an incision to the recipient plant. Grafting has also been tried in recent years in the animal kingdom, but with limited success between donor and recipient due to rejection by the recipient's immune system.

The next advance, which for a while received great publicity, was the procedure called Cloning. Because each cell—let us say a human cell—contains all the genetic data necessary to reproduce that human, it has the potential for giving rise, within a female egg, to the birth of a being identical to its parent. In theory, cloning offers a way to produce an endless number of Einsteins or, heaven help us, Hitlers.

Experimentally the possibilities of cloning began to be tested with plants, as an advanced method to replace grafting. Indeed, the term *cloning* comes from the Greek *klon* which means "twig." The procedure began with the notion of implanting just one desired cell from the donor plant in the recipient plant. The technique then advanced to the stage where no recipient plant was needed at all; all that had to be done was to nourish the desired cell in a solution of nutrients until it began to grow, divide, and eventually form the whole plant. In the 1970s one of the hopes pinned on this process was that whole forests of trees identical to a desired species will be created in test tubes, then shipped in a parcel to the desired location to be planted and grow.

Adapting this technique from plants to animals proved more tricky. First, cloning involves asexual reproduction. In animals that reproduce by fertilizing an egg with a sperm, the reproductive cells (egg and sperm) differ from all other cells in that they do not contain all the *pairs* of chromosomes (which carry the genes as on stems) but only *one set* each. Thus, in a fertilized human egg ("ovum") the forty-six chromosomes that constitute the required twenty-three pairs are provided half by the mother (through the ovum) and half by the father (in the sperm). To achieve cloning, the chromosomes in the ovum must be removed surgically and a complete set of pairs inserted instead, not from a male sperm but from any other human cell. If all succeeds and the egg, nestled in the womb, becomes first an embryo, then a fetus and then a baby—the baby will be identical to the person from whose single cell it has grown.

There were other problems inherent in the process, too technical to detail here, but they were slowly overcome with the aid of experimentation, improved instruments, and progress in understanding genetics. One intriguing finding that aided the experiments was that the younger the source of the transplanted nucleus the better the chances of success. In 1975 British scientists succeeded in cloning frogs from tadpole cells; the procedure required the removal of a frog egg's nucleus and its replacement with a tadpole cell's nucleus. This was achieved by microsurgery, possible because the cells in question are considerably larger than, say, human cells. In 1980 and 1981 Chinese and American scientists claimed to have cloned fish with similar techniques; flies were also experimented on.

When the experiments shifted to mammals, mice and rabbits were chosen because of their short reproductive cycles. The problem with mammals was not only the complexity of their cells and cell nuclei but also the need to nestle the fertilized egg in a womb. Better results were obtained when the egg's nucleus was not removed surgically but was inactivated by radiation; even better results followed when this nucleus was "evicted" chemically and the new nucleus also introduced chemically; the procedure, developed through experiments on rabbit eggs by J. Derek Bromhall of Oxford University, became known as Chemical Fusion.

Other experiments relating to the cloning of mice seemed

to indicate that for a mammal's egg to be fertilized, to start dividing, and, even more important, to begin the process of differentiation (into the specialized cells that become the different parts of the body), more than the donor's set of chromosomes is needed. Experimenting at Yale, Clement L. Markert concluded that there was something in the male sperm that promoted these processes, something beside the chromosomes; that ''the sperm might also be contributing some unidentified spur that stimulates development of the egg.''

In order to prevent the sperm's male chromosomes from merging with the egg's female chromosomes (which would have resulted in a normal fertilization rather than in cloning), one set had to be removed surgically just before the merger began and the remaining set ''excited'' by physical or chemical means to double itself. If the sperm's chromosomes were chosen for the latter role, the embryo might become either male or female; if the egg's set were chosen and duplicated, the embryo could only be female. While Markert was continuing his experiments on such methods of nuclear transfer, two other scientists (Peter C. Hoppe and Karl Illmensee) announced in 1977 the successful birth, at the Jackson Laboratory in Bar Harbor, Maine, of seven ''single-parent mice.'' The process, however, was more accurately designated parthenogenesis, ''virgin birth,'' than cloning; since what the experimenters did was to cause the chromosomes in the egg of a female mouse to double, keep the egg with the full set of chromosomes in certain solutions, and then, after the cell had divided several times, introduce the self-fertilized cell into the womb of a female mouse. Significantly, the recipient mouse had to be a different female, not the mouse whose own egg had been used.

Quite a stir was caused early in 1978 by the publication of a book that purported to relate how an eccentric American millionaire, obsessed by the prospect of death, sought immortality by arranging to be cloned. The book claimed that the nucleus of a cell taken from the millionaire was inserted into a female egg, which was carried through pregnancy to a successful birth by a female volunteer; the boy, fit and healthy in all respects, was reported at the time of publication to have been fourteen months old. Though written as a factual report, the tale was received with disbelief. The scientific community's

skepticism stemmed not from the impossibility of the feat—
indeed, that it would one day be possible almost all concerned
agreed—but from doubts whether the feat could have been
achieved by an unknown group in the Caribbean when the best
researchers had only, at that time, achieved the virgin birth of
mice. There was also doubt about the successful cloning of a
male adult, when all the experiments had indicated that the
older the donor's cell, the lower the chances of success.

With the memory of the horrors inflicted on Mankind by
Nazi Germany in the name of a "master race" still fresh, even
the possibility of cloning selected humans for evil purposes (a
theme of Ira Levin's best-selling novel *The Boys from Brazil*)
was reason enough to dampen interest in this avenue of genetic
manipulation. One alternative, which substituted the "Should
man play God?" outcry with what one might call the "Can
science play husband?" idea, was the process that led to the
phenomenon of "Test-tube babies."

Research conducted at Texas A & M University in 1976
showed that it was possible to remove an embryo from a mammal (a baboon, in that instance) within five days of ovulation
and reimplant it in the uterus of another female baboon in a
transfer that led to a successful pregnancy and birth. Other
researchers found ways to extract the eggs of small mammals
and fertilize them in test tubes. The two processes, that of
Embryo Transfer and In vitro Fertilization, were employed in
an event that made medical history in July, 1978, when Louise
Brown was born at the Oldham and District General Hospital
in northwest England. The first of many other test-tube babies,
she was conceived in a test tube, not by her parents but by
techniques employed by Doctors Patrick Steptoe and Robert
Edwards. Nine months earlier they had used a device with a
light at its end to suck out a mature egg from Mrs. Brown's
ovary. Bathed in a dish containing life-support nutrients, the
extracted egg was "mixed"—the word was used by Dr. Edwards—with the husband's sperm. Once a sperm succeeded
in fertilizing the egg, the egg was transferred to a dish containing other nutrients, where it began to divide. After fifty
hours it had reached an eight-celled division; at that point, the
egg was re-implanted in Mrs. Brown's womb. With care and
special treatment, the embryo developed properly; a caesarean

delivery completed the feat, and a couple who before this could not have a child because of the wife's defective fallopian tubes now had a normal daughter.

"We have a girl and she's perfect!" the gynecologist who performed the caesarean delivery shouted as he held up the baby.

"I have created, my hands have made it!" Ninti cried out as she delivered the Adam by caesarean section, an eon earlier. . . .

Also reminiscent of the ancient reports of the long road of trial and error taken by Enki and Ninti was the fact that the Baby Louise "breakthrough" about which the media went wild (Fig. 55) came after twelve years of trial and error, in the course of which fetuses and even babies turned out defective. Undoubtedly unbeknown to the doctors and researchers was the fact that, in discovering also that the addition of *blood* serum to the mixture of nutrients and sperm was essential to

Figure 55

success, they were following the very same procedures that Enki and Ninti had employed. . . .

Although the feat gave new hope to barren women (it also opened the way to surrogate motherhood, embryo freezing, semen banks, and new legal entanglements), it was just a distant cousin of the feat accomplished by Enki and Ninti. Yet it had to employ the techniques of which we have read in the ancient texts—just as the scientists engaged in nucleus transfers have found that the male donor must be young, as the Sumerian texts have stressed.

The most obvious difference between the test-tube baby variants and what the ancient texts describe is that in the former the natural process of procreation is emulated: human male sperm fertilize a human female egg that then develops in the womb. In the case of the creation of The Adam, the genetic material of two different (even if not dissimilar) species was mixed to create a new being, positioned somewhere between the two "parents."

In recent years modern science has made substantial advances in such genetic manipulation. With the aid of increasingly sophisticated equipment, computers, and ever-more minute instruments, scientists have been able to "read" the genetic code of living organisms, up to and including that of Man. Not only has it become possible to read the A-G-C-T of DNA and the A-G-C-U "letters" of the genetic "alphabet," but we can now also recognize the three-letter "words" of the genetic code (like AGG, AAT, GCC, GGG—and so on in myriad combinations) as well as the segments of the DNA strands that form genes, each with its specific task—for example, to determine the color of the eyes, to direct growth, or to transmit a hereditary disease. Scientists have also found that some of the code's "words" simply act to instruct the replication process where to start and when to stop. Gradually, scientists have become able to transcribe the genetic code to a computer screen and to recognize in the printouts (Fig. 56) the "stop" and "go" signs. The next step was to tediously find out the function of each segment, or gene—of which the simple *E. coli* bacterium has about 4,000 and human beings well over 100,000. Plans are now afoot to "map" the

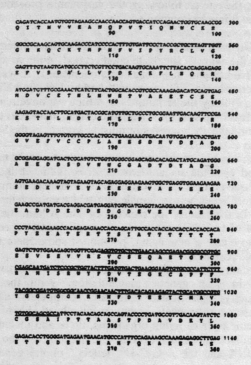

Figure 56

complete human genetic makeup ("Genome"); the enormity
of the task, and the extent of the knowledge already gained,
can be appreciated by the fact that if the DNA in all human
cells were extracted and put in a box, the box need be no bigger
than an ice cube; but if the twisting strands of DNA were
stretched out, the string would extend 47 million miles. . . .

In spite of these complexities, it has become possible, with
the aid of enzymes, to cut DNA strands at desired places,
remove a "sentence" that makes up a gene, and even insert
into the DNA a foreign gene; through these techniques an
undesired trait (such as one that causes disease) can be removed

or a desired one (such as a growth-hormone gene) added. The advances in understanding and manipulating this fundamental chemistry of life were recognized in 1980 with the award of the Nobel prize in chemistry to Walter Gilbert of Harvard and Frederick Sanger of Cambridge University for the development of rapid methods for reading large segments of DNA, and to Paul Berg of Stanford University for pioneering work in ''gene splicing.'' Another term used for the procedures is ''Recombinant DNA technology,'' because after the splicing, the DNA is recombined with newly introduced segments of DNA.

These capabilities have made possible gene therapy, the removal from or correction within human cells of genes causing inherited sicknesses and defects. It has also made possible Biogenetics: inducing, through genetic manipulation, bacteria or mice to manufacture a needed chemical (such as insulin) for medical treatment. Such feats of recombinant technology are possible because all the DNA in all living organisms on Earth is of the same makeup, so that a strand of bacteria DNA will accept (''recombine'' with) a segment of human DNA. (Indeed, American and Swiss researchers reported in July 1984 the discovery of a DNA segment that was common to human beings, flies, earthworms, chickens, and frogs—further corroboration of the single genetic origin of all life on Earth.)

Hybrids such as a mule, which is the progeny of a donkey and a horse, can be born from the mating of the two because they have similar chromosomes (hybrids, however, cannot procreate). A sheep and a goat, though not too distant relatives, cannot naturally mate; however, because of their genetic kinship, experiments have brought them together to form (in 1983) a ''geep'' (Fig. 57)—a sheep with its woolly coat but with a goat's horns. Such mixed, or ''mosaic,'' creatures are called chimeras, after the monster in Greek mythology that had the forepart of a lion, the middle of a goat, and the tail of a dragon (Fig. 58). The feat was attained by ''Cell Fusion,'' the fusing together of a sheep embryo and a goat embryo at the stage of their early divisions into four cells each, then incubating the mixture in a test tube with nutrients until it was time to transfer the mixed embryo to the womb of a sheep that acted as a surrogate mother.

In such cell fusions, the outcome (even if a viable offspring

Figure 57

Figure 58

is born) cannot be predicted; it is totally a matter of chance which genes will end up where on the chromosomes, and what traits—"images" and "likenesses"—will be picked up from which cell donor. There is little doubt that the monsters of Greek mythology, including the famous Minotaur (half bull, half man) of Crete, were recollections of the tales transmitted to the Greeks by Berossus, the Babylonian priest, and that his sources were the Sumerian texts concerning the trial-and-error experiments of Enki and Ninti which produced all kinds of chimeras.

The advances in genetics have provided biotechnology with other routes than the unpredictable chimera route; it is evident that in doing so, modern science has followed the alternate (though more difficult) course of action undertaken by Enki and Ninti. By cutting out and adding on pieces of the genetic strands, or Recombinant Technology, the traits to be omitted, added, or exchanged can be specified and targeted. Some of the landmarks along this progress in genetic engineering were the transfer of bacterial genes to plants to make the latter resistant to certain diseases and, later (in 1980), of specific bacteria genes into mice. In 1982 growth genes of a rat were spliced into the genetic code of a mouse (by teams headed by Ralph L. Brinster of the University of Pennsylvania and Richard D. Palmiter of Howard Hughes Medical Institute), resulting in the birth of a "Mighty Mouse" twice the size of a normal mouse. In 1985 it was reported in *Nature* (June 27) that experimenters at various scientific centers had succeeded in inserting functioning *human* growth genes into rabbits, pigs, and sheep; and in 1987 (*New Scientist*, September 17) Swedish scientists likewise created a Super-Salmon. By now, genes carrying other traits have been used in such "trans-genic" recombinations between bacteria, plants, and mammals. Techniques have even progressed to the artificial manufacture of compounds that perfectly emulate specific functions of a given gene, mainly with a view to treating diseases.

In mammals, the altered fertilized female egg ultimately must be implanted in the womb of a surrogate mother—the function that was assigned, according to the Sumerian tales, to the "Birth Goddesses." But before that stage, a way had to be found to introduce the desired genetic traits from the male donor into the egg of the female participant. The most common method is micro-injection, by which a female egg, already fertilized, is extracted and injected with the desired added genetic trait; after a short incubation in a glass dish, the egg is reimplanted in a female womb (mice, pigs, and other mammals have been tried). The procedure is difficult, has many hurdles, and results in only a small percentage of successes— but it works. Another technique has been the use of viruses, which naturally attack cells and fuse with their genetic cores: the new genetic trait to be transferred into a cell is attached by complex ways to a virus, which then acts as the carrier; the problem here is that the choice of the site on the chromosome stem to which the gene is to be attached is uncontrollable, and in most cases chimeras have resulted.

In June 1989 a report in *Cell* by a team of Italian scientists headed by Corrado Spadafora of the Institute of Biomedical Technology in Rome announced success in using sperm to act as the carriers of the new gene. They reported procedures whereby sperm were induced to let down their natural resistance to foreign genes; then, after being soaked in solutions containing the new genetic material, the sperm incorporated the genetic material into their cores. The altered sperm were then used to impregnate female mice; the offspring contained the new gene in their chromosomes (in this case a certain bacterial enzyme).

The use of the most natural medium—sperm—to carry genetic material into a female egg astounded the scientific community in its simplicity and made front-page news even in *The New York Times*. A follow-up study in *Science* of August 11, 1989, reported mixed successes by other scientists in duplicating the Italian technique. But all the scientists involved in recombinant technologies concurred that, with some modifications and improvements, a new technique—and the most simple and natural one—has been developed.

Some have pointed out that the ability of sperm to take up foreign DNA was suggested by researchers as early as 1971, after experiments with rabbit sperm. Little is it realized that the technique had been reported even earlier, in Sumerian texts describing the creation of The Adam by Enki and Ninti, who had mixed the Apewoman's egg in a test tube with the sperm of a young Anunnaki in a solution also containing blood serum.

In 1987 the dean of anthropology at the University of Florence, Italy, raised a storm of protests by clergymen and humanists when he revealed that ongoing experiments could lead to the "creation of a new breed of slave, an anthropoid with a chimpanzee mother and a human father." One of my fans sent me the clipping of the story with the comment, *"Well, Enki, here we go again!"*

This seems to best sum up the achievements of modern microbiology.

SARAH - ABRAHAMS 1/2 sister & wife

WASPS, MONKEYS,
AND BIBLICAL PATRIARCHS

Much of what has happened on Earth, and especially its earliest wars, stemmed from the Succession Code of the Anunnaki that deprived the firstborn son of the succession if another son was born to the ruler by a half sister.

The same succession rules, adopted by the Sumerians, are reflected in the tales of the Hebrew Patriarchs. The Bible relates that Abraham (who came from the Sumerian capital city of Ur) asked his wife Sarah (a name that meant "Princess") to identify herself, when meeting foreign kings, as his sister rather than as his wife. Though not the whole truth it was not a lie, as explained in Genesis 20:12: "Indeed she is my sister, the daughter of my father but not the daughter of my mother, and she became my wife."

Abraham's successor was not the firstborn Ishmael, whose mother was the handmaiden Hagar, but Isaac, the son of the half sister Sarah, though he was born much later.

The strict adherence to these succession rules in antiquity in all royal courts, whether in Egypt of the Old World or in the Inca empire in the New World, suggest some "bloodline," or genetic, assumption that appears odd and contrary to the belief that mating with close relatives is undesirable.

But did the Anunnaki know something modern science has yet to discover?

In 1980 a group led by Hannah Wu at Washington University found that, given a choice, female monkeys preferred to mate with half brothers. "The exciting thing about this experiment," the report stated, "is that although the preferred half brothers shared the same father, they had different mothers." *Discover* magazine (December 1988) reported studies showing that "male wasps ordinarily mate with their sisters." Since one male wasp fertilizes many females, the preferential mating was found to be with *half* sisters: same father but different mother.

It appears thus that there was more than whim to the succession code of the Anunnaki.

9

THE MOTHER CALLED EVE

By tracing Hebrew words in the Bible through their Akkadian stem to their Sumerian origin it has been possible to understand the true meaning of biblical tales, especially those in the Book of Genesis. The fact that so many Sumerian terms had more than one meaning, mostly but not always derived from a common original pictograph, constitutes a major difficulty in understanding Sumerian and requires reading them carefully in context. On the other hand, the propensity of Sumerian writers to use that for frequent plays of words, makes their texts an intelligent reader's joy.

Dealing, for example, with the biblical tale of the "upheavaling" of Sodom and Gomorrah in *The Wars of Gods and Men*, I pointed out that the notion that Lot's wife was turned into a "pillar of salt" when she stayed back to watch what was happening, in fact meant "pillar of vapor" in the original Sumerian terminology. Since salt was obtained in Sumer from vapor-filled swamps, the original Sumerian term NI.MUR came to mean both "salt" and "vapor." Poor Lot's wife was vaporized, not turned into salt, by the nuclear blasts that caused the upheaval of the cities of the plain.

Regarding the biblical tale of Eve, it was the great Sumerologist Samuel N. Kramer who first pointed out that her name, which meant in Hebrew "She who has life," and the tale of her origin from Adam's rib in all probability stemmed from the Sumerian play on the word TI, which meant both "life" and "rib."

Some other original or double meanings in the creation tales have already been mentioned in a previous chapter. More can be gleaned about "Eve" and her origins from comparisons of the biblical tales with the Sumerian texts and an analysis of Sumerian terminology.

The genetic manipulations, we have seen, were conducted by Enki and Ninti in a special facility called, in the Akkadian versions, *Bit Shimti*—"House where the wind of life is breathed in"; this meaning conveys a pretty accurate idea of what the purpose of the specialized structure, a laboratory, was. But here we have to invite into the discussion the Sumerian penchant for word play, thereby throwing fresh light on the source of the tale of Adam's rib, the use of clay, and the breaths of life.

The Akkadian term, as earlier stated, was a rendering of the Sumerian SHI.IM.TI. a compound word in which each of the three components conveyed a meaning that combined with, strengthened, and expanded the other two. SHI stood for what the Bible called *Nephesh*, commonly translated "soul" but more accurately meaning "breath of life." IM had several meanings, depending on the context. It meant "wind," but it could also mean "side." In astronomical texts it denoted a satellite that is "by the side" of its planet; in geometry it meant the side of a square or triangle; and in anatomy it meant "rib." To this day the parallel Hebrew word *Şela* means both the side of a geometric shape and a person's rib. And, lo and behold, IM also had a totally unrelated fourth meaning: "clay." . . .

As if the multiple meanings "wind"/"side"/"rib"/"clay" of IM were not enough, the term TI added to the Sumerians' linguistic fun. It meant, as previously mentioned, both "life" and "rib"—the latter being the parallel of the Akkadian *şilu*, from which came the Hebrew *Şela*. Doubled, TI.TI meant "belly"—that which held the fetus; and, lo and behold, in Akkadian *titu* acquired the meaning "clay," from which the Hebrew word *Tit* has survived. Thus, the component TI of the laboratory's Sumerian name, SHI.IM.TI, we have the meanings "life"/"clay"/"belly"/"rib."

In the absence of the original Sumerian version from which the compilers of Genesis might have obtained their data, one cannot be sure whether they had chosen the "rib" interpretation because it was conveyed by both IM and TI or because it gave them an opening to making a social statement in the ensuing verses:

And Yahweh Elohim caused a deep sleep
upon the Adam, and he slept.
And He took one of his ribs
and closed up the flesh in its place.
And Yahweh Elohim constructed of the rib
which He had taken from the Adam a woman,
and He brought her to the Adam.
And the Adam said,
"This is now bone of my bones,
flesh of my flesh."

Therefore is the being called *Ish-sha* ["Woman"]
because out of *Ish* ["Man"] was this one taken.
Therefore doth a man leave his father and his mother
and shall cleave unto his wife
to become as one flesh.

This tale of the creation of Man's female counterpart relates
how the Adam, having already been placed in the E.DIN to
till it and tend its orchards, was all alone. "And Yahweh
Elohim said, it is not good that the Adam is by himself; let
me make him a mate." This obviously is a continuation of the
version whereby The Adam alone was created, and not part of
the version whereby Mankind was created male and female
right away.

In order to resolve this seeming confusion, the sequence of
creating the Earthlings must be borne in mind. First the male
lulu, "mixed one" was perfected; then the fertilized eggs of
Apewoman, bathed and mixed with the blood serum and sperm
of a young Anunnaki, were divided into batches and placed in
a "mold," where they acquired either male or female characteristics. Reimplanted in the wombs of Birth Goddesses, the
embryos produced seven males and seven females each time.
But these "mixed ones" were hybrids, which could not procreate (as mules cannot). To get more of them, the process
had to be repeated over and over again.

At some point it became apparent that this way of obtaining
the serfs was not good enough; a way had to be found to get
more of these humans without imposing the pregnancies and
deliveries on female Anunnaki. That way was a second genetic

manipulation by Enki and Ninti, giving The Adam the ability to procreate on his own. To be able to have offspring, Adam had to mate with a fully compatible female. How and why she was brought into being is the story of the Rib and of the Garden of Eden.

The tale of the Rib reads almost like a two-sentence summary of a report in a medical journal. In no uncertain terms it describes a major operation of the kind that makes headlines nowadays, when a close relative (for example, a father or a sister) donates an organ for transplant. Increasingly, modern medicine resorts to the transplantation of bone marrow when the malady is a cancer or affects the immune system.

The donor in the biblical case is Adam. He is given general anesthesia and is put to sleep. An incision is made and a rib is removed. The flesh is then pulled together to close up the wound, and Adam is allowed to rest and recover.

The action continues elsewhere. The Elohim now use the piece of bone to construct a woman; not to create a woman, but to "construct" one. The difference in terminology is significant; it indicates that the female in question already existed but required some constructive manipulation to become a mate for Adam. Whatever was needed was obtained from the rib, and the clue to what the rib supplied lies in the other meanings of IM and TI—life, belly, clay. Was an extract of Adam's bone marrow implanted in that of a female Primitive Worker's "clay" through her belly? Regrettably, the Bible does not describe what was done to the female (named Eve by Adam), and the Sumerian texts that have surely dealt with this point have not been found so far. That something of the kind did exist is certain from the fact that the best available translation of the *Atra Hasis* text into Early Assyrian (about 850 B.C.) contains lines that parallel some of the biblical verses about a man leaving his father's house and becoming as one with his wife as they lie in bed together. The tablet that carries this text is too damaged, however, to reveal all that the Sumerian original text had to say.

But we do know nowadays, thanks to modern science, that sexuality and the ability to procreate lie in human chromosomes; each person's cell contains twenty-three pairs—in the case of a woman a pair of X chromosomes and in the case of

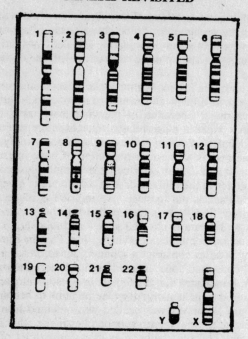

Figure 59

men one *X* and one *Y* chromosome (Fig. 59). However, the reproductive cells (female egg, male sperm) each contain only one set of chromosomes, not pairs. The pairing takes place when the egg is fertilized by the sperm; the embryo thus has the twenty-three pairs of chromosomes, but only half of them come from the mother and only half from the father. The mother, having two *X* chromosomes, always contributes an *X*. The father, having both an *X* and a *Y*, may end up contributing either one; if it is an *X*, the baby will be female; if a *Y*, it will be a male.

The key to reproduction thus lies in the fusion of the two single sets of chromosomes; if their number and genetic code differ, they will not combine and the beings will not procreate. Since both female and male Primitive Workers already existed, their sterility was not due to the lack of *X* or *Y* chromosomes. The need for a *bone*—the Bible stresses that Eve was "bone of the bones" of Adam—suggests that there was a need to overcome some immunological rejection by the female Primitive Workers of the males' sperms. The operation carried out by the Elohim overcame this problem. Adam and Eve discovered their sexuality, having acquired "knowing"—a biblical term that connoted sex for the purpose of procreation ("And Adam *knew* Eve his wife and she conceived and gave birth to Cain."). Eve, as the tale of the two of them in the Garden of Eden relates, was thenceforth able to become pregnant by Adam, receiving from the deity a blessing combined with a curse: "In suffering shalt thou bear children."

With that, "The Adam," Elohim said, "has become as one of us." He was granted "Knowing." *Homo sapiens* was able to procreate and multiply on his own. But though he was given a good measure of the genetic makeup of the Anunnaki, who made Man in their image and after their likeness even in this respect of procreation, one genetic trait was not transmitted. That was the longevity of the Anunnaki. Of the fruit of the "Tree of Life," partaking of which would have made Man live as long as the Anunnaki, he was not even to taste. This point is clearly spelled out in the Sumerian tale of *Adapa*, the Perfect Man created by Enki:

> Wide understanding he perfected for him. . . .
> Wisdom he had given him. . . .
> To him he had given Knowing;
> Eternal life he had not given him.

Ever since publication of *The 12th Planet* in 1976, I have spared no effort to explain the seeming "immortality" of the "gods." Using flies in my home as an example, I have been wont to say that if flies could talk, Papa Fly would tell Son Fly, "You know, this man here is immortal; as long as I have lived, he has not aged at all; my father told me that his father, all our forefathers as far as we can remember, have seen this man the way he is: ever-living, immortal!"

My "immortality" (in the eyes of the talking flies) is, of course, simply a result of the different life cycles. Man lives so many decades of years; flies count their lives in days. But what are all these terms? A "day" is the time it takes our planet to complete one revolution about its axis; a "year" is the time it takes our planet to complete one orbit around the Sun. The length of time activities by the Anunnaki took on Earth was counted in *sars*, each one equivalent to 3,600 Earth-years. A *sar*, I have suggested, was the "year" on Nibiru—the time it took that planet to complete one orbit around the Sun. So when the Sumerian King Lists reported, for example, that one leader of the Anunnaki administered one of their cities for 36,000 years, the text actual states *ten sars*. If a single generation for Man is twenty years, there would be 180 generations of Man's progeny in one Anunnaki "year"—making them appear to be Forever Living, "immortal."

The ancient texts make clear that this longevity was not passed on to Man, but intelligence was. This implies a belief or knowledge, in antiquity, that the two traits, intelligence and longevity, could somehow be bestowed upon or denied to Man by those who had genetically created him. Not surprisingly, perhaps, modern science agrees. "Evidence amassed over the past 60 years suggests that there is a genetic component to intelligence," *Scientific American* reported in its March 1989 issue. Besides giving examples of geniuses in various fields who had bequeathed their talents to children and grandchildren, the article highlighted a report by researchers from the University of Colorado at Boulder and Pennsylvania State University (David W. Fulker, John C. DeFries, and Robert Plomin), who had established a "close biological correlation" in mental abilities attributable to genetic heredity. *Scientific American* headlined the article, "More Evidence Links Genes and Intelligence." Other studies, recognizing that "memories are made of molecules," have led to the suggestion that if computers are ever to match human intelligence, they ought to be "molecular computers." Updating suggestions made in this direction by Forrest Carter of the Naval Research Laboratories in Washington, D.C., John Hopfield of Caltech and AT&T's Bell Laboratories outlined in 1988 (*Science*, vol. 241) a blueprint for a "biological computer."

Evidence has also been mounting for the genetic source of the life cycles of living organisms. The various stages in the life of insects and the length of time they live are clearly genetically orchestrated. So is the fact that so many creatures—but not mammals—die after reproducing. Octupuses, for example, it was discovered (by Jerome Wodinsky of Brandeis University) are genetically programmed to "self-destruct" after reproduction through chemicals found in their optical glands. The studies were carried out in the course of research on the aging process in animals, not on the life of octupuses per se. Many other studies have shown that some animals possess the capacity to repair damaged genes in their cells and thus halt or reverse the aging process. Every species clearly has a life span fixed by its genes—a single day for the mayfly, about six years for a frog, a limit of about fifteen for a dog. Nowadays the human limit lies somewhere not much beyond one hundred years but in earlier times human life spans were much longer.

According to the Bible, Adam lived to be 930 years old, his son Seth 912 years, and *his* son Enosh, 905. Although there is reason to believe that the editors of Genesis reduced by a factor of 60 the much greater life spans reported in the Sumerian texts, the Bible does acknowledge that mankind had much longer lifetimes before the Deluge. Patriarchal life spans began to shorten as the millennia raced on. Terah, Abraham's father, died at the age of 205. Abraham lived 175 years; his son Isaac died at age 180. Isaac's son Jacob lived to be 147 but Jacob's son passed away at age 110.

While it is believed the genetic errors that accumulate as DNA keeps reproducing itself in the cells contribute to the aging process, scientific evidence indicates the existence of a biological "clock" in all creatures, a basic, built-in genetic trait that controls the life span of each species. What that gene or group of genes is, what makes it tick, what triggers it to "express" itself, are still matters of intense research. But that the answer lies in the genes has been shown by numerous studies. Some, on viruses, show that they possess fragments of DNA that can literally "immortalize" them.

Enki must have known all that, so that when it came to perfecting The Adam—creating a true, procreating *Homo sapiens*—he gave Adam intelligence and "Knowing," but not the full longevity that the Anunnaki genes possessed.

As Mankind keeps distancing itself from the days of its creation as a *Lulu*, a "mixed" being who carried the genetic heritage of both the Earth and the Heavens, the shortening of its average life span might be seen as a symptom of the minute loss, from generation to generation, of what some consider "divine" elements and the increasing preponderance of the "animal which is within us." The existence in our genetic makeup of what some call "nonsense" DNA—segments of DNA that seem to have lost their purpose—is an apparent leftover from the original "mixing." The two independent, though connected, parts of the brain—one more primitive and emotional, the other newer and more rational—are another attestation to the mixed genetic origin of Mankind.

The evidence that corroborates the ancient tales of creation, massive as it has been so far, does not end with genetic manipulation. There is more to come, and it is all above Eve!

Modern anthropology, with the aid of fossil finds by paleontologists and advances in other fields of science, has made great strides in tracing back the origin of Man. By now the question "Where did we come from?" has been clearly answered: Mankind arose in southeastern Africa.

The story of Man, we now know, did not begin with Man; the "chapter" that tells of the group of mammals called "Primates" takes us back some forty-five or fifty million years, when a common ancestor of monkeys, apes, and Man appeared in Africa. Twenty-five or thirty million years later—that is how slowly the wheels of evolution turn—a precursor of the Great Apes branched off the primate line. In the 1920s fossils of this early ape, "Proconsul," were found by chance on an island in Lake Victoria (see map), and the find eventually attracted to the area the best-known husband-wife team of paleontologists, Louis S. B. and Mary Leakey. Besides Proconsul fossils they also discovered in the area remains of *Ramapithecus*, the first erect ape or manlike primate; it was some fourteen million years old—some eight or ten million years up the evolutionary tree from Proconsul.

These discoveries meant more than finding a few fossils; they unlocked the door to nature's secret laboratory, the hideaway where Mother Nature keeps forging ahead with the ev-

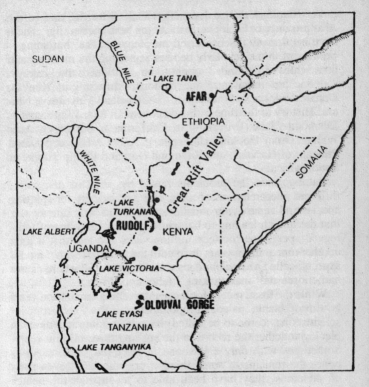

Figure 60

olutionary march that has led from mammal to primate to great apes to hominids. The place was the rift valley that slashes through Ethiopia, Kenya, and Tanzania—part of the rift system that begins in the Jordan Valley and the Dead Sea in Israel, includes the Red Sea, and runs all the way to southern Africa (map, Fig. 60).

Numerous fossil finds have been made at sites that the Leakeys and other paleoanthropologists have made famous. The richest finds have been in Olduvai Gorge in Tanzania; near

Lake Rudolf (renamed Lake Turkana) in Kenya; and in the Afar province of Ethiopia, to name the best-known sites. There have been many discoverers from many nations, but some—prominent in the scholarly debates regarding the meaning and time scales of the finds—ought to be mentioned: the Leakeys' son Richard (curator of the National Museums of Kenya), Donald C. Johanson (curator at the Cleveland Museum of Natural History at the time of his discoveries), Tim White, and J. Desmond Clark (University of California at Berkeley), Alan Walker (John Hopkins University), Andrew Hill and David Pilbeam of Harvard, and Raymond Dart and Phillip Tobias of South Africa.

Putting aside the problems raised by pride of discovery, different interpretations of finds, and a propensity for splitting species and genuses into smaller subdivisions, it is safe to state that the branch leading to humans separated from that of four-legged apes some fourteen million years ago and that it took another nine million years or so until the first apes with hominid aspects, called *Australopithecus*, showed up—all where nature had chosen its "man-making" laboratory to be.

While the fossil record for those intervening ten million years is almost blank, paleoanthropologists (as the new group of scientists has come to be called) have been quite ingenious in piecing together the record in the ensuing three million years. Sometimes with only a jawbone, a fractured skull, a pelvis bone, the remains of some fingers, or, with luck, even parts of skeletons, they have been able to reconstruct the beings these fossils represented; with the aid of other finds, such as animal bones or stones crudely shaped to serve as tools, they have determined the developmental stage and customs of the beings; and by dating the geologic strata in which the fossils are found, they have been able to date the fossils themselves.

Among the outstanding road markers have been such finds as skeletal parts of a female nicknamed "Lucy" (who might have looked like the hominid in Fig. 61)—believed to have been an advanced Australopithecus who lived some 3.5 million years ago; a fossil known by its catalog number as "Skull 1470" of a male from perhaps 2 million years ago and considered by its finders to be a "near man," or *Homo habilis* ("Handy Man")—a term to whose implications many object;

Lucy?

Homo erectus

Figure 61

and skeletal remains of a "strapping young male" cataloged WT.15000 of a *Homo erectus* from about 1.5 million years ago, probably the first true hominid. He ushered in the Old Stone Age; he began to use stones as tools, and migrated via the Sinai peninsula, which acts as a land bridge between Africa and Asia, to southeast Asia on the one hand and to southern Europe on the other.

The trail of the *Homo* genus is lost after that; the chapter between about 1.5 million years to about 300,000 years ago is missing, except for traces of *Homo erectus* on the peripheries of this hominid's migrations. Then, about 300,000 years ago, without any evidence of gradual change, *Homo sapiens* made his appearance. At first it was believed that *Homo sapiens neanderthalis*, Neanderthal man (so named after the site of his first discovery in Germany), who came into prominence in Europe and parts of Asia about 125,000 years ago, was the ancestor of the Cro-Magnons, *Homo sapiens sapiens*, who took over the lands about 35,000 years ago. Then it was held that the more "brutish" and thus "primitive" Neanderthal stemmed from a different *Homo sapiens* branch, that Cro-Magnon had developed somewhere on his own. Now it is known that the latter notion is more correct, but not entirely. Related but not the offspring of each other, the two lines of *Homo sapiens* lived side by side as far back as 90,000 or even 100,000 years ago.

The evidence was found in two caves, one on Mount Carmel and the other near Nazareth, in Israel; they are among a number of caves in the area where prehistoric man had made himself a home. The first finds in the 1930s were believed to be about 70,000 years old and only of Neanderthal Man, thus fitting well with the theories then held. In the 1960s a joint Israeli-French team reexcavated the cave at Qafzeh, the one near Nazareth, and discovered that the remains were not only of Neanderthals but also of Cro-Magnon types. In fact, the layering indicated that Cro-Magnons had used the cave *before* the Neanderthals—a fact that pushed back the appearance of the Cro-Magnons from the supposed 35,000 years ago to well before 70,000 years ago.

Themselves incredulous, the scientists at Hebrew University in Jerusalem turned for verification to the remains of rodents found in the same layers. Their examination gave the same incredible date: Cro-Magnons, *Homo sapiens sapiens*, who were not supposed to have made an appearance before 35,000 years ago, had reached the Near East and settled in what is now Israel more than 70,000 years ago. Moreover, for a long time they shared the area with the Neanderthals.

At the end of 1987 the finds at Qafzeh and Kebara, the cave on Mount Carmel, were dated by new methods, including Thermoluminescence, a technique that gives reliable dates much further back than the 40,000-to-50,000–year limit of radiocarbon dating. As reported in two issues (vols. 330 and 340) of *Nature* by the leader of the French team, Helene Vallades of the National Research Center at Gif sur Yvette, the results showed without doubt that both Neanderthals *and* Cro-Magnons dwelt in the area between 90,000 and 100,000 years ago (scientists now use 92,000 years as the mean date). These dings were confirmed later at another site in the Galilee.

Devoting an editorial in *Nature* to the findings, Christopher

Stringer of the British Museum acknowledged that the conventional view that Neanderthals preceded Cro-Magnons had to be discarded. Both lines appeared to stem from an earlier form of *Homo sapiens*. "Wherever the original 'Eden' for modern humans might have been," the editorial stated, it now appeared that for some reason Neanderthals were the first to migrate northward, about 125,000 years ago. Joined by his colleague, Peter Andrews, and Ofer Bar-Yosef of Hebrew University and Harvard, they forcefully argued for an "Out of Africa" interpretation of these finds. A northward migration by these first *Homo sapiens* from an African birthplace was confirmed by the discovery (by Fred Wendorf of Southern Methodist University, Dallas) of a Neanderthal skull near the Nile in Egypt that was 80,000 years old.

"Does it all mean an earlier dawn for humans?" a *Science* headline asked. As scientists from other disciplines joined the search, it became clear the answer was yes. The Neanderthals, it was determined, were not just visitors to the Near East but long-time dwellers there. And they were not the primitive brutes that earlier notions had made them out to be. They buried their dead in rituals that indicated religious practices and "at least one type of spiritually motivated behavior that allies them with modern humans" (Jared M. Diamond of the University of California Medical School at Los Angeles). Some, as the discoverer of Neanderthal remains at the Shanidar cave, Ralph S. Solecki of Columbia University, believe that the Neanderthals knew how to use herbs for healing—60,000 years ago. Skeletal finds in the Israeli caves convinced anatomists that, contrary to previously held theories, Neanderthals could speak: "Fossil brain casts show a well-developed language area," stated Dean Falk of the State University of New York at Albany. And "Neanderthal's brain was bigger than ours . . . he was not dull-witted and inarticulate," concluded neuroanatomist Terrence Deacon of Harvard.

All these recent discoveries have left no doubt that Neanderthal man was without doubt a *Homo sapiens*—not an ancestor of Cro-Magnon man but an earlier type from the same human stock.

In March 1987 Christopher Stringer of the British Museum, along with a colleague, Paul Mellars, organized a conference

at Cambridge University to update and digest the new findings
concerning "The Origins and Dispersal of Modern Man." As
reported by J. A. J. Gowlett in *Antiquity* (July 1987), the con-
ferees first considered the fossil evidence. They concluded that
after a hiatus of 1.2 to 1.5 million years by *Homo erectus,
Homo sapiens* made a sudden appearance soon after 300,000
years ago (as evidenced by fossil remains in Ethiopia, Kenya,
and South Africa). Neanderthals "differentiated" from those
early *Homo sapiens* ("Wise man") about 230,000 years ago
and may have begun their northward migrations 100,000 years
later, perhaps coinciding with the appearance of *Homo sapiens
sapiens*.

The conference also examined other lines of evidence, including the brand-new data provided by the field of biochemistry. Most exciting were the findings based on genetics. The
ability of geneticists to trace parentage through comparisons
of DNA "sentences" has been proven in paternity lawsuits.
It was inevitable that the new techniques would be extended
to trace not only child-parent relationships but also whole lin-
eages of species. It was this new science of molecular genetics
that enabled Allan C. Wilson and Vincent M. Sarich (both of
the University of California at Berkeley) to establish with great
accuracy that hominids differentiated from apes about 5 million, not 15 million years ago, and that the hominids' closest
"next of kin" were chimpanzees and not gorillas.

Because a person's DNA keeps getting mixed by the genes
of the generational fathers, comparisons of the DNA in the
nucleus of the cell (which come half from mother, half from
father) do not work well after several generations. It was discovered, however, that in addition to the DNA in the cell's
nucleus, some DNA exists in the mother's cell but outside the
nucleus in bodies called "mitochondria" (Fig. 62). This DNA
does not get mixed with the father's DNA; instead, it is passed
on "unadulterated" from mother to daughter to granddaughter,
and so on through the generations. This discovery, by Douglas
Wallace of Emory University in the 1980s, led him to compare
this "mtDNA" of about 800 women. The surprising conclusion, which he announced at a scientific conference in July
1986, was that the mtDNA in all of them appeared to be so
similar that these women must have all descended from a single
female ancestor.

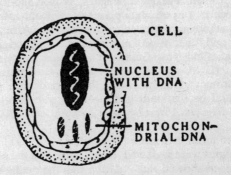

Figure 62

The research was picked up by Wesley Brown of the University of Michigan, who suggested that by determining the rate of natural mutation of mtDNA, the length of time that had passed since this common ancestor was alive could be calculated. Comparing the mtDNA of twenty-one women from diverse geographical and racial backgrounds, he came to the conclusion that they owed their origin to "a single mitochondrial Eve" who had lived in Africa between 300,000 and 180,000 years ago.

These intriguing findings were taken up by others, who set out to search for "Eve." Prominent among them was Rebecca Cann of the University of California at Berkeley (later at Hawaii University). Obtaining the placentas of 147 women of different races and geographical backgrounds who gave birth at San Francisco hospitals, she extracted and compared their mtDNA. The conclusion was that they all had a common female ancestor who had lived between 300,000 and 150,000 years (depending on whether the rate of mutation was 2 percent or 4 percent per million years). "We usually assume 250,000 years," Cann stated.

The upper limit of 300,000 years, paleoanthropologists noted, coincided with the fossil evidence for the time *Homo sapiens* made his appearance. "What could have happened 300,000 years ago to bring this change about?" Cann and Allan Wilson asked, but they had no answer.

To further test what has come to be called the "Eve Hypothesis," Cann and her colleagues, Wilson and Mark Stoneking, proceeded to examine placentas of about 150 women in America whose ancestors came from Europe, Africa, the Middle East, and Asia, as well as placentas from aborigine women in Australia and New Guinea. The results indicated that the African mtDNA was the oldest and that all those different women from various races and the most diverse geographic and cultural backgrounds had the same *sole female ancestor who had lived in Africa between 290,000 and 140,000 years ago.*

In an editorial in *Science* (September 11, 1987) in which all these findings were reviewed, it was stated that the overwhelming evidence showed that "Africa was the cradle of modern humans. . . . The story molecular biology seems to be telling is that modern humans evolved in Africa about 200,000 years ago."

These sensational findings—since then corroborated by other studies—made worldwide headlines. "The question Where did we come from? has been answered" the *National Geographic* (October, 1988) announced: out of southeastern Africa. "The Mother of Us All" has been found, headlined the *San Francisco Chronicle*. "Out of Africa: Man's Route to Rule the World," announced the London *Observer*. *Newsweek* (January 11, 1988) in what was to be its best-selling issue ever depicted an "Adam" and an "Eve" with a serpent on its front cover, headlining it "The Search for Adam and Eve."

The headline was appropriate, for as Allan Wilson observed, "Obviously where there was a mother there had to be a father."

All these very recent discoveries go a long way indeed in confirming the biblical claim regarding the first couple of *Homo sapiens*:

> And Adam called his wife's name *Chava*
> ["She of Life"—"Eve" in English]
> for she was the mother of all who live.

Several conclusions are offered by the Sumerian data. First, the creation of the *Lulu* was the result of the mutiny of the

Anunnaki about 300,000 years ago. This date as the upper limit for the first appearance of *Homo sapiens* has been corroborated by modern science.

Second, the forming of the *Lulu* had taken place "above the Abzu," north of the mining area. This is corroborated by the location of the earliest human remains in Tanzania, Kenya, and Ethiopia—north of the gold-mining areas of southern Africa.

Third, the full emergence of the first type of *Homo sapiens*, the Neanderthals—about 230,000 years ago—falls well within the 250,000 years suggested by the mtDNA findings for the data of "Eve," followed later by the emergence of *Homo sapiens sapiens*, "modern Man."

There is no contradiction at all between these later dates and the 300,000-year date of the mutiny. Bearing in mind that these were Earth-years, whereas for the Anunnaki 3,600 Earth-years amounted to only one of theirs, we should first recall that a period of trial and error followed the decision to "create the Adam," until the "perfect model" was achieved. Then, even after the Primitive Workers were brought forth, seven males and seven females at a time, pregnancies by Birth Goddesses were required, as the new hybrid was unable to procreate.

Clearly, the tracing of mtDNA accounts for the "Eve" who could bear children, not a female *Lulu* unable to procreate. The granting to mankind of this ability, it was shown earlier, took place as a result of a second genetic manipulation by Enki and Ninti which, in the Bible, is reflected in the story of Adam, Eve, and the Serpent in the Garden of Eden.

Did that *second* genetic manipulation take place about 250,000 years ago, the data for "Eve" suggested by Rebecca Cann, or 200,000 years ago, as the article in *Science* prefers?

According to the Book of Genesis, Adam and Eve began to have children only after their expulsion from "Eden." We know nothing of whether Abel, their second son who was killed by his elder brother Cain, had any offspring. But we do read that Cain and his descendants were ordered to migrate to far-away lands. Were these descendants of the "accursed line of Cain" the migrating Neanderthals? It is an intriguing possibility that must remain a speculation.

What seems certain is that the Bible does recognize the final emergence of *Homo sapiens sapiens*, modern human beings. It tells us that the third son of Adam and Eve, Seth, had a son named Enosh, of whom the lineage of Mankind is descended. Now, *Enosh* in Hebrew means "human, human being"—you and me. It was in the time of Enosh, the Bible states, that "men began to call the name of Yahweh. It was then, in other words, that fully civilized Man and religious worship were established.

With that, all the aspects of the ancient tale stand corroborated.

THE EMBLEM OF ENTWINED SERPENTS

In the biblical tale of Adam and Eve in the Garden of Eden, the antagonist of the Lord God who had caused them to acquire "knowing" (the ability to procreate) was the Serpent, *Nahash* in Hebrew.

The term has two other meanings: "he who knows secrets" and "he who knows copper." These other meanings or word plays are found in the Sumerian epithet BUZUR for Enki, which meant "he who solves secrets" and "he of the metal mines." I have therefore suggested in previous writings that, in the original Sumerian version, the "Serpent" was Enki. His emblem was entwined serpents; it was the symbol of his "cult center" Eridu (a), of his African domains in general (b), and of the pyramids in particular (c); and it appeared on Sumerian illustrations on cylinder seals of the events described in the Bible.

What did the emblem of entwined serpents—the symbol for medicine and healing to this very day—represent? The discovery by modern science of the double-helix structure of DNA (see Fig. 49) offers the answer: the Entwined Serpents emulated the structure of the genetic code, the secret knowledge of which enabled Enki to create The Adam and then grant Adam and Eve the ability to procreate.

The emblem of Enki as a sign of healing was invoked by Moses when he made a *nahash nehosheth*—a "copper serpent"—to halt an epidemic afflicting the Israelites. Was the involvement of copper in the triple meanings of the term and in the making of the copper serpent by Moses due to some unknown role of copper in genetics and healing?

Recent experiments, conducted at the universities of Minnesota and St. Louis, suggest that it is indeed so. They showed that radionucleide copper–62 is a "positron-emitter," valuable in imaging blood flow, and that other copper compounds can carry pharmaceuticals to living cells, including brain cells.

10

WHEN WISDOM WAS
LOWERED FROM HEAVEN

The Sumerian King Lists—a record of rulers, cities, and events arranged chronologically—divide prehistory and history into two distinct parts: first the long record of what had happened before the Deluge, then what transpired after the Deluge. One was the time when the Anunnaki "gods" and then their sons by the "daughters of Man," the so-called demigods, ruled upon the Earth; the other was when human rulers—kings selected by Enlil—were interposed between the "gods" and the people. In both instances the institution of an organized society and orderly government, "Kingship," was stated to have been "lowered from heaven"—the emulation on Earth of the societal and governmental organization on Nibiru.

"When kingship was lowered from heaven," begins the Sumerian King List, "kingship was in Eridu. In Eridu, Alulim became king and ruled 28,800 years." After listing the other antediluvial rulers and cities, the text states that "then the Flood swept over the Earth." And it continues: "After the Flood had swept over the Earth, when kingship was lowered again from heaven, kingship was in Kish." From then on, the lists take us into historical times.

Although the subject of this volume is what we call Science and the ancients called Wisdom, a few words about "Kingship"—the good order of things, an organized society and its institutions—will not be out of place, because without them no scientific progress or the dissemination and preservation of "Wisdom" could be possible. "Kingship" was the "portfolio" of Enlil, the Chief Administrator of the Anunnaki on Earth. It is noteworthy that as in so many scientific fields where we still live off and build upon the Sumerian bequests, so does the institution of kings and kingship still exist, having served Mankind for so many millennia. Samuel N. Kramer, in *History Begins at Sumer*, listed scores of "firsts" begun there, including a bicameral chamber of elected (or selected) deputies.

Various aspects of an organized and orderly society were incorporated into the concept of kingship, first and foremost among them the need for justice. A king was required to be "righteous" and to promulgate and uphold the laws, for Sumerian society was one that lived by the law. Many have learnt in school of the Babylonian king Hammurabi and his famous law code, dating back to the second millenium B.C.; but at least two thousand years before him Sumerian kings had already promulgated codes of law. The difference was that Hammurabi's was a code of crime and punishment: if you do this, your punishment will be that. The Sumerian law codes, on the other hand, were codes of just behavior; they stated that "you should not take away a widow's donkey" or delay the wages of a day laborer. The Bible's Ten Commandments were, like the Sumerian codes, not a list of punishments but a code of what is right to do and what is wrong and should not be done.

The laws were upheld by a judicial administration. It is from Sumer that we have inherited the concept of judges, juries, witnesses, and contracts. The unit of society we call the "family," based on a contractual marriage, was instituted in Sumer; so were rules and customs of succession, of adoption, of the rights of widows. The rule of law was also applied to economic activities: exchange based on contracts, rules for employment, wages, and—how else—taxation. We know much of Sumer's foreign trade, for example, because there had been a customs station at a city called Drehem where meticulous records were kept of all commercial movements of goods and animals.

All that and more came under the umbrella of "Kingship." As the sons and grandchildren of Enlil entered the stage of relations between Man and his gods, the functions of kingship and the supervision of kings were gradually handed over to them, and Enlil as the All Beneficent became a cherished memory. But to this day what we call a "civilized society" still owes its foundations to the time when "kingship was lowered from heaven."

"Wisdom"—sciences and the arts, the activities that required know-how—were the domain first of Enki, the Chief
Scientist of the Anunnaki, and later on, of his children.

We learn from a text scholars call "Inanna and Enki: The
Transfer of the Arts of Civilization" that Enki possessed certain
unique objects called ME—a kind of computer or data disks—
which held the information needed for the sciences, the han-
dicrafts, and the arts. Numbering more than a hundred, they
included such diverse subjects as writing, music, metalwork-
ing, construction, transportation, anatomy, medical treatments,
flood control, and urban decay; also, as other lists make clear,
astronomy, mathematics, and the calendar.

Like Kingship, Wisdom was "lowered to Earth from
Heaven," granted to Mankind by the Anunnaki "gods." It
was by their sole decision that scientific knowledge was passed
on to Mankind, usually through the medium of selected individuals; the instance of Adapa, to whom Enki granted "wide
understanding," has already been mentioned. As a rule, however, the chosen person belonged to the priesthood—another
"first" that stayed with Mankind for millennia through the
Middle Ages, when priests and monks were still also the scientists.

Sumerian texts tell of Enmeduranki who was groomed by
the gods to be the first priest, and relate how the gods

Showed him how to observe oil and water,
secrets of Anu, Enlil and Enki.
They gave him the Divine Tablet,
the engraved secrets of Heaven and Earth.
They taught him how to make calculations with numbers.

These brief statements disclose considerable information.
The first subject Enmeduranki was taught, the knowledge of
"oil and water," concerned medicine. In Sumerian times phy-
sicians were called either an A.ZU or a IA.ZU, meaning "One
who knows water" and "One who knows oil," and the difference was the method by which they administered medica-
ments: mixed and drunk down with water, or mixed with oil
and administered by an enema. Next, Enmeduranki was given
a "divine," or celestial, tablet on which were engraved the

"secrets of Heaven and Earth"—information about the planets and the Solar System and the visible constellations of stars, as well as knowledge about "Earth sciences"—geography, geology, geometry and—since the *Enuma elish* was incorporated into the temple rituals on New Year's Eve—cosmogony and evolution. And, to be able understand all that—the third subject, mathematics: "calculations with numbers."

In Genesis the story of the antediluvial patriarch called Enoch is summed up in the statement that he did not die but was taken up to the Lord when he was 365 years old (a number that corresponds to the number of days in a year); but considerably more information about Enoch is provided in the Book of Enoch (of which several renderings have been found), which was not made part of the Bible. In it the knowledge imparted by angels to Enoch is described in much detail; it included mining and metallurgy and the secrets of the Lower World, geography and the way Earth is watered, astronomy and the laws governing celestial motions, how to calculate the calendar, knowledge of plants and flowers and foods and so on—all shown to Enoch in special books and on "heavenly tablets."

The biblical Book of Proverbs devotes a good deal of its teachings to Man's need for Wisdom and to the realization that it is granted by God only to the righteous, "for it is the Lord who giveth wisdom." The many secrets of Heaven and Earth that Wisdom encompasses are highlighted in an Ode to Wisdom found in chapter 8 of Proverbs. The Book of Job likewise extols the virtues of Wisdom and all the abundance Man can obtain by it, but pointedly asks: "But whence cometh Wisdom, and where is the source of Understanding?" To which the answer is, "It is God who understands the way thereof"; the Hebrew word translated "God" is *Elohim*, the plural term first used in the creation tales. It is certain that the inspiration for these two biblical books, if not their actual source, was Sumerian and Akkadian texts of proverbs and of the Sumerian equivalent of the Book of Job; the latter, interestingly, was titled "I Will Praise the Lord of Wisdom."

There was no doubt in ancient times that scientific knowledge was a gift and a teaching from the "gods"—the Anunnaki, *Elohim*—to Mankind. The assertions that astronomy was a major subject are self-evident statements, since, as must be evident from earlier chapters in this book, the astounding knowledge in Sumerian times of the complete Solar System and the cosmogony that explained the origin of Earth, the asteroid belt, and the existence of Nibiru could have come only from the Anunnaki.

While I have seen a gratifying increase—to some extent, I would like to think, due to my writings—in the recognition of the Sumerian contribution to the beginnings and concept of laws, medical treatment, and cuisine, the parallel recognition of the immense Sumerian contribution to astronomy has not come about; this, I suspect, because of the hesitation in crossing the "forbidden threshold" of the inevitable next step: if you admit what the Sumerians knew about celestial matters, you must admit the existence not only of Nibiru but also of its people, the Anunnaki. . . . Nevertheless, this "fear of crossing" (a nice play on words, since Nibiru's name meant "Planet of the Crossing" . . .) in no way negates the fact that modern astronomy owes to the Sumerians (and through them, to the Anunnaki) the basic concept of a spherical astronomy with all its technicalities; the concept of an ecliptic as the belt around the Sun in which the planets orbit; the grouping of stars into constellations; the grouping of the constellations seen in the ecliptic into the Houses of the Zodiac; and the application of the number 12 to these constellations, to the months of the year, and to other celestial, or "divine," matters. This emphasis on the number 12 can be traced to the fact that the Solar System has twelve members, and each leading Anunnaki was assigned a celestial counterpart, forming a pantheon of twelve "Olympians" who were also each assigned a constellation and a month. Astrologers certainly owe much to these celestial divisions, since in the planet Nibiru astrologers find the twelfth member of the Solar System that they have been missing for so long.

As the Book of Enoch details and as the biblical reference to the number 365 attests, a direct result of the knowledge of the interrelated motions of the Sun, the Moon, and the Earth was the development of the calendar: the counting of the days (and their nights), the months, and the years. It is now generally recognized that the Western calendar we use nowadays harkens back to Mankind's first-ever calendar, the one known as the

Calendar of Nippur. Based on the alignment of its start with the spring equinox in the zodiac of Taurus, scholars have concluded that this calendar was instituted at the beginning of the fourth millennium B.C. Indeed, the very concept of a calendar that is coordinated with the Earth-Sun occurrences of the equinoxes (the time the Sun crosses the equator and day and night are equal) or, alternatively, with the solstices (when the Sun appears to have reached its farthest point north or south)—concepts that are found in all calendars in both the Old World and the New World—come to us from Sumer.

The Jewish calendar, as I have repeatedly pointed out in books and articles, still adheres to the calendar of Nippur not only in its form and structure but also in its count of years. In A.D. 1990 the Jewish calendar counts the year 5750; and it is not from "the creation of the world," as the explanation has been, but from the start of the calendar of Nippur in 3760 B.C.

It was in that year, I have suggested in *The Lost Realms*, that Anu, Nibiru's king, came to Earth on a state visit. His name, AN in Sumerian and *Anu* in Akkadian, meant "heaven," "The Heavenly One," and was a component of numerous astronomical terms, such as AN.UR ("celestial horizon") and AN.PA ("point of zenith"), as well as being a component of the name "Anunnaki," "Those Who From Heaven to Earth Came." Archaic Chinese, whose syllables were written and pronounced in a manner that reveals their Sumerian origin, used for example the term *kuan* to denote a temple that served as an observatory; the Sumerian kernel of the term, KU.AN, had meant "opening to the heavens." (The Sumerian origin of Chinese astronomy and astrology was discussed by me in the article "The Roots of Astrology," which appeared in the February 1985 issue of *East-West Journal*). Undoubtedly, the Latin *annum* ("year") from which the French *année* ("year"), the English *annual* ("yearly"), and so on stem from the time when the calendar and the count of years began with the state visit of AN.

The Chinese tradition of combining temples with observatories has, of course, not been limited to China; it harkens back to the ziggurats (step pyramids) of Sumer and Babylon. Indeed, a long text dealing with that visit by Anu and his spouse Antu to Sumer relates how the priests ascended to the ziggurat's

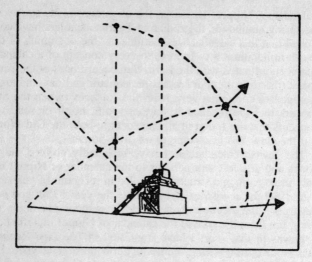

Figure 63

topmost level to observe the appearance of Nibiru in the skies.
Enki imparted the knowledge of astronomy (and of other sciences) to his firstborn son Marduk, and the renowned ziggurat
of Babylon, built there after Marduk gained supremacy in Mesopotamia, was built to serve as an astronomical observatory
(Fig. 63).

Enki bestowed the "secrets" of the calendar, mathematics,
and writing on his younger son Ningishzidda, whom the Egyp-
tians called Thoth. In *The Lost Realms* I present substantial
evidence to show that he was one and the same Mesoamerican
god known as Quetzalcoatl, "The Plumed Serpent." This
god's name, which means (in Sumerian) "Lord of the Tree of
Life," reflected the fact that it was to him that Enki entrusted
medical knowledge, including the secret of reviving the dead.
A Babylonian text quotes the exasperated Enki as telling Marduk he had taught him enough, when Marduk also wanted to
learn the secret of reviving the dead. That the Anunnaki could
achieve that feat (at least in so far as their own were concerned)

Figure 64

is clear from a text titled "The Descent of Inanna to the Lower World," where she was put to death by her own sister. When her father appealed to Enki to revive the goddess, Enki directed at the corpse "that which pulsates" and "that which radiates" and brought her back to life. A Mesopotamian depiction of a patient on a hospital table shows him receiving radiation treatment (Fig. 64).

Putting aside the ability to revive the dead (which is mentioned as fact in the Bible), it is certain that the teaching of anatomy and medicine was part of priestly training, as stated in the Enmeduranki text. That the tradition continued into later times is clear from Leviticus, one of the Five Books of Moses, which contains extensive instructions by Yahweh to the Israelite priests in matters of health, medical prognosis, treatment and hygiene. The dietary commandments regarding "appropriate" (*kosher*) and non-appropriate foods undoubtedly stemmed from health and hygienic considerations rather than from religious observance; and many believe that the important requirement of circumcision was also rooted in medical reasons. These instructions were not unlike those in numerous earlier Mesopotamian texts that served as medical manuals for the A.ZUs and IA.ZUs, which instructed the physician-priests to first observe the symptoms; next stated which remedy had to be applied; and then gave a list of the chemicals, herbs, and other pharmaceutical ingredients from which the medicines were to be prepared. That the Elohim were the source of these teachings should come as no surprise when we recall the medical, anatomical, and genetic feats of Enki and Ninti.

Basic to the science of astronomy and the workings of the calendar, as well as to commerce and economic activity, was the knowledge of mathematics—the "making of calculations with numbers," in the words of the Enmeduranki text.

The Sumerian numbers system is called sexagesimal, meaning "base 60." The count ran from 1 to 60, as we now do with 1 to 100. But then, where we say "two hundred," the Sumerians said (or wrote) "2 *gesh*," meaning 2 x 60, which equaled 120. When in their calculations the text said "take half" or "take one-third," the meaning was one-half of 60 = 30, one-third of 60 = 20. This might seem to us, reared on the decimal system ("times 10"), which is geared to the number of fingers on our hands, cumbersome and complicated; but to a mathematician, the sexagesimal system is a delight.

The number 10 is divisible by very few other whole numbers (by 2 and 5 only, to be precise). The number 100 is divisible only by 2, 4, 5, 10, 20, 25, and 50. But 60 is divisible by 2, 3, 4, 5, 6, 10, 12, 15, 20, and 30. Inasmuch as we have inherited the Sumerian 12 in our counting of the daily hours, 60 in our counting of time (60 seconds in a minute, 60 minutes in an hour), and 360 in geometry (360 degrees in a circle), the sexagesimal system is still the only perfect one in the celestial sciences, in time reckoning, and in geometry (where a triangle has angles adding up to 180 degrees and a square's angles add up to 360 degrees). In both theoretical and applied geometry (such as the measuring of field areas) this system made it possible to calculate the areas of diverse and complex shapes (Fig. 65), the volumes of vessels of all kinds (needed to hold grains or oil or wine), the length of canals, or the distances between planets.

When record keeping began, a stylus with a round tip was used to impress on wet clay the various symbols that stood for the numbers 1, 10, 60, 600, and 3,600 (Fig. 66a). The ultimate numeral was 3,600, signified by a large circle; it was called SAR (*Shar* in Akkadian)—the "princely," or "royal," num-

Figure 65

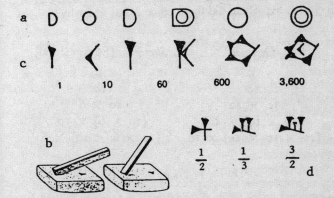

Figure 66

ber, the number of Earth-years it took Nibiru to complete one orbit around the Sun.

With the introduction of cuneiform ("wedge-shaped") writing, in which scribes used a wedge-shaped stylus (Fig. 66b), the numerals were also written in wedge-shaped signs (Fig. 66c). Other cuneiform signs denoted fractions or multiples (Fig. 66d); together with combination signs that instructed the calculator to add, subtract, divide, or multiply, problems in arithmetic and algebra that would baffle many of today's students were correctly solved. These problems included the squaring, cubing, or finding the square root of numbers. As shown by F. Thureau-Dangin in *Textes mathematiques Babyloniens*, the ancients followed prescribed formulas, with two or even three unknowns, that are still in use today.

Although dubbed "sexagesimal," the Sumerian system of numeration and mathematics was in reality not simply based on the number 60 but on a combination of 6 and 10. While in the decimal system each step up is accomplished by multiplying the previous sum by 10 (Fig. 67a), in the Sumerian system the numbers increased by *alternate* multiplications: once by 10, then by 6, then by 10, then again by 6 (Fig. 67b). This method has puzzled today's scholars. The decimal system is obviously geared to the ten digits of the human hands (as the numbers, too, are still called), so the 10 in the Sumerian system can be understood; but where did the 6 come from, and why?

a. *Decimal*	b. *Sumerian* (Sexagesimal)
1	1
10	10
10 × 10	10 × 6
(10 × 10) × 10	(10 × 6) × 10
(10 × 10 × 10) × 10	(10 × 6 × 10) × 6

Figure 67

There have been other puzzles. Among the thousands of mathematical tablets from Mesopotamia, many held tables of ready-made calculations. Surprisingly, however, they did not run from smaller numbers up (like 1, 10, 60, etc.) but ran down, starting from a number that can only be described as astronomical: 12,960,000. An example quoted by Th.G. Pinches (*Some Mathematical Tablets of the British Museum*) began with the following lines at the top:

1.	12960000	its ⅔ part	8640000
2.		its half part	6480000
3.		its third "	4320000
4.		its fourth "	3240000

and continued all the way down through "its 80th part 180000" to the 400th part "[which is] 32400." Other tablets carried the procedure down to the 16,000th part (equals 810), and there is no doubt that this series continued downward to 60, the 216,000th part of the initial number 12,960,000.

H.V. Hilprecht (*The Babylonian Expedition of the University of Pennsylvania*), after studying thousands of mathematical tablets from the temple libraries of Nippur and Sippar and from the library of the Assyrian king Ashurbánipal in Nineveh, concluded that the number 12,960,000 was literally astronomical—that it stemmed from the phenomenon of Precession, which retards the zodiac constellation against which the Sun rises by a full House once in 2,160 years. The complete circle of the twelve Houses, by which the Sun returns to its original background spot, thus takes 25,920 years; the number 12,960,000 represented five hundred such complete Precessional circles.

It was incredible to learn, as Hilprecht and others have, that the Sumerians were not only aware of the phenomenon of precession but also knew that a shift from House to House in the zodiac required 2,160 years; it was doubly incomprehensible that they chose as the base of their mathematics a number representing *five hundred* complete twelve-House cycles, *each one* of which required the fantastic (as far as human beings are concerned) time span of 25,920 years. In fact, while modern astronomy accepts the existence of the phenomenon and its periods as calculated in Sumer, there is no scientist now or in former times who can or could confirm from personal experience the shift of even one House (a shift to Aquarius is now anticipated); and all the scientists put together have yet to witness one complete cycle. Still, there it is in the Sumerian tablets.

It seems to me that a solution to all these puzzles can be found if modern science will accept the existence of Nibiru and its Anunnaki as fact. Since it was they who had granted mathematical "wisdom" to Mankind, the astronomical base number and the sexagesimal system were developed by the Anunnaki for their own use and from their own viewpoint—and then were scaled down to human proportions.

As Hilprecht has correctly suggested, the number 12,960,000 indeed stemmed from astronomy—the time (25,920 years) required for a full precessional cycle. But that cycle could be broken down to more human-sized proportions, that of the precessional shift by one zodiacal House. Although a complete shift in 2,160 years was also beyond an Earthling's lifetime, the gradual shift of one degree every 72 years was an observable phenomenon (which the astronomer-priests witnessed and dealt with). This was the "earthly" element in the formulation.

Then there was the orbital period of Nibiru, which the Anunnaki knew equaled 3,600 Earth-years. Here, then, were two basic and immutable phenomena, cycles of a certain length that combined the movements of Nibiru and Earth in a ratio of 3,600:2,160. This ratio can be reduced to 10:6. Once in 21,600 years, Nibiru completed six orbits around the Sun and Earth shifted ten zodiacal houses. *This, I suggest, created the 6 x 10 x 6 x 10 system of alternating counting that is called "sexagesimal."*

The sexagesimal system, as has been noted, still lies at the core of modern astronomy and time-keeping. So has the legacy of the 10:6 ratio of the Anunnaki. Having perfected architecture and the eye-pleasing plastic arts, the Greeks devised a canon of proportions called the Golden Section. They held that a perfect and pleasing ratio of the sides of a temple or great chamber was reached by the formula $AB:AP = AP:PB$, which gives a ratio of the long part or side to the shorter one of 100 to 61.8 (feet, cubits, or whatever unit of measure is chosen). It seems to me that architecture owes the debt for this Golden

Section not to the Greeks but to the Anunnaki (via the Sumerians), for this ratio is really the 10:6 ratio on which the sexagesimal system was based.

The same can be said of the mathematical phenomenon known as the Fibonacci Numbers, wherein a series of numbers grows in such a way that each successive number (e.g., 5) is the sum of its two preceding numbers (2 + 3); then 8 is the sum of 3 + 5, and so on. The fifteenth century mathematician Lucas Pacioli recognized the algebraic formula for this series and called the quotient—1.618—the Golden Number and its reciprocal—0.618—the Divine Number. Which brings us back to the Anunnaki. . . .

Having explained how, in my opinion, the sexagesimal system was devised, let us look at what Hilprecht concluded was the upper base of the system, the number 12,960,000.

It is easy to show that this number is simply the square of the real basic number of the Anunnaki—3,600—which is the length in Earth-years of Nibiru's orbit. (3,600 x 3,600 = 12,960,000). It was from dividing 3,600 by the earthly ten that the easier-to-handle number of 360 degrees in a circle was obtained. The number 3,600, in turn, is the square of 60; this relationship provided the number of minutes in an hour and (in modern times) the number of seconds in a minute, and of course the basic sexagesimal number.

The zodiacal origin of the astronomical number 12,960,000 can, I believe, explain a puzzling biblical statement. It is in Psalm 90 that we read that the Lord—the reference is to the "Celestial Lord"—who has had his abode in the heavens for countless generations and from the time "before the mountains were brought forth, before Earth and continents were created," considers a thousand years to be merely a single day:

> A thousand years in thine eyes
> are but a day, a yesterday past.

Now if we divide the number 12,960,000 by 2,160 (the number of years to achieve a shift from one zodiac House), the result is 6,000—a thousand times six. Six as a number of "days" is not unfamiliar—we came upon it at the beginning of Genesis and its six days of creation. Could the psalmist have seen the mathematical tablets in which he would have found the line listing "12,960,000 the 2160th part of which is a thousand times six"? It is indeed intriguing to find that the Psalms echo the numbers with which the Anunnaki had toyed.

In Psalm 90 and other relevant psalms, the Hebrew word translated as "generation" is *Dor*. It stems from the root *dur*, "to be circular, to cycle." For human beings it does mean a generation; but for celestial bodies it means a cycle around the sun—an orbit. It is with this understanding that the true meaning of Psalm 102, the moving prayer of a mortal to the Everlasting One, can be grasped:

> But thou, O Lord, shalt abide forever,
> and thy remembrance from cycle to cycle.
>
> For He hath looked down from his sanctuary on high:
> From Heaven did Yahweh behold the Earth.
>
> I say, my God,
> "Do not ascend me in the midst of my days,"
> thou whose years are in a cycle of cycles.
>
> Thou art unchanged;
> Thine years shall have no end.

Relating it all to the orbit of Nibiru, to its cycle of 3,600 Earth-years, to the precessional retardation of Earth in *its* orbit around the Sun—this is the secret of the Wisdom of Numbers that the Anunnaki lowered from Heaven to Earth.

Before Man could "calculate with numbers," the other two of the "three Rs"—reading and 'riting—had to be mastered. We take it for granted that Man can speak, that we have languages by which to communicate to our fellow men (or clansmen). But modern science has not held it so; in fact, until quite recently, the scientists dealing with speech and languages believed that "Talking Man" was a rather late phenomenon that may have been one reason the Cro-Magnons—who could speak and converse with each other—took over from the nonspeaking Neanderthals.

This was not the biblical view. The Bible took it for granted, for example, that the Elohim who were on Earth long before The Adam could speak and address each other. This is apparent from the statement that The Adam was created as a result of a discussion among the Elohim, in which it was said, "Let us make The Adam in our image and after our likeness." This implies not only the ability to speak but also a language with which to communicate.

Let us now look at The Adam. He is placed in the Garden of Eden and is told what to eat and what to avoid. The instructions were understood by The Adam, as the ensuing conversation between the Serpent and Eve makes clear. The Serpent (whose identity is discussed in *The Wars of Gods and Men*) "said unto the woman: Hath Elohim indeed said, Ye shall not eat of all the trees in the garden?" Eve says yes, the fruit of one tree was forbidden on penalty of death. But the Serpent assures the woman it is not so, and she and Adam eat of the forbidden fruit.

A lengthy dialogue then ensues. Adam and Eve hide when they hear the footsteps of Yahweh, "strolling in the garden in the cool of the day." Yahweh calls out to Adam, "Where are you?" and the following exchange takes place:

Adam: "I heard the sound of you in the garden and I was afraid because I am naked, and I hid."

Yahweh: "Who told you that you are naked? Did you eat of the tree of which I ordered you not to eat?"

Adam: "The woman whom you placed with me, she is the one who gave me of the tree, and I ate."

Yahweh: [to the woman] "What have you done?"

Woman: "The serpent beguiled me, and I ate."

This is quite a conversation. Not only the Deity can speak; Adam and Eve can also speak and understand the Deity's language. So, in what language did they converse, for there must have been one (according to the Bible). If Eve was the

First Mother, was there a First Language—a Mother Tongue?

Again, scholars began by differing with the Bible. They assumed that language was a cultural heritage rather than an evolutionary trait. It was assumed that Man progressed from groans to meaningful shouts (on seeing prey or sensing danger) to rudimentary speech as he formed clans. From words and syllables, languages were born—many languages, arising simultaneously as clans and tribes formed.

This theory of the origin of languages not only ignored the significance of the biblical tales of the Elohim and of the incident in the Garden of Eden; it denied the biblical assertion that prior to the incident of the Tower of Babel ''the whole Earth was of one language and of one kind of words''; that it was a deliberate act of the Elohim to disperse Mankind all over the Earth and ''confuse'' its language ''that they may not understand one another's speech.''

It is gratifying to note that in recent years, modern science has come around to the belief that there was indeed a Mother Tongue; and that both types of *Homo sapiens*—Cro-Magnon and Neanderthal—could talk from the very beginning.

That many languages have words that sound the same and have similar meanings has long been recognized, and that certain languages can therefore be grouped into families has been an accepted theory for over a century, when German scholars proposed naming these language families ''Indo-European,'' ''Semitic,'' ''Hamitic,'' and so on. But this very grouping held the obstacle to the recognition of a Mother Tongue, because it was based on the notion that totally different and unrelated groups of languages developed independently in different ''core zones'' from which migrants carried their tongues to other lands. Attempts to show that there are apparent word and meaning similarities even between distant groups, such as the writings in the nineteenth century by the Reverend Charles Foster (*The One Primeval Language*, in which he pointed to the Mesopotamian precursors of Hebrew) were dismissed as no more than a theologian's attempt to elevate the status of the Bible's language, Hebrew.

It was mainly advances in other fields, such as anthropology, biogenetics, and the Earth sciences, as well as computerization, that opened new avenues of study of what some call "linguistic genetics." The notion that languages developed rather late in Man's march to civilization—at one point the beginning of languages (not just speech) was put at only five thousand years ago—obviously had to be amended and the date pushed back to much earlier times when archaeological finds showed that the Sumerians could already write six thousand years ago. As the dates of ten thousand and twelve thousand years ago were being considered, the search for points of similarity, speeded up by computers, led scholars to the discovery of protolanguages and thus to larger and less numerous groupings.

Searching for an early affiliation for the Slavic languages, Soviet scientists under the leadership of Vladislav Illich-Svitych and Aaron Dolgopolsky suggested, in the 1960s, a proto-language they termed *Nostratic* (from the Latin "Our Language") as the core of most European (including Slavic) languages. Later on they presented evidence for a second such proto-language, which they termed *Dene-Caucasian*, as the core tongue of the Far Eastern languages. Both began, they estimated from linguistic mutations, about twelve thousand years ago. In the United States, Joseph Greenberg of Stanford University and his colleague Merritt Ruhlen suggested a third proto-language, *Amerind*.

Without dwelling on the significance of the fact, it behooves me to mention that the date of about twelve thousand years ago would put the period of the appearance of these protolanguages somewhere around the immediate aftermath of the Deluge, which in *The 12th Planet* was shown to have occurred about thirteen thousand years ago; that also conforms to the biblical notion that post-Diluvial Mankind divided into three branches, descended from the three sons of Noah.

Meanwhile, archaeological discoveries kept pushing back the time of human migrations, and this was especially significant in regard to the arrival of migrants in the Americas. When a time of twenty thousand years or even thirty thousand years ago was suggested, Joseph Greenberg created a sensation when he demonstrated in 1987 *(Language in the Americas)* that the hundreds of tongues in the New World could be grouped into just three families, which he termed *Eskimo-Aleut, Na-Dene*, and *Amerind*. The greater significance of his conclusions was that these three in turn were brought to the Americas by migrants from Africa, Europe, Asia, and the Pacific and thus in effect were not true proto-languages but offshoots of Old World ones. The protolanguage he called ''Na-Dene,'' Greenberg suggested, was related to the Dene-Caucasian group of the Soviet scholars. This family, Merritt Ruhlen wrote in *Natural History* (March 1987), appears to be ''genetically closest'' to the group of languages that include ''the extinct languages Etruscan and *Sumerian*.'' Eskimo-Aleut, he wrote, is most closely related to the Indo-European languages. (Readers wishing to know more about the earliest arrivals in the Americas may want to read *The Lost Realms*, Book IV of ''The Earth Chronicles'' series).

But did true languages begin only about twelve thousand years ago—only after the Deluge? It is not only according to the Bible that language existed at the very beginning of *Homo sapiens* (Adam and Eve), but also the fact that Sumerian texts repeatedly refer to inscribed tablets that dated from before the Deluge. The Assyrian king Ashurbanipal boasted that, knowledgeable as Adapa, he could read ''tablets from before the Deluge.'' If so, there had to be true language even much earlier.

Discoveries by paleontologists and anthropologists make linguists push their estimations back in time. The discoveries in the Kebara cave, mentioned earlier, indeed forced a complete reevaluation of previous timetables.

Among the finds in the cave was an astounding clue. The skeletal remains of a sixty-thousand-year-old Neanderthal included an intact hyoid bone—the first ever to be discovered. This horned-shaped bone which lies between the chin and the larynx (voice box) anchors the muscles that move the tongue, lower jaw, and larynx and makes human speech possible (Fig. 68).

Combined with other skeletal features, the hyoid bone offered unequivocal proof that Man could speak as he does today at least sixty thousand years ago and probably much earlier. Neanderthal Man, the team of six international scientists led by Baruch Arensburg of Tel-Aviv University stated in *Nature* (April 27, 1989), ''had the morphological basis for human speech capability.''

If so, how could Indo-European, whose origins are traceable

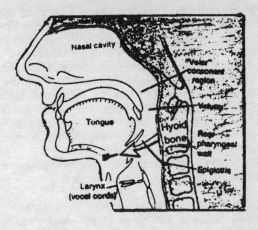

Figure 68

to only a few thousand years ago, be given such a prominent position on the language tree? Less inhibited about lowering the claims for Indo-European than their Western colleagues, Soviet scholars continued to search audaciously for a proto-proto language. Spearheading the search for a Mother Tongue have been Aaron Dolgopolsky, now at Haifa University in Israel, and Vitaly Shevoroshkin, now at the University of Michigan. It was primarily on the latter's initiative that a "breakthrough" conference was held at the University of Michigan in November 1988. Titled "Language and Prehistory," the conference brought together, from seven countries, more than forty scholars from the fields of linguistics, anthropology, archaeology, and genetics. The consensus was that there had been a "mono-genesis" of human languages—a Mother Tongue in a "proto-proto-proto stage" at a time about 100,000 years ago.

Still, scientists from other fields relating to the anatomy of speech, such as Philip Lieberman of Brown University and Dean Falk of the State University of New York at Albany, see speech as a trait of *Homo sapiens* from the very first appearance of these "Thinking/Wise Men." Brain specialists such as Ronald E. Myers of the National Institute of Communicative Disorders and Strokes believe that "human speech developed spontaneously, unrelated to the crude vocalization of other primates," as soon as humans acquired their two-part brains.

And Allan Wilson, who had participated in the genetic research leading to the "One-Mother-of-All" conclusion, put speech back in the mouth of "Eve": "The human capacity for language may have come from a genetic mutation that occurred in a woman who lived in Africa 200,000 years ago," he announced at a meeting in January 1989 of the American Association for the Advancement of Science.

"Gift of Gab Goes Back to Eve," one newspaper headlined the story. Well, to Eve *and* Adam, according to the Bible.

And so we arrive at the last of the Rs—writing.

It is now believed that many of the shapes and symbols found in Ice Age caves in Europe, attributed to Cro-Magnons living during the period of between twenty thousand and thirty thousand years ago, represent crude pictographs—"picture writing." Undoubtedly, Man learned to write long after he began to speak. The Mesopotamian texts insist that there was writing before the Deluge, and there is no reason to disbelieve this. But the first writing discovered in modern times is the early Sumerian script which was pictographic. It took but a few centuries for this script to evolve into the cuneiform script (Fig. 69), which was the means of writing in all the ancient languages of Asia until it was finally replaced, millennia later, by the alphabet.

At first glance cuneiform script looks like an impossible hodgepodge of long, short, and just wedge-point markings (Fig. 70). There are hundreds of cuneiform symbols, and how on Earth the ancient scribes could remember how to write them and what they meant is baffling—but not more so than the Chinese language signs are to a non-Chinese. Three generations of scholars have been able to arrange the signs in a logical order and, as a result, have come up with lexicons and dictionaries of the ancient languages—Sumerian, Babylonian, Assyrian, Hittite, Elamite and so on—that used cuneiform.

But modern science reveals that there was more than some logical order to creating such a diversity of signs.

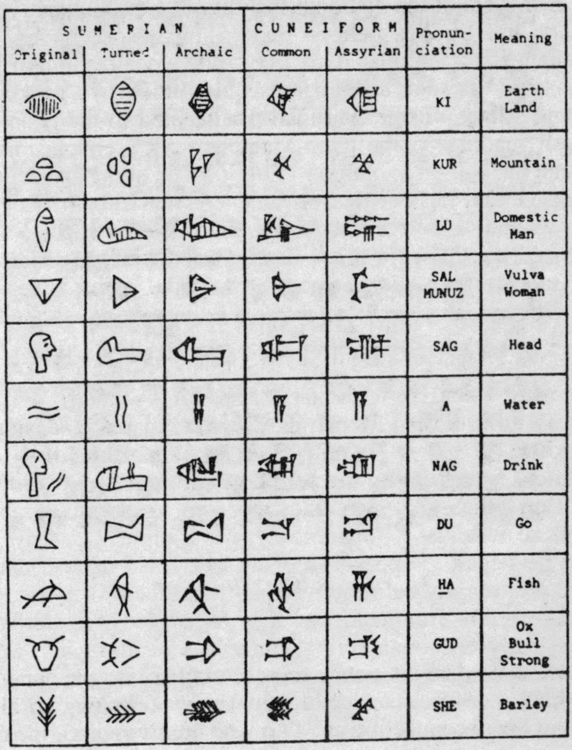

SUMERIAN			CUNEIFORM		Pronun-ciation	Meaning
Original	Turned	Archaic	Common	Assyrian		
					KI	Earth Land
					KUR	Mountain
					LU	Domestic Man
					SAL MUNUZ	Vulva Woman
					SAG	Head
					A	Water
					NAG	Drink
					DU	Go
					HA	Fish
					GUD	Ox Bull Strong
					SHE	Barley

Figure 69

Mathematicians, especially those dealing with graph theory—the study of points joined by lines—are familiar with the Ramsey Graph Theory, named for Frank P. Ramsey, a British mathematician who, in a paper read to the London Mathematical Society in 1928, suggested a method of calculating the number of various ways in which points can be connected and the shapes resulting therefrom. Applied to games and riddles as well as to science and architecture, the theory offered by Ramsey made it possible to show, for ex-

Figure 70

ample, that when six points representing six people are joined
by either red lines (connecting any two who know each other)
or blue lines (connecting any two who are strangers), the result
will always be either a red or a blue triangle. The results of
calculating the possibilities for joining (or not joining) points
can best be illustrated by some examples (Fig. 71). Underlying
the resulting graphs (i.e., shapes) are the so-called Ramsey
Numbers, which can be converted to graphs connecting a certain number of dots. I find that this results in dozens of
"graphs" whose similarity to the Mesopotamian cuneiform
signs is undeniable (Fig. 72).

The almost one hundred signs, only partly illustrated here,
are simple graphs based on no more than a dozen Ramsey
Numbers. So, if Enki or his daughter Nidaba, the Sumerian
"goddess of writing," had known as much as Frank Ramsey,
they must have had no problem in devising for the Sumerian

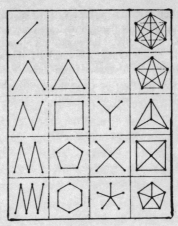

Figure 71

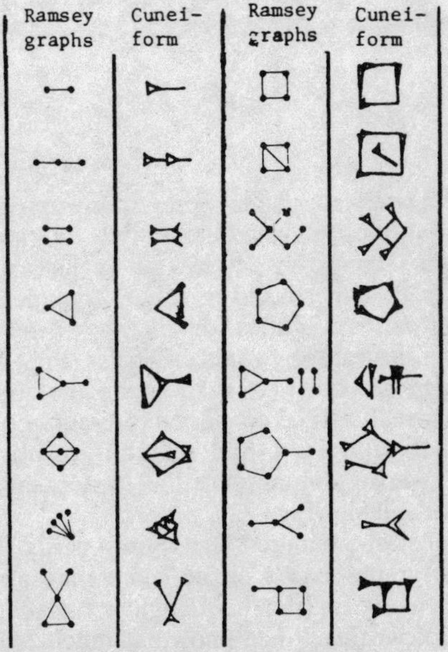

Ramsey graphs	Cunei-form	Ramsey graphs	Cunei-form

Figure 72

scribes a mathematically perfect system of cuneiform signs.

"I will greatly bless thee, and I will exceedingly multiply thy seed as the stars of the heavens," Yahweh told Abraham. And with this single verse, several of the elements of the knowledge that was lowered from heaven were expressed: speech, astronomy, and the "counting with numbers."

Modern science is well on its way to corroborating all that.

THE FRUITS OF EDEN

What was the Garden of Eden, remembered in the Bible for its variety of vegetation and as the place where still-unnamed animals were shown to Adam?

Modern science teaches that Man's best friends, the crops and animals we husband, were domesticated soon after 10000 B.C. Wheat and barley, dogs and sheep (to cite some examples) in their domesticated and cultivable forms appeared, then, within no more than two thousand years. This, it is admitted, is a fraction of the time that natural selection alone would require.

Sumerian texts offer an explanation. When the Anunnaki landed on Earth, they state, there were none of such "domesticated" crops and animals; it was the Anunnaki who brought them forth, in their "Creation Chamber." Together with *Lahar* ("woolly cattle") and *Anshan* ("grains") they also brought forth "vegetation that luxuriates and multiplies." It was all done in the *Edin*; and after The Adam was created, he was brought there to tend it all.

The amazing Garden of Eden was thus the bio-genetic farm or enclave where "domesticated" crops, fruits, and animals were brought forth.

After the Deluge (about thirteen thousand years ago) the Anunnaki provided Mankind with the crop and animal seeds, which they had preserved, to get started again. But this time, Man himself had to be the husbandman. The Bible confirms this and attributes to Noah the honor of having been the first husbandman. It also states that the first cultivated food after the Deluge was the grape. Modern science confirms the grape's antiquity; science has also discovered that besides being a nourishing food, the grape's wine is a strong gastrointestinal medicine. So, when Noah drank the wine (in excess), he was, in a manner of speaking, taking his medicine.

11

A SPACE BASE ON MARS

Having been to the Moon, Earthlings are eager to set foot on Mars.

It was on the occasion of the twentieth anniversary of the first landing by Man on the Moon that the President of the United States outlined his country's stepping stones to Earth's nearest outer planet. Speaking at the National Air and Space Museum in Washington and flanked by the three Apollo—11 astronauts—Neil A. Armstrong, Edwin E. Aldrin, Jr., and Michael Collins—President George Bush outlined America's way stations to Mars. First, progress from the shuttlecraft program to the emplacement in permanent Earth orbit of a Space Station, where the larger vehicles necessary for the onward flights would be assembled. Then would come the establishment of a space base on the Moon, where materials, equipment, and fuels necessary for the long space voyages would be developed and tested, and experience would be gained in Man's living and working for extended periods in outer space. And finally, the actual expedition to Mars.

Vowing to make the United States "a spacefaring nation," the goal, the President said, will be "back to the Moon, back to the future . . . and then, a journey into tomorrow, to another planet: a manned mission to Mars."

"Back to the future." The choice of words may or may not have been coincidental; the premise that going to the future involves going back to the past might have been more than a speech writer's choice slogan.

For there is evidence that "A Space Base on Mars," this chapter's heading, should apply not to the discussion of future plans but to a disclosure of what has already taken place in the past: *Evidence that a space base existed on the planet Mars in antiquity; and what is even more startling, that it might have been reactivated before our very eyes.*

If Man is to venture from planet Earth into space, it is only logical and technologically called for to make Mars the first planet on the outbound voyage. The road to other worlds must have way stations due to the laws of celestial motion, the constraints of weight and energy, the requirements for human survival, and limitations on human physical and mental endurance. A spaceship capable of carrying a team of astronauts to Mars and back might have to weigh as much as four million pounds. Lifting such a massive vehicle off the surface of Earth (a planet with a substantial gravitational pull, compared with its immediate neighbors) would require a commensurately large load of fuel that, together with the tanks to hold it, would further increase the lift-off weight and make the launch impractical. (U.S. space shuttles now have a payload capacity of sixty-five thousand pounds.)

Such lift-off and fuel problems would be greatly reduced if the spaceship will be assembled in weightless orbit around the Earth. This scenario envisions an orbiting, manned space station, to which shuttle craft will ferry the knocked-down spaceship. Meanwhile, astronauts stationed on the Moon at a permanent space base would develop the technology required for Man's survival in space. Man and vehicle would then be joined for the voyage to Mars.

The round trip may take between two and three years, depending on the trajectory and Earth-Mars alignments. The length of stay on Mars will also vary according to these constraints and other considerations, beginning with no stay at all (just several orbits around Mars) to a long stay in a permanent colony served or sustained by shifts of spacecraft and astronauts. Indeed, many advocates of "The Case for Mars," as this approach has come to be called after several scientific conferences on the subject, consider a manned mission to Mars justified only if a permanent space base is established there, both as a prelude to manned missions to even more distant planets and as the forerunner of a colony, a permanent settlement of Earthlings on a new world.

The progression from shuttlecraft to an orbiting space station to landings on the Moon and the establishment of a space base thereon, all as stepping-stones or way stations toward a landing on Mars, has been described in scenarios that read like science fiction but are based on scientific knowledge and attainable technology. Based on the Moon and on Mars, even a colony on Mars, have been in the planning for a long time and are deemed entirely feasible. Sustaining human life and activity on the Moon is certainly challenging, but the studies show how it could be achieved. The tasks are more challenging for Mars, since resupply from Earth (as the Moon projects envision) is more difficult and costly. Nevertheless, the vital resources needed by Man to survive and function are available on Mars, and scientists believe that Man could live "off the land" there.

Mars, it has been concluded, is habitable—because *it was habitable in the past.*

Mars appears nowadays as a cold, half-frozen planet inhospitable to anything living upon its surface, with bitter-cold winters and temperatures rising above freezing only at the equator in the warmest season, with vast areas covered either with permafrost or with rusted iron rocks and gravel (which give the planet its reddish hue), with no liquid water to sustain life or oxygen to breathe. But not so long ago in geological terms, it was a planet with relatively pleasant seasons, flowing water, oceans and rivers, cloudy (blue!) skies, and perhaps— just perhaps—even some forms of indigenous simple plant life.

All the various studies converge toward the conclusion that Mars is now going through an ice age, not unlike the ice ages that Earth has experienced periodically. The causes of Earth's ice ages, attributed to many factors, are now believed to stem from three basic phenomena that relate to Earth's orbit around the Sun. The first is the configuration of the orbit itself: the orbit, it has been concluded, changes from more circular to more elliptical in a cycle of about one hundred thousand years; this brings the Earth at times closer to the Sun and at times farther away from it. Earth has seasons because the axis of Earth is not perpendicular to its orbital plane (ecliptic) but is tilted, bringing the northern hemisphere under a stronger in- fluence of the Sun's during the (northern) summer and the southern hemisphere to its winter, and vice versa (Fig. 73); but this tilt, now about 23.5 degrees, is not stable; the Earth,

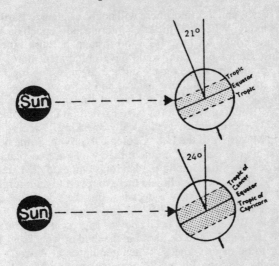

Figure 73

like a rolling ship, changes its tilt by about 3 degrees back and forth in a cycle that takes about forty-one thousand years to complete. The greater the tilt the more extreme are the winters and summers; air and water flows change and aggravate the climatic changes that we call "ice ages" and "interglacial" warm periods. A third contributing cycle is that of the Earth's wobble as it spins, its axis forming an imaginary circle in the heavens; this is the phenomenon of Precession of the Equinoxes, and the duration of this cycle is about twenty-six thousand years.

The planet Mars is also subject to all three cycles, except that its larger orbit around the Sun and greater tilt differential cause more extreme climatic swings. The cycle, as we have mentioned, is believed to last some fifty thousand years on Mars (although shorter and longer durations have also been suggested).

When the next Martian warm period, or interglacial, arrives, the planet will literally flow with water, its seasons will not be as harsh, and its atmosphere will not be as alien to Earthlings as it is today. When was the last "interglacial" epoch on Mars? The time could not have been too distant, because otherwise the dust storms on Mars would have obliterated more, if not most, of the evidence on its surface of once-flowing rivers, ocean shorelines, and lake basins; and there would not be as much water vapor still in the Martian atmosphere as is found today. "Running water must have existed on the red planet in relatively recent times, geologically speaking," according to Harold Masursky of the U.S. Geological Survey. Some believe the last change occurred no more than ten thousand years ago.

Those who are planning the landings and extended stays on Mars do not expect the climate there to revert to an interglacial epoch within the next two decades; but they do believe that the basic requirements for life and survival on Mars are locally available. Water, as has been shown, is present as permafrost in vast areas and could be found in the mud of what from space appear to be dry riverbeds. When geologists at Arizona State University working for NASA were suggesting Mars landing sites to Soviet scientists, they pointed to the great canyon in the Lunae Planum basin as a place where a roving vehicle "could visit former riverbeds and dig into the sediments of a delta where an ancient river flowed into a basin," and find there liquid water. Aquifers—subterranean water pools—are a sure source of water in the opinion of many scientists. New analyses of data from spacecraft as well as from Earth-based instruments led a team headed by Robert L. Huguenin of the University of Massachusetts to conclude, in June 1980, that two concentrations of water evaporation on Mars south of its equator suggest the existence of vast reservoirs of liquid water just a few inches below the Martian surface. Later that year Stanley H. Zisk of the Haystack Observatory in Westford, Massachusetts, and Peter J. Mouginis-Mark of Brown University, Rhode Island, reported in *Science and Nature* (November 1980) that radar probing of areas in the planet's southern hemisphere indicated "moist oases" of "extensive liquid water" beneath the surface. And then, of course, there is all the water captured in the ice cap of the northern pole, which melts around its rims during the northern summer, creating large, visible darkish patches (Fig. 74). Morning fogs

U.S. Geological Survey

Figure 74

and mists that have been observed on Mars suggest to scientists the existence of dew, a source of water for many plants and animals on Earth in arid areas.

The Martian atmosphere, at first sight inhospitable and even poisonous to Man and life, could in fact be a source of vital resources. The atmosphere has been found to contain some water vapor, which could be extracted by condensation. It could also be a source of oxygen for breathing and burning. It consists on Mars primarily of carbon dioxide (CO_2) with small percentages of nitrogen, argon, and traces of oxygen (Earth's atmosphere consists primarily of nitrogen, with a large percentage of oxygen and small amounts of other gases). The process of converting carbon dioxide (CO_2) to carbon monoxide (CO), thereby releasing oxygen (CO + O) is almost elementary and could easily be performed by astronauts and settlers. Carbon monoxide can then serve as a simple rocket fuel.

The planet's reddish-brown, or "rusty," hue is also a clue to the availability of oxygen, for it is the result of the actual rusting of iron rocks on Mars. The product is iron oxide—iron that has combined with oxygen. On Mars it is of a type called limonite, a combination of iron oxide (Fe_2O_3) with several molecules of water (H_2O); with the proper equipment, the plentiful oxygen could be separated and extracted. The hydrogen obtainable by breaking down water into its component elements could be used in the production of foods and useful materials, many of which are based on hydrocarbons (hydrogen-carbon combinations).

Although the Martian soil is relatively high in salts, scientists believe it could be washed with water sufficiently to the point where patches would be suitable for plant cultivation in greenhouses; local foods could thus be grown, especially from seeds of salt-resistant strains of grains and vegetables; human waste could be used as fertilizer, as it is used in many Third World countries on Earth. Nitrogen, needed by plants and fertilizers, is in short supply on Mars but not absent: the atmosphere, though 95 percent carbon dioxide, does contain almost 3 percent nitrogen. The greenhouses for growing all this food would be made of inflatable plastic domes; electricity would be obtained from solar-powered batteries; the rover vehicles will also be solar-powered.

Another source not just of water but also of heat on Mars is indicated by the past volcanic activity there. Of several notable volcanoes, the one named Olympus, after the Greek mountain of the gods, dwarfs anything on Earth or even in the Solar System. The largest volcano on Earth, Mauna Loa in Hawaii, rises 6.3 miles; Olympus Mons on Mars towers 15 miles above the surrounding plain; its crater's top measures 45 miles across. The volcanoes of Mars and other evidence of volcanic activity on the planet indicate a hot molten core and thus the possible existence of warm surface spots, hot-water springs, and other phenomena resulting from internally generated heat.

With a day almost exactly the length of a day on Earth, seasons (although about twice as long as Earth's), equatorial regions, icy northern and southern poles, water resources that once were seas and lakes and rivers, mountain ranges and plains, volcanoes and canyons, Mars is Earthlike in so many ways. Indeed, some scientists believe that Mars, although created at the same time as the other planets 4.6 billion years ago, is at the stage Earth was at its beginnings, before plant life began to emit oxygen and change Earth's atmosphere. This notion has served as a basis for the suggestion by proponents of the Gaia Theory of how Man might "jump the gun" on Martian evolution by bringing life to it; for they hold that it was Life that made Earth hospitable to life.

Writing in *The Greening of Mars*, James Lovelock and Michael Allaby employed science fiction to describe how microorganisms and "halocarbon gases" would be sent from Earth to Mars in rockets, the former to start the biological chain and the latter to create a shield in the Martian atmosphere. This shield of halocarbon gases, suspended in the atmosphere above the now cold and arid planet, would block the dissipation into space of the warmth Mars receives from the Sun and its own internal heat and would create an artificially induced "greenhouse" effect. The warming and the thickened atmosphere would release Mars's frozen waters, enhance plant growth, and thereby increase the planet's oxygen supply. Each step in this artificially induced evolution would strengthen the process; thus will the bringing of Life to Mars make it hospitable to life.

The suggestion by the two scientists that the transformation of Mars into a habitable planet—they called the process "Terra forming"—should begin with the creation of an artificial shield to protect the planet's dissipating heat and water vapor by artificially suspending a suitable material in the planet's atmosphere was made by them in 1984.

Whether by coincidence or not, it was once again a case of modern science catching up with ancient knowledge. For, in *The 12th Planet* (1976), it was described how the Anunnaki came to Earth about 450,000 years ago in order to obtain gold—needing the metal to protect life on their planet Nibiru by suspending gold particles as a shield in its dwindling atmosphere, to reverse the loss of heat, air, and water.

The plans proposed by the advocates of the Gaia Hypothesis are based on an assumption and a presumption. The first, that Mars does not have life-forms of its own; the second, that people from one planet have the right to introduce their life-forms to another world, whether or not it has its own life.

But does Mars have life on it or, as some prefer to ask, did it have life on it in its less harsh epochs? The question has preoccupied those who have planned and executed the various missions to Mars; and after all the scanning and photographing and probing, it is evident that Life as it has blossomed on Earth—trees and forests, bushes and grasses, flying birds and roaming animals—is just not there. But what about lesser life-forms—lichens or algae or the lowly bacteria?

Although Mars is much smaller than Earth (its mass is about a tenth that of Earth, its diameter about half) its surface, now all dry land, is about the same area as the dry-land portion of Earth's surface. The area to be explored is thus the same as the area on Earth with all its continents, mountains, valleys, equatorial and polar zones; its warm and the cold places; its humid regions and the dry desert ones. When an outline of the United States, coast to coast, is superimposed on the face of Mars (Fig. 75), the scope of the exploration and the variety of terrains and climates to contend with can well be appreciated.

No wonder when then that the first successful unmanned Mars probes, *Mariners 4, 6,* and *7* (1965–69), which photographed parts of the planet's surface in the course of flybys, revealed a planet that was heavily cratered and utterly desolate, with little sign of any geologic activity in its past. As it happened, the pictures were almost all of the cratered highlands in the southern hemisphere of Mars. This image, of a planet not only without life on it but itself a lifeless and dead globe, changed completely when *Mariner 9* went into orbit around Mars in 1971 and surveyed almost its entire surface. It showed a living planet with a history of geologic activity and volcanism, with plains and mountains, with canyons in which America's Grand Canyon could be swallowed without a trace, and

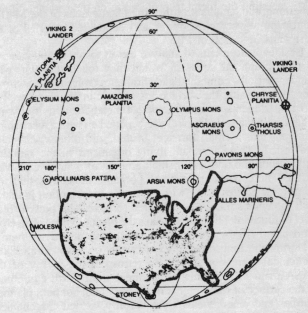

Figure 75

the marks of flowing water. It was not only a living planet but one that could have life upon it.

The search for life on Mars was thus made a prime objective of the Viking missions. *Viking 1* and *Viking 2* were launched from Cape Canaveral in the summer of 1975 and reached their destination in July and August of 1976. Each consisted of an Orbiter that remained in orbit around the planet for ongoing observation, and of a Lander that was lowered to the planet's surface. Although to ensure safe landings, relatively flat sites in the northern hemisphere, not too distant from each other, were selected for the touchdowns, "biological criteria" (i.e., the possibility of life) "dominated the decision regarding the latitude at which the spacecraft would land." The orbiters have provided a rich array of data about Mars that is still being studied and analyzed, with new details and insights constantly emerging; the landers sent thrilling photographs of the Martian landscape at very close range and conducted a series of experiments in search of Life.

Besides instruments to analyze the atmosphere and cameras to photograph the areas in which they touched down, each Lander carried a combined gas-chromatograph/mass-spectrometer for analyzing the surface for organic material, as well as three instruments designed to detect metabolic activity by any organism in the soil. The soil was scooped up with a mechanical arm, put into a small furnace, heated, and otherwise treated and tested. There were no living organisms in the samples; only carbon dioxide and a small amount of water vapor were found. There were not even the organic molecules that impacting meteorites bring with them; the presumption is that if such molecules had been delivered to Mars, the present high level of ultraviolet light that strikes the planet, whose protective atmosphere is now almost gone, must have destroyed them.

During the long days of experiments on Mars, drama and excitement were not absent. In retrospect the ability of the NASA team to manipulate and direct from Earth equipment on the surface of Mars seems like a fairy tale; but both planned routines and emergencies were adroitly tackled. Mechanical arms failed to work but were fixed by radio commands. There were other malfunctions and adjustments. There was breathtaking suspense when the gas-exchange experiments detected a burst of oxygen; there was the need to have *Viking 2* instruments confirm or disprove the results of experiments carried out by those of *Viking 1* that left open the question of whether changes in the scooped-up soil samples were organic or chemical, biological or inanimate. *Viking 2* results confirmed the reactions of *Viking 1* experiments: when gases were mixed or when soil was added to a ''nutrient soup,'' there were marked changes in the level of carbon dioxide; but whether the changes represented a chemical reaction or a biological response remained a puzzle.

As eager as scientists were to find life on Mars, and thereby find support for their theories of how life on Earth began spontaneously from a primordial soup, most had to conclude regretfully that no evidence of life on Mars was found. Norman Horowitz of Caltech summed up the prevailing opinion when he stated (in *Scientific American*, November 1977) that "at least those areas on Mars examined by the two spacecraft are not habitats of life. Possibly the same conclusion applies to the entire planet, but that is an intricate problem that cannot yet be addressed."

In subsequent years, in laboratory experiments in which the soil and conditions on Mars were simulated as best as the researchers could, the reactions indicated biological responses. Especially intriguing were experiments conducted in 1980 at the Space Biology Laboratory of Moscow University: when Earthly life-forms were introduced into a simulated Martian environment, birds and mammals expired in a few seconds, turtles and frogs lived many hours, insects survived for weeks—but fungi, lichens, algae, and mosses quickly adapted themselves to the new environment; oats, rye, and beans sprouted and grew but could not reproduce.

Life, then, could take hold on Mars; but had it? With 4.6 billion years at the disposal of evolution on Mars, where are not merely some microorganisms (which may or may not exist) but higher life-forms? Or were the Sumerians right in saying that life sprouted on Earth so soon after its formation only because the "Seed of Life" was brought to it, by Nibiru?

While the soil of Mars still keeps its riddle of whether or not its test reactions were chemical and lifeless or biological and caused by living organisms, the rocks of Mars challenge us with even more enigmatic puzzles.

One can begin with the mystery of Martian rocks found not on Mars but on Earth. Among the thousands of meteorites found on Earth, eight that were discovered in India, Egypt, and France between 1815 and 1865 (known as the SNC group, after the initials of the sites' names) were unique in that their age was only 1.3 billion years, whereas meteorites are generally 4.5 billion years old. When several more were discovered in Antarctica in 1979, the gaseous composition of the Martian atmosphere was already known; comparisons revealed that the SNC meteorites contained traces of isotopic Nitrogen–14, Argon–40 and 36, Neon–20, Krypton–84, and Xenon–13 almost identical to the presence of these rare gases on Mars.

How did these meteorites or rocks reach Earth? Why are they only 1.3 billion years old? Did a catastrophic impact on

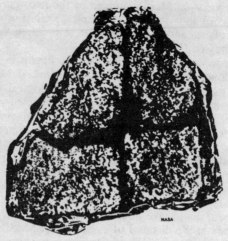

Figure 76

Mars cause them to somehow defy its gravity and fly off to Earth?

The rocks discovered in Antarctica are even more puzzling. A photograph of one of them, released by NASA and published in *The New York Times* of September 1, 1987, shows it to be not "football sized" as these rocks had been described, but rather a broken-off block (Fig. 76) of four bricklike, *artificially shaped and angled stones fitted together*—something one would expect to find in pre-Inca ruins in Peru's Sacred Valley (Fig. 77) but not on Mars. Yet all tests on the rock (it is no longer referred to as a meteorite) attest to its Martian origin.

To compound the mystery, photographs of the Martian surface have revealed features that, on seeing them, astronomers dubbed "Inca City." Located in the planet's southern part, they represent a series of steep walls made up of squarish or rectangular segments (Fig. 78 is from *Mariner–9* photographic frame 4212–15). John McCauley, a NASA geologist, commented that the "ridges" were "continuous, show no breaching, and stand out among the surrounding plains and small hills like walls of an ancient ruin."

Figure 77

Figure 78

This immense wall or series of connected shaped stone blocks bears a striking resemblance to such colossal and enigmatic structures on Earth as the immense wall of gigantic stone blocks that forms the base of the vast platform at Baalbek in Lebanon (Fig. 79) or to the cruder but equally impressive zigzagging parallel stone walls of Sacsahuaman above Cuzco in Peru (Fig.

Figure 79

80). In *The Stairway to Heaven* and *The Lost Realms*, I have attributed both structures to the Anunnaki/Nefilim. The features on Mars might perhaps be explained as natural phenomena, and the size of the blocks, ranging from three to five miles in length, might very well indicate the hand of nature rather than of people, of whatever provenance. On the other hand, since no plausible natural explanation has emerged, they might be

Figure 80

the remains of artificial structures—if the "giants" of Near Eastern and Andean lore had also visited Mars. . . .

The notion of "canals" on Mars appeared to have been laid to rest when—after decades of ridicule—scientists suggested that what Schiaparelli and Lowell had observed and mapped were in fact channels of dried-up rivers. Yet other features were found on the Martian surface that defy easy explanation. These include white "streaks" that run in *straight lines* for endless miles—sometimes parallel, sometimes at angles to each other, sometimes crossing other, narrower "tracks" (Fig. 81 is a sketched-over photo). Once again, the NASA teams suggested that windblown dust storms may have caused these features. This may be so, although the regularity and especially the intersecting of the lines seem to indicate an artificial origin. Searching for a comparable feature on Earth, one must look to the famous Nazca lines in southern Peru (Fig. 82) which have been attributed to "the gods."

Both the Near East and the Andes are known for their various pyramids—the immense and unique ones at Giza, the stepped pyramids or ziggurats of Mesopotamia and of the early American civilizations. As pictures taken by the *Mariner* and *Viking*

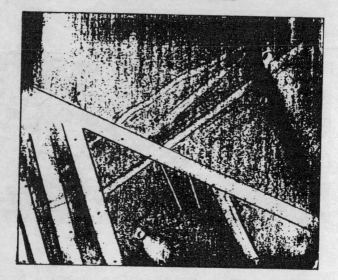

Figure 81

cameras seem to show, even pyramids, or what look like pyramids, have been seen on Mars.

What appear to be three-sided pyramids in the Elysium (map, Fig. 83) plateau in the region called Trivium Charontis were first noticed on *Mariner–9* frames 4205–78, taken on February 8, 1972 and 4296–23, taken six months later. Attention was focused on two pairs of "tetrahedron pyramidal structures," to use the cautious scientific terminology; one pair were huge pyramids, while the other pair were much smaller, and they seemed to be laid out in a rhombus-shaped pattern (Fig. 84). Here again, the size of the "pyramids"—the larger are each two miles across and half a mile high—suggests that they are natural phenomena, and a study in the journal *Icarus* (vol. 22, 1974, by Victor Ablordeppy and Mark Gipson) offered four theories to explain these formations naturally. David Chandler (*Life on Mars*) and astronomer Francis Graham (in *Frontiers of Science*, November–December 1980), among others, showed the flaws in each theory. The fact that the features

Figure 82

were photographed six months apart, at different sunlights and angles, and yet show their accurate terrahedral shapes, convinces many that they are artificial structures, even if we do not understand the reason for their great size. "Given the present lack of any easily acceptable explanation," Chandler wrote, "there seems to be no reason to exclude from consideration the most obvious conclusion of all: perhaps they were

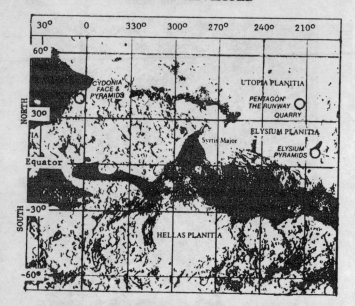

Figure 83

built by intelligent beings." And Francis Graham, stating that
"the conjecture that these are buildings of an ancient race of
Martians must take its place among the theories of their origin," wondered whether future explorers might discover in
these structures inner chambers, buried entrances, or inscriptions that might have withstood "ten thousand millennia of
wind erosion."

More "pyramids" with varying numbers of smooth sides
have been discerned by researchers who have scanned the Martian photographs. Interest, and controversy, have focused
mainly on an area named Cydonia (see map, Fig. 83) because
a group of what may be artificial structures appears to be
aligned with what some called a Martian "sphinx" to the east
of these structures, as can be readily seen in the panoramic
NASA photo 035-A-72 (Plate E). What is noticeable is a rock
with the features of a well-proportioned human face, seemingly
of a man wearing some kind of a helmet (Fig. 85), with a

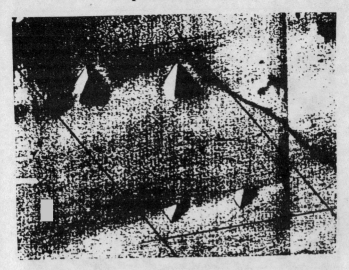

Figure 84

Figure 85

Plate E

slightly open mouth and with eyes that look straight out at the
viewer—if the viewer happens to be in the skies above Mars.
Like the other "monuments"—the features that resemble artificial structures—on Mars, this one, too, is of large proportions: the Face measures almost a mile from top to bottom and
has been estimated to rise almost half a mile above the surrounding plateau, as can be judged by its shadow.

Although it is said that the NASA scientist who examined
the photographs received from the *Viking 1* Orbiter on July
25, 1976, "almost fell out of his chair" when he saw this
frame and that appropriate "Oh, my God" or expressions to
that effect were uttered, the fact is that the photograph was
filed away with the thousands of other *Viking* photographs
without any further action because the similarity to a human
face was deemed just a play of light and shadows on a rock

eroded by natural forces (water, wind). Indeed, when some newsmen who happened to see the transmitted image wondered whether it in fact showed a human face, the chief scientist of the Mission asserted that another photograph, taken a few hours later, did not show such a feature at all. (Years later NASA acknowledged that that was an incorrect and misleading statement and an unfortunate one, because the fact was that the area fell into darkness of night "a few hours later" and there did exist other photographs clearly showing the Face.)

Three years later Vincent DiPietro, an electrical engineer and imaging specialist, who remembered seeing the "Face" in a popular magazine, came face-to-face with the Martian image as he was thumbing through the archives of the National Space Science Data Center. The *Viking* photo, bearing the catalog number 76-A-593/17384, was simply titled "HEAD." Intrigued by the decision to keep the photo in the scientific data center under that tantalizing caption—the "Head" whose very existence had been denied—he embarked, together with Greg Molenaar, a Lockheed computer scientist, on a search for the original NASA image. They found not one but two, the other being image 070-A-13 (Plate F). Subsequent searches came up with more photos of the Cydonia area taken by different *Viking* Orbiter cameras and from both the right and left sides of the features (there are eleven by now). The Face as well as more pyramidlike and other puzzling features could be seen on all of them. Using sophisticated computer enhancement and imaging techniques, DiPietro and Molenaar obtained enlarged and clearer images of the Face that convinced them it had been artificially sculpted.

Armed with their findings, they attended the 1981 The Case for Mars conference but instead of acclaiming them the assembled scientists cold-shouldered their assertions—undoubtedly because they would have to draw the conclusion that the Face was the handiwork of intelligent beings, "Martians" who had inhabited the planet; and that was a totally unacceptable proposition. Publishing their findings privately (*Unusual Mars Surface Features*) DiPietro and Molenaar took great pains to dissociate themselves from "wild speculations" regarding the origin of the unusual features. All they claimed, the book's epilogue stated, was "that the features do not seem natural and

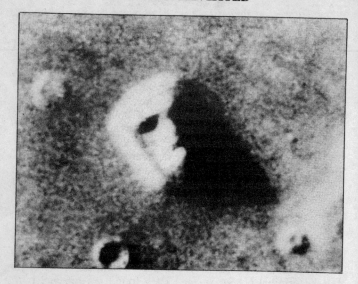

Plate F

warrant further investigation.'' NASA scientists, however, strongly rejected any suggestion that future missions should include a visit to the Face, since it was clearly just a rock shaped by the forces of nature so that it resembled a human face.

The cause of the Face on Mars was thereafter taken up primarily by Richard C. Hoagland, a science writer and one-time consultant at the Goddard Space Flight Center. He organized a computer conference titled The Independent Mars Investigation Team with the purpose of having the features and all other pertinent data studied by a representative group of scientists and specialists; the group eventually included Brian O'Leary, a scientist-astronaut, and David Webb, a member of the U.S. President's Space Commission. In their conclusions they not only concurred with the view that the ''Face'' and ''pyramids'' were artificial structures, they also suggested that other features on the surface on Mars were the handiwork of intelligent beings who had once been on Mars.

I was especially intrigued by the suggestion in their reports that the orientation of the Face and the principal pyramid indicated they were built about half a million years ago in alignment with sunrise at solstice time on Mars. When Hoagland and his colleague Thomas Rautenberg, a computer specialist, sought my comments on their photographic evidence, I pointed out to them that the Anunnaki/Nefilim, according to my conclusions in *The 12th Planet*, had first landed on Earth about 450,000 years ago; it was, perhaps, no coincidence that Hoagland and Rautenberg's dating of the monuments on Mars coincided with my timetable. Although Hoagland was careful to hedge his bets, he did devote many pages in his book *The Monuments of Mars* to my writings and to the Sumerian evidence concerning the Anunnaki.

The publicity accorded the findings of DiPietro, Molenaar, and Hoagland has caused NASA to insist that they were wrong. In an unusual move, the National Space Flight Center in Greenbelt, Maryland, which supplies the public with copies of NASA data, has been enclosing along with the "Face" photographs copies of rebuttals of the unorthodox interpretations of the images. These rebuttals include a three-page paper dated June 6, 1987, by Paul Butterworth, the Center's Resident Planetologist. He states that "there is no reason to believe that this particular mountain, which is similar to tens of thousands of others on the planet, is not the result of the natural geological processes which have produced all the other landforms on Mars. Among the huge numbers of mountains on Mars it is not surprising that some should remind us of more familiar objects, and nothing is more familiar than the human face. I am still looking for the 'Hand on Mars' and the 'Leg on Mars'!"

"No reason to believe" that the feature is other than natural is, of course, not a factual argument in disproving the opposite position, whose proponents contend that they do have reason to believe the features are artificial structures. Still, it is true that on Earth there are hills or mountains that give the appearance of a sculpted human or animal head although they are the work of nature alone. This, I feel, might well be a valid argument regarding the "pyramids" on the Elysium plateau or the "Inca City." But the Face and some features near it, especially those with straight sides, remain a challenging enigma.

A scientifically significant study by Mark J. Carlotto, an optics scientist, was published in the May 1988 issue of the prestigious journal *Applied Optics*. Using computer graphic techniques developed in optical sciences, Carlotto employed four frames from NASA images, taken by the *Viking* Orbiter with different cameras during four different orbits, to recreate a three-dimensional representation of the Face. The study provided detailed information about the complex optical procedures and mathematical formulations of the three-dimensional analysis, and Carlotto's conclusions were that the "Face" was indeed a bisymmetrical human face, with another eye socket in the shaded part and a "fine structure of the mouth suggesting teeth." These, Carlotto stated, "were facial features and not a transient phenomenon" or a trick of light and shadow. "Although the *Viking* data are not of sufficient resolution to permit the identification of possible mechanisms of origin for these objects, *the results to date suggest that they may not be natural*."

Applied Optics deemed the study important enough to make it its front-cover feature, and the scientific journal *New Scientist* devoted a special report to the published paper and to an interview with its author. The journal echoed his suggestion that "at the very least these enigmatic objects"—the Face and the adjoining pyramidal features that some had dubbed "The City"—"deserve further scrutiny by future Mars probes, such as the 1988 Soviet Phobos mission or the U.S. Mars Observer."

The fact that the controlled Soviet press has published and republished articles by Vladimir Avinksy, a noted researcher in geology and mineralogy, that support the non-natural origin of the monuments, surely indicates the Soviet aerospace attitudes on the matter—a subject that will be dealt with at greater length later on. Noteworthy here are two points made by Dr. Avinsky. He suggests (in published articles and privately delivered papers) that in considering the enormous size of the

Martian formations, one must bear in mind that due to the low gravity of Mars a man could perform gigantic tasks on it; and he attaches great importance to the dark circle that is clearly seen in the flat area between the Face and the pyramids. While NASA scientists dismissed it as "a water spot on the lens of the *Viking* Orbiter," Avinsky considers it "the centre of the entire composition" of the "Martian complex" and its layout (Fig. 86).

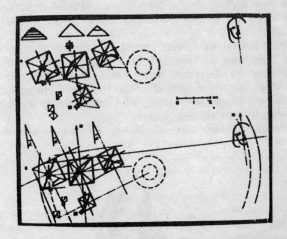

Figure 86

Unless it is assumed that Earthlings possessed, tens of thousands or even half a million years ago, a high civilization and a sophisticated technology that enabled them to engage in space travel, arrive on Mars and, among other things, put up monuments on it, including the Face, only two other alternatives logically remain. The first is that intelligent beings had evolved on Mars who not only could engage in megalithic construction but also happened to look like us. But in the absence even of microorganisms in the soil of Mars, nor evidence of plant and animal life that among other things could provide the humanlike Martians with nourishment, the rise of a Martian population akin to Earthlings and one that even duplicated the structural forms found on Earth seems highly improbable.

The only remaining plausible alternative is that someone, neither from Earth nor from Mars, capable of space travel half a million years ago, had visited this part of the Solar System and had stayed; and then left behind monuments, both on Earth and on Mars. The only beings for which evidence has been found—in the Sumerian and biblical texts and in all the ancient "mythologies"—are the Anunnaki from Nibiru. We know how they looked: they looked like us because they made us look like them, in their image and after their likeness, to quote Genesis.

Their humanlike visages appear in countless ancient depictions, including the famous Sphinx at Giza (Fig. 87). Its face, according to Egyptian inscriptions, was that of *Hor-em-Akhet*, the "Falcon-god of the Horizon," an epithet for Ra, the firstborn son of Enki, who could soar to the farthest heavens in his Celestial Boat.

The Giza Sphinx was so oriented that its gaze was aligned

Figure 87

precisely eastward along the thirtieth parallel toward the space-port of the Anunnaki in the Sinai Peninsula. The ancient texts attributed communications functions to the Sphinx (and the purported subterranean chambers under it):

> A message is sent from heaven;
> it is heard in Heliopolis and is repeated in Memphis
> by the Fair of Face.
> It is composed in a dispatch by the writing of Thoth
> with regard to the city of Amen. . . .
> The gods are acting according to command.

The reference to the message-transmitting role of the "Fair of Face"—the sphinx at Giza—raises the question of what the purpose of the Face on Mars was; for, if it was indeed the handiwork of intelligent beings, then by definition they did not expend the time and effort to create the Face without a logical reason. Was the purpose, as the Egyptian text suggests, to send the "message from Heaven" to the sphinx on Earth, a "command" according to which the gods acted, sent from one Face to another Fair-of-Face?

If such was the purpose of the Face on Mars, then one would indeed expect to find pyramids nearby, as one finds at Giza; there, three unique and exceptional pyramids, one smaller and two colossal, rise in symmetry with each other and with the Sphinx. Interestingly, Dr. Avinsky discerns three true pyramids in the area adjoining the Face on Mars.

As the ample evidence presented in the volumes of "The Earth Chronicles" series indicates, the Giza pyramids were not the handiwork of Pharaohs but were constructed by the Anunnaki. Before the Deluge their spaceport was in Meso-potamia, at Sippar ("Bird City"). After the Deluge the space-port was located in the Sinai Peninsula, and the two great pyramids of Giza, two artificial mountains, served as beacons for the Landing Corridor whose apex was anchored on Mount Ararat, the Near East's most visible natural feature. If this was also the function of the pyramids in the Cydonia area, then some correlation with that most conspicuous natural feature on Mars, Olympus Mons, might eventually be found.

When the principal center of gold production by the Anunnaki shifted from southeast Africa to the Andes, their metallurgical center was established on the shores of Lake Titicaca, at what is nowadays the ruins of Tiahuanacu and Puma-Punku. The principal structures in Tiahuanacu, which was connected to the lake by canals, were the "pyramid" called Akapana, a massive mound engineered to process ores, and the Kalasasaya, a square, "hollowed-out" structure (Fig. 88) that served astronomical purposes; its orientation was aligned with the solstices. Puma-Punku was situated directly on the lakeshore; its principal structures were "golden enclosures" built of immense stone blocks that stood alongside an array of zigzagging piers (Fig. 89).

Of the unusual features the orbiting cameras captured on the face of Mars, two appear to me to be almost certainly artificial—*and both seem to emulate structures found on the shores*

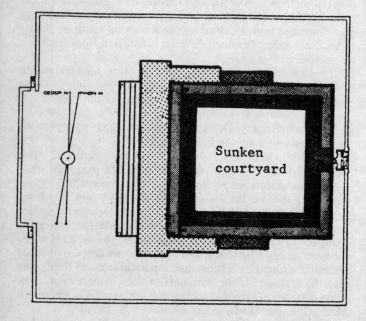

Figure 88

of Lake Titicaca in the Andes. One, which is akin to the Kalasasaya, is the first feature west of the Face on Mars, just above (north of) the mysterious darkish circle (see Plate E). As an enlargement thereof indicates (Plate G), its still-standing southern part consists of two distinct massive walls, perfectly straight, meeting at an angle that appears sharp because of the photographic angle but is in fact a true right angle. The structure—which could not possibly be natural no matter how far the imagination is stretched—appears to have collapsed, in its

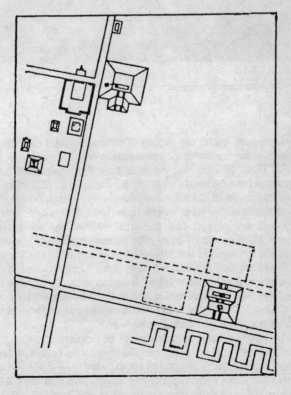

Figure 89

Plate G

northern part, under the impact of a huge boulder that dropped on it in some catastrophic circumstances.

The other feature that could not be the product of natural erosion is found directly south of the Face, in an area of chaotic features, some of which have amazingly straight sides (Plate M). Separated by what might have been a channel or waterway—all are agreed that the area was on the shores of an ancient Martian sea or lake—the prominent feature's side that faces the channel is not straight but is outfitted with a series of "indentations" (Plate H). One must keep in mind that all these photographs were taken from an altitude of about one thousand two hundred miles above the Martian surface; what we observe, then, may well have been an array of large piers—just as one finds at Puma-Punku.

The two features, which cannot be explained away as the result of the play of light and shadow, thus bear similarities to the facilities and structures on the shores of Lake Titicaca. In this they not only support my suggestion that they are the remains of structures put up by the same visitors—the An-

Plate H

unnaki—they also offer a hypothesis for explaining their purpose and possible function. This conclusion is further supported by features that can be seen in the Utopia area: a pentagonal structure (enhanced NASA frame 086-A-07) and a "runway" next to what some deem evidence of mining (NASA frame 086-A-08)—Plates I and J.

The spaceports of the Anunnaki on Earth, judging by Sumerian and Egyptian records, consisted of a Mission Control Center, Landing Beacons, an underground silo, and a large, flat plain whose natural surface served as runways. The Mission Control Center and certain Landing Beacons were some distance away from the spaceport proper where the runways were situated; when the spaceport was in the Sinai Peninsula, Mission Control Center was in Jerusalem and the Landing Beacons were in Giza, Egypt (the underground silo in the Sinai is depicted in Egyptian tomb drawings—see vignette at end of this chapter—and was destroyed by nuclear weapons in 2024 B.C.). In the Andes, the Nazca lines, I believe, represent the visual

Plate I

evidence for the use of that perfect, arid plain as runways for
space shuttle takeoffs and landings. The inexplicable criss-
crossing lines on the surface of Mars, the so called "tracks"
(see Fig. 81) could well represent the same kind of evidence.

There are also what appear to be true tracks on the Martian
surface. From the air they look like the markings made by a
pointed object on a linoleum floor, more or less straight
"scratches" left on the Martian plain. These markings have
been explained away as geological features, that is, natural
cracks in the Martian surface. But as can be seen in NASA
frame 651-A-06 (Plate K), the "cracks," or tracks, appear to
lead from an elevated structure of a geometric design with

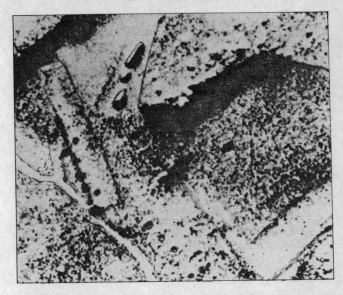

Plate J

straight sides and pierlike "teeth" on one side—a structure now mostly buried under windblown sands—to the shores of what evidently was once a lake. Other aerial photographs (Fig. 90) show some tracks on an escarpment above the great canyon in the Valles Marineris near the Martian equator; these tracks not only follow the contours of the terrain but also crisscross each other in a pattern that could hardly be natural.

It has been pointed out that if an alien spacecraft were to search for signs of life on Earth in areas of the Earth's surface outside the cities, what would give away the presence of intelligent beings on Earth would be the tracks we call "roads" and the rectilinear patterns of agricultural lands. NASA itself has supplied what might amount to evidence of deliberate agricultural activity on Mars. Frame 52-A-35 (Plate L) shows a

Plate K

series of parallel grooves resembling contoured farmland—as one would find in the high mountains of Peru's Sacred Valley. The photo caption prepared by the NASA News Center in Pasadena, California, when the photograph was released on August 18, 1976, stated thus:

> Peculiar geometric markings, so regular that they appear almost artificial can be seen in this Mars picture taken by Viking Orbiter 1 on August 12 from a range of 2053 kilometers (1273 miles).
>
> The contoured markings are in a shallow depression or basin, possibly formed by wind erosion. The markings—about one kilometer (one-half mile) from crest to crest—are low ridges and valleys and may be related to the same erosion process.
>
> The parallel contours look very much like an aerial view of plowed ground.

Figure 90

Plate L

The feature's similarity to a "farmer's field after plowing" was noticed as soon as the image was received, and the comment of Michael Carr, head of the imaging team, was, "we're getting some strange things, it's very puzzling . . . it's hard to think of a natural cause because the stripes are so regular." Not surprising, perhaps, was the location: the Cydonia region, site of the Face and other enigmatic features!

In the Elysium region, where some identify the group of three-sided pyramids, surface features that resemble an area of artificial irrigation have been seen (Plate M). Scientific studies explain the features (called by some a "waffle pattern") as "meltwater deposits with outflow channels" resulting naturally from interactions between volcanic activity and ground ice which caused these "collapse features." On the other hand, the features resemble recently discovered evidence of agricultural practices by ancient civilizations in Mesoamerica and South America, which attained large crop yields in rainless areas but with substantial subsurface water resources by raising

Plate M

crops on "islands" surrounded by irrigation canals. Were it not for all the other evidence and enigmatic features, the complex natural-process explanation might have been accepted; with all the other evidence one may well prefer to see in these photographs further proof of humanlike activities on Mars.

Since the Anunnaki counted the planets from the outside inward, Mars was the sixth planet; and the Sumerians depicted it accordingly by the symbol of a six-pointed star (just as Earth, the seventh planet, was depicted as a seven-pointed star or simply by seven dots). Using these symbols as a clue, we can now turn to examine an amazing Sumerian depiction on a cylinder seal (Fig. 91). It shows a spacecraft, with its solar panels and antennas extended, passing between the sixth and the seventh planets, that is, between Mars and Earth (the seven-dot symbol for Earth is accompanied by the symbol of the Moon's crescent). A winged Anunnaki (a way to depict the members of the Anunnaki corps of astronauts) holding an instrument is greeting another one who is obviously on Mars who wears a helmet to which some equipment is attached and holds an instrument. They seem to be telling each other, "The spaceship is now on its way from Mars to Earth." (The double-fish symbol below the spacecraft stands for the zodiac of Pisces).

lists, written on clay tablets, have been found by archaeologists. As was the custom then, the names were epithets whose

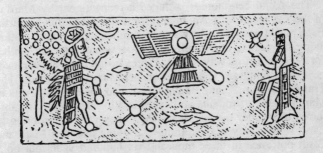

Figure 91

meaning conveyed information regarding the named person or object. One epithet for Mars was *Simug*, meaning "smith," honoring the god Nergal with whom the planet was associated in Sumerian times. A son of Enki, he was in charge of African domains that included the gold-mining areas. Mars was also called UTU.KA.GAB.A, meaning "Light Established at the Gate of the Waters," which can be interpreted either as its position next to the asteroid belt that separated the Lower Waters from the Upper Waters, or as a source of water for the astronauts as they passed beyond the more hazardous and less hospitable giant planets Saturn and Jupiter.

Even more interesting are Sumerian planetary lists that describe the planets as the Anunnaki passed them during a space journey to Earth. Mars was called MUL APIN—"Planet Where the Right Course is Set." It was so named also on an amazing circular tablet which copied nothing less than a route map for the journey from Nibiru to Earth by Enlil, graphically showing the "right turn" at Mars.

Even more enlightening as to what role Mars, or the space facilities upon it, had played in the journeys of the Anunnaki to Earth is the Babylonian text concerning the *Akitu* festival. Borrowed from ancient Sumerian traditions, it outlined the rituals and symbolic procedures during the ten days of the New Year ceremonies. In Babylon the principal deity who took over the supremacy from the earlier ones was Marduk; part of the transfer of the supremacy to him was the renaming by the Babylonians of the Planet of the Gods from the Sumerian *Nibiru* to the Babylonian *Marduk*.

The Akitu ceremonies included a reenactment by Marduk of the voyages of the Anunnaki from Nibiru/Marduk to Earth. Each planet passed on the way was symbolized by a way station along the course of the religious processions, and the epithet for each planet or way station expressed its role, appearance, or special features. The station/planet Mars was termed "The Traveler's Ship," and I have taken it to mean that it was at Mars that the astronauts and cargo coming from Nibiru transferred to smaller spacecraft in which they were transported to Earth (and vice versa), coming and going between Mars and Earth not once in three thousand six hundred years but on a more frequent schedule. Nearing Earth, these transporters linked up with the Earth orbiting station(s) manned by the Igigi; the actual landing on and takeoff from Earth were performed by smaller shuttlecraft that glided down to the natural "runways" and took off by soaring upward as they increased power.

Planners of the forthcoming steps into space by Mankind envision almost the same sequence of different vehicles as the best way to overcome the constraints of Earth's gravity, making use of the weightlessness of the orbiting station and the lower gravity of Mars (and, in their plans, also of the Moon). In this, once again, modern science is only catching up with ancient knowledge.

Coupled with these ancient texts and depictions, the photographic data from the surface of Mars, and the similarities between the Martian structures and those on Earth erected by the Anunnaki all lead to one plausible conclusion:

Mars, some time in its past, was the site of a space base.

And there is also evidence suggesting that *the ancient space base has been reactivated—in our very own time, in these very days.*

A DRAWING THAT DREW ATTENTION

When the Egyptian viceroy Huy died, his tomb was decorated with scenes of his life and work as governor of Nubia and the Sinai during the reign of the renowned Pharaoh Tut-Ankh-Amen. Among the drawings was that of a rocketship with its shaft in an underground silo and its conical command module above ground, among palm trees and giraffes.

The drawing, which was reproduced in *The 12th Planet* together with a comparable Sumerian pictograph of a spacecraft that designated the Anunnaki, caught the eye of Stuart W. Greenwood, an aerospace engineer then conducting research for NASA. Writing in *Ancient Skies* (July–August 1977), a publication of the Ancient Astronaut Society, he found in the ancient drawing aspects indicating knowledge of a sophisticated technology and drew attention in particular to four "highly suggestive features": (1) The "airfoil cross-section surrounding the rocket," which appears suitable for "the walls of a duct used for the development of thrust";

Space Ship - Rocket.

(2) The rocket head above ground, "reminiscent of the Gemini space capsule even to the appearance of the windows and (3) the charred surface and blunt end"; and (4) The unusual spike, which is like spikes tested by NASA for reducing the drag on the space capsule without success, but which in the drawing suggests it was retractable and thus could overcome the overheating problem that NASA was unable to solve.

He estimated that "if the relative locations of the rocket-head and shaft shown in the drawing are those applying during operation within the atmosphere, the inclined shock wave from the nose of the rockethead would touch the duct 'lip' at about Mach–3 (3 times the speed of sound)."

12

PHOBOS: MALFUNCTION OR STAR WARS INCIDENT?

On October 4, 1957, the Soviet Union launched Earthlings' first artificial satellite, *Sputnik 1*, and set Mankind on a road that has led Man to the Moon and his spacecraft to the edge of the Solar System and beyond.

On July 12, 1988, the Soviet Union launched an unmanned spacecraft called *Phobos 2* and may have provided Mankind with its first Star Wars incident—not the "Star Wars" nickname of America's Strategic Defense Initiative (SDI), but *a war with people from another world*.

Phobos 2 was one of two unmanned satellites, the other being *Phobos 1*, that were set off from Earth in July 1988, headed toward the planet Mars. *Phobos 1*, reportedly because of a radio command error, was lost two months later. *Phobos 2* arrived safely at Mars in January 1989 and entered into orbit around Mars as the first step at its destination toward its ultimate goal—to transfer to an orbit that would make it fly almost in tandem with the Martian moonlet called Phobos (hence the spacecraft's name) and explore the moonlet with highly sophisticated equipment that included two packages of instruments to be placed on the moonlet's surface.

All went well until *Phobos 2* aligned itself with Phobos, the Martian moonlet. Then, on March 28, 1989, the Soviet mission control center acknowledged sudden communication "problems" with the spacecraft; and Tass, the official Soviet news agency, reported that "*Phobos 2* failed to communicate with Earth as scheduled after completing an operation yesterday around the Martian moon Phobos. Scientists at mission control have been unable to establish stable radio contact."

These admissions left the impression that the problem was not incurable and were accompanied by assurances that mission control scientists were engaged in maneuvers to reestablish contact with the spacecraft. Soviet space program officials as well as many Western specialists were aware that the Phobos mission represented an immense investment in terms of finance, planning, effort, and prestige. Although launched by the Soviets, the mission in reality represented an international effort on an unprecedented scale, with more than thirteen European countries (including the European Space Agency and major French and West German scientific institutions) participating officially and British and American scientists participating "personally" (with their governments' knowledge and blessing). It was thus understandable that the "problem" was at first represented as a break in communications that could be overcome in a matter of days. Soviet television and press reports played down the seriousness of the occurrence, emphasizing that attempts were being made to reestablish links with the spacecraft. In fact, American scientists associated with the program were not officially informed of the nature of the problem and were led to believe that the communications breakdown was caused by the malfunction of a low-power backup transmitting unit that had been in use since the principal transmitter had failed earlier.

But on the next day, while the public was still being reassured that a resumption of contact with the spacecraft was achievable, a high-ranking official at Glavkosmos, the Soviet space agency, hinted that there indeed was no such hope. "Phobos 2 is ninety-nine percent lost for good," Nikolai A. Simyonov said; on that day, his choice of words—not that *contact* with the spacecraft was lost but that the *spacecraft itself* was "lost for good"—was not paid any particular heed.

On March 30, in a special report from Moscow to *The New York Times*, Esther B. Fein mentioned that *Vremya*, the main evening news program on Soviet television, "rapidly rattled off the bad news about *Phobos*" and focused its report instead on the successful research the spacecraft had already accomplished. Soviet scientists appearing on the program "displayed some of the space images, but said it was still not clear what clues they offered to understanding Mars, Phobos, the Sun and interplanetary space."

What "images" and what "clues" were they talking about?

This became clearer the following day, when reports published in the European press (but for some reason not in the U.S. media) spoke of an "unidentified object" that was seen "in the final pictures taken by the spaceship," which showed an "inexplicable" object or "elliptical shadow" on Mars.

This was an avalanche of puzzling words out of Moscow!

The Spanish daily *La Epoca*, for example (Fig. 92), headlined the dispatch by the Moscow correspondent of the European news agency EFE "*Phobos 2 Captured Strange Photos of Mars Before Losing Contact With Its Base*." The text of the dispatch, in translation, read as follows:

The TV newscast "Vremya revealed yesterday that the space probe *Phobos 2*, which was orbiting above Mars when Soviet scientists lost contact with it on Monday, had photographed an unidentified object on the Martian surface seconds before losing contact.

The TV broadcast devoted a long segment to the strange pictures taken by the spaceship before losing contact, and

Figure 92

showed the two most important pictures, in which a large shadow is visible in one of the pictures and in the other.

Scientists characterized the final picture taken by the spaceship, in which the thin ellipse can be clearly seen, as "inexplicable."

The phenomenon, it was stated, could not be an optical illusion because it was captured with the same clarity both by color cameras as well as by cameras taking infrared images.

One of the members of the Permanent Space Commission who had worked around the clock to reestablish contact with the lost space probe stated on Soviet television that in the opinion of the commission's scientists the object "looked like a shadow on the surface of Mars."

According to calculations by researchers from the Soviet Union the "shadow" that the last photo taken by *Phobos 2* shows is some twenty kilometers [about 12.5 miles] long.

A few days earlier, the spaceship had already recorded an identical phenomenon, except that in that instance the "shadow" was between twenty-six to thirty kilometers [about 16 to 19 miles] long.

The reporter from "Vremya" asked one of the members of the special commission if the shape of the "phenomenon" didn't suggest to him a space rocket, to which the scientist responded, "This is to fantasize."

[Here follow details of the mission's original assignments.]

Needless to say, this is an amazing and literally "out of this world" report that raises as many questions as it answers. The loss of contact with the spacecraft was associated, by implication if not in so many words, with the observation by the spacecraft of "an object on the Martian surface seconds before." The culprit "object" is described as "a thin ellipse" and is also called "a phenomenon" as well as "a shadow." It was observed at least twice—the report does not state whether in the same location on the surface of Mars—and is capable of changing its size: the first time it was about 12.5 miles long; the second and fatal time, about 16 to 19 miles long. And when the "Vremya" reporter wondered whether it was a "space rocket," the scientist responded, "This is to fantasize." So, what was—or is—it?

The authoritative weekly *Aviation Week & Space Technology*, in its issue of April 3, 1989, printed a report of the incident based on several sources in Moscow, Washington, and Paris (the authorities in the last being deeply involved because an equipment malfunction would have reflected badly on the French contribution to the mission, whereas an "act of God" would exonerate the French space industry). The version given *AW&ST* treated the occurrence as a "communications problem" that remained unresolved in spite of a week of attempts to "re-establish contact." It included the information that program officials at the Soviet Space Research Institute in Moscow said that the problem occurred "after an imaging and data-gathering session," following which *Phobos 2* had to change the orientation of its antenna. "The data-gathering segment itself apparently proceeded as planned, but reliable contact with *Phobos 2* could not be established afterward." At the time, the spacecraft was in a near-circular orbit around Mars and in the phase of "final preparations for the encounter with Phobos" (the moonlet).

While this version attributed the incident to a "loss-of-communications" problem, a report a few days later in *Science* (April 7, 1989) spoke of "the apparent loss of *Phobos 2*"— loss of the spacecraft itself, not just of the communications link with it. It happened, the prestigious journal stated, "on 27 March as the spacecraft turned from its normal alignment with Earth to image the tiny moon Phobos that was the primary mission target. When it came time for the spacecraft to turn itself and its antenna automatically back toward Earth, nothing was heard."

The journal then continued with a sentence that remains as inexplicable as the whole incident and the "thin ellipse" on the surface of Mars. It states:

A few hours later, a weak transmission was received, but controllers could not lock onto the signal. Nothing was heard during the next week.

Now, as a rereading of all the previous reports and statements will confirm, the incident was described as a sudden and total loss of the "communications link." The reason given was that the spacecraft, having turned its antennas *to scan Phobos*, failed to turn its antenna back toward Earth due to some unknown reason. But if the antenna remained stuck in a position facing away from Earth, how could "a weak transmission" be received "a few hours later"? And if the antenna did in fact turn itself back toward Earth properly, what caused the abrupt silence for several hours, followed by the transmission of a signal too weak to be locked onto?

The question that arises is indeed a simple one: Was the spacecraft Phobos 2 hit by "something" that put it out of commission, except for a last gasp in the form of a weak signal hours later?

There was one more report, from Paris, in *AW&ST* of April 10, 1989. Soviet space scientists, it said, suggested that *Phobos 2* "did not stabilize itself on the proper orientation to have the high-gain antenna pointing earthward." This obviously puzzled the editors of the magazine because, its report said, the *Phobos 2* spacecraft was "three-axis stabilized" by technology developed for the Soviet Venera spacecraft, which had performed perfectly on Venus missions.

The mystery thus is, what caused the spacecraft to destabilize itself? Was it a malfunction, or was there an extraneous cause—perhaps an impact?

The weekly's French sources provided this tantalizing detail:

> One controller at the Kaliningrad control center said the limited signals received after conclusion of the imaging session gave him the impression he was "tracking a spinner."

Phobos 2, in other words, acted as if it was in a spin.

Now, what was *Phobos 2* "imaging" when the incident occurred? We already have a good idea from the "Vremya" and European press agency reports. But here is what the *AW&ST* report from Paris states, quoting Alexander Dunayev, chairman of the Soviet Glavkosmos space administration:

> One image appears to include an odd-shaped object between the spacecraft and Mars. It may be debris in the orbit of Phobos or could be *Phobos 2*'s autonomous pro-

pulsion sub-system that was jettisoned after the spacecraft was injected into Mars orbit—we just don't know.''

This statement must have been made with quite a tongue-in-cheek attitude. The Viking orbiters left no debris in Mars orbit, and we know of no other ''debris'' resulting from Earth-originated activities. The other ''possibility,'' that the object orbiting Mars between the planet and the spacecraft *Phobos 2* was a jettisoned part of the spacecraft, can be readily dismissed once one looks at the shape and structure of *Phobos 2* (Fig. 93); none of its parts had the shape of a ''thin ellipse.'' Moreover, it was disclosed on the ''Vremya'' program that the ''shadow'' was 12.5, 16, or 19 *miles* long. Now, it is true that an object can throw a shadow much longer than itself, depending on the angle of sunlight; still, a part of *Phobos 2* that was only a few *feet* in length could hardly throw a shadow measured in miles. Whatever had been observed was neither debris nor a jettisoned part.

At the time I wondered why the official speculation omitted what was surely the most natural and believable third possibility, that what had been observed was indeed a shadow—but the shadow of Phobos, the Martial moonlet itself. It has

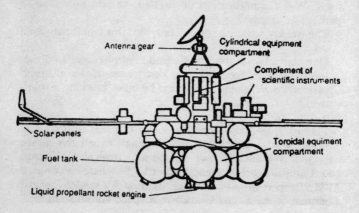

Figure 93

most often been described as "potato-shaped" (Fig. 94) and measures about seventeen miles across—just about the size of the "shadow" mentioned in the initial reports. In fact, I recalled seeing a *Mariner 9* photograph of an eclipse on Mars caused by the shadow of Phobos. Couldn't that be, I thought, what the fuss was all about, at least regarding the "apparition," if not what had caused the spacecraft, *Phobos 2*, to be lost?

The answer came about three months later. Pressed by their international participants in the Phobos missions to provide more definitive data, the Soviet authorities released the taped television transmission *Phobos 2* sent in its last moments—

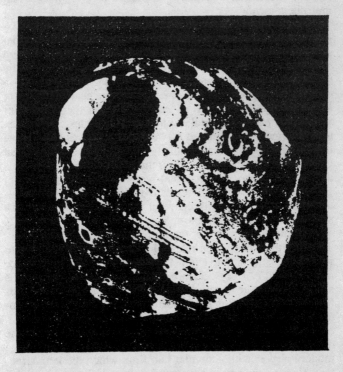

Figure 94

except for the last frames, taken just seconds before the spacecraft fell silent. The television clip was shown by some TV stations in Europe and Canada as part of weekly "diary" programs, as a curiosity and not as a hot news item.

The television sequence thus released focused on two anomalies. The first was a network of straight lines in the area of the Martian equator; some of the lines were short, some longer, some thin, some wide enough to look like rectangular shapes "embossed" in the Martian surface. Arranged in rows parallel to each other, the pattern covered an area of some six hundred square kilometers (more than two hundred thirty square miles). The "anomaly" appeared to be far from a natural phenomenon.

The television clip was accompanied by a live comment by Dr. John Becklake of England's Science Museum. He described the phenomenon as very puzzling, because the pattern seen on the surface of Mars was photographed not with the spacecraft's optical camera but with its infrared camera—a camera that takes pictures of objects using the heat they radiate, and not by the play of light and shadow on them. In other words, the pattern of parallel lines and rectangles covering an area of almost two hundred fifty square miles was a source of heat radiation. It is highly unlikely that a natural source of heat radiation (a geyser or a concentration of radioactive minerals under the surface, for example) would create such a perfect geometric pattern. When viewed over and over again, the pattern definitely looks artificial; but what it was, the scientist said, "I certainly don't know."

Since no coordinates for the precise location of this "anomalous feature" have been released publicly, it is impossible to judge its relationship to another puzzling feature on the surface of Mars that can be seen in *Mariner 9* frame 4209–75. It is also located in the equatorial area (at longitude 186.4) and has been described as "unusual indentations with radial arms protruding from a central hub" caused (according to NASA scientists) by the melting and collapse of permafrost layers. The design of the features, bringing to mind the structure of a modern airport with a circular hub from which the long structures housing the airplane gates radiate, can be better visualized when the photograph is reversed (showing depressions as protrusions—Fig. 95).

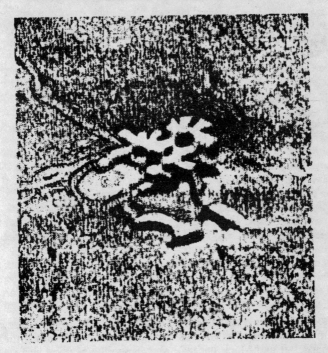

Figure 95

We now come to the second "anomaly" shown on the television segment. Seen on the surface of Mars was a clearly defined dark shape that could indeed be described, as it was in the initial dispatch from Moscow, as a "thin ellipse" (Plate N is a still from the Soviet television clip). It was certainly different from the shadow of Phobos recorded eighteen years earlier by *Mariner 9* (Plate O). The latter cast a shadow that was a rounded ellipse and fuzzy at the edges, as would be cast by the uneven surface of the moonlet. The "anomaly" seen in the *Phobos 2* transmission was a thin ellipse with very sharp rather than rounded points (the shape is known in the diamond trade as a "marquise") and the edges, rather than being fuzzy,

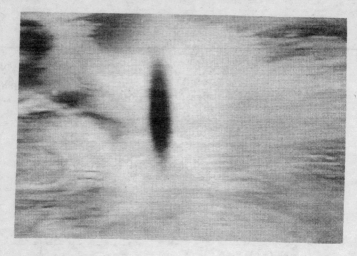

Plate N

stood out sharply against a kind of halo on the Martian surface. Dr. Becklake described it as "something that is between the spacecraft and Mars, because we can see the Martian surface below it," and stressed that the object was seen both by the optical and the infrared (heat-seeking) camera.

All these reasons explain why the Soviets have not suggested that the dark, "thin ellipse" might have been the shadow of the moonlet.

While the image was held on the screen, Dr. Becklake explained that it was taken as the spacecraft was aligning itself with Phobos (the moonlet). "As the last picture was halfway through," he said, "they [Soviets] *saw something which should not be there.*" The Soviets, he went on to state, "have not yet released this last picture, and we won't speculate on what it shows."

Since the last frame or frames have not yet been publicly released even a year after the incident, one can only speculate, surmise, or believe rumors, according to which the last frame,

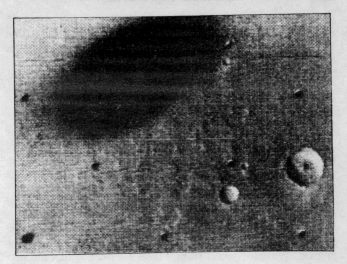

Plate O

halfway through its transmission, shows the "something that should not be there" *rushing toward* Phobos 2 *and crashing into it*, abruptly interrupting the transmission. Then there was, according to the reports mentioned earlier, a weak burst of transmission some hours later, too garbled to be clear. (This report, incidentally, belies the initial explanation that the space-craft could not turn its antennas back to an Earth-transmitting position).

In the October 19, 1989 issue of *Nature*, Soviet scientists published a series of technical reports on the experiments *Phobos 2* did manage to conduct; of the thirty-seven pages, a mere three paragraphs deal with the spacecraft's loss. The report confirms that the spacecraft was spinning, either because of a computer malfunction or because *Phobos 2* was "impacted" by an unknown object (the theory that the collision was with "dust particles" is rejected in the report).

So what was it that collided or crashed into *Phobos 2*, the "something that should not be there"? What do the last frame or frames, still secret, show? In his careful words to *AW&ST*, the chairman of the Soviet equivalent of NASA referred to that last frame when he tried to explain the sudden loss of contact, saying,

> "One image appears to include an odd-shaped object between the spacecraft and Mars."

If not "debris," or "dust," or a "jettisoned part of *Phobos 2*," what was the "object" that all accounts of the incident now admit collided with the spacecraft—an object with an impact strong enough to put the spacecraft into a spin, an object whose image was captured by the last photographic frames?

"We just don't know," said the chief of the Soviet space program.

But the evidence of an ancient space base on Mars and the odd-shaped "shadow" in its skies add up to an awesome conclusion: What the secret frames hide is evidence that the loss of *Phobos 2* was not an accident but an *incident*.

Perhaps the first incident in a Star Wars—the shooting down by Aliens from another planet of a spacecraft from Earth intruding on their Martian base.

Has it occurred to the reader that the Soviet space chief's answer, "We just don't know" what the "odd-shaped object between the spacecraft and Mars" was, is tantamount to calling it a UFO—an Unidentified Flying Object?

For decades now, ever since the phenomenon of what was first called Flying Saucers and later UFOs became a worldwide enigma, no self-respecting scientist would touch the subject even with a ten foot pole—except, that is, to ridicule the phenomenon and whoever was foolish enough to take it seriously.

The "modern UFO era," according to Antonio Huneeus, a science writer and internationally known lecturer on UFOs, began on June 24, 1947, when Kenneth Arnold, an American pilot and businessman, sighted a formation of nine silvery disks flying over the Cascade Mountains in the state of Washington. The term "Flying Saucer" that then came into vogue was based on Arnold's description of the mysterious objects.

While the "Arnold incident" was followed by alleged sightings across the United States and other parts of the world, the UFO case deemed most significant and one still discussed (and dramatized on television) is the alleged crash of an "alien spacecraft" on July 2, 1947—a week after the Arnold sighting—on a ranch near Roswell, New Mexico. That evening a bright, disk-shaped object was seen in the area's skies; the next day a rancher, William Brazel, discovered scattered wreckage in his field northwest of Roswell. The wreckage and the "metal" of which it was made looked odd, and the discovery was reported to the nearby Army Air Corps base at Roswell Field (which then had the world's only nuclear-weapons squadron.) Major Jesse Marcel, an intelligence officer, together with an officer from the counterintelligence corps, went to examine the debris. The pieces, engineered in various shapes, looked and felt like balsa wood but were not wood; they would neither burn nor bend, no matter how the investigators tried. On some beam-shaped pieces there were geometric markings that were later referred to as "hieroglyphics." On returning to the base, the officer in charge instructed the base's public relations officer to notify the press (in a release dated July 7, 1947) that AAF personnel had retrieved parts of a "crashed flying saucer." The release made headline news in *The Roswell Daily Record* (Fig. 96) and was picked up by a press wire service in Albuquerque, New Mexico. Within hours a new official statement, superseding the first, claimed instead that the debris was part of a fallen weather balloon. Newspapers printed the retraction; and, according to some reports, radio stations were ordered to stop broadcasting the first version by being told, "Cease transmission. National security item. Do not transmit."

In spite of the revised version and ensuing official denials of any "flying saucer" incident at Roswell, many of those personally involved in that incident persist, to this very day, in adhering to the first version. Many also assert that at a nearby crash site of another "flying saucer" (in an area west of Socorro, New Mexico), civilian witnesses had seen not only the wreckage but also several bodies of dead humanoids. These bodies, as well as bodies allegedly of "aliens" who crashed after these two events, have been variously reported to have

Figure 96

undergone examination at Wright-Patterson Air Force Base in Ohio. According to a document known in UFO circles as *MJ-12* or *Majestic–12* (the two, some claim, are not identical), President Truman formed, in September, 1947, a blue-ribbon, top-secret committee to deal with the Roswell and related incidents, but the authenticity of this document remains unverified. What is known for a fact is that Senator Barry Goldwater, who either chaired or was a senior member of U.S. Senate committees on Intelligence, Armed Services, Tactical Warfare, Science, Technology, and Space and others with a bearing on the subject, was repeatedly refused admission to a so-called Blue Room at that air base. "I have long ago given up acquiring access to the so-called blue room at Wright-Patterson, as I have had one long string of denials from chief after chief," he wrote to an inquirer in 1981. "This thing has gotten so highly classified . . . it is just impossible to get anything on it."

Reacting to continued reporting of UFO sightings and unease about excessive official secrecy, the U.S. Air Force conducted several investigations of the UFO phenomenon through such projects as Sign, Grudge, and Blue Book. Between 1947 and 1969 about thirteen thousand reports of UFOs were investigated, and they were by and large dismissed as natural phenomena, balloons, aircraft, or just imagination. Some seven hundred sightings, however, remained unexplained. In 1953, the U.S. Central Intelligence Agency's Office of Scientific Intelligence convened a panel of scientists and government officials. Known as the Robertson Panel, the group spent a total of twelve hours viewing UFO films and studying case histories and other information and found that "reasonable explanations could be suggested for most sightings." The evidence presented, it was reported, showed how the remaining cases could not be explained by probable causes, "leaving 'extra-terrestrials' as the only remaining explanation in many cases," although, the panel noted, "present astronomical knowledge of the solar system makes the existence of intelligent beings . . . elsewhere than on the Earth extremely unlikely."

While official "debunking" of UFO reports continued (another investigation along the same lines and with similar conclusions was the officially commissioned Scientific Study of Unidentified Flying Objects by the University of Colorado, conducted from 1966 to 1969), the number of sightings and "encounters" continued to rise, and civilian amateur investigative groups have sprung up in numerous countries. The encounters are now classified by these groups; those of the "second kind" are instances where physical evidence (landing markings or interference with machinery) is left behind by the UFOs; and those of the "third kind," where contact takes place with the UFO's occupants.

Descriptions of the UFOs once were varied, from "flying saucers" to "cigar-shaped." Now most describe them as circular in construction and, when landing, as resting on three or four extended legs. Descriptions of the occupants also are more uniform: "humanoids" three to four feet tall, with large, hairless heads and very big eyes (Fig. 97a, b). According to a purported eye-witness report by a military intelligence officer who saw "recovered UFOs and alien bodies" at a "secret base in Arizona," the humanoids "were very, very white; there were no ears, no nostrils. There were only openings: a very

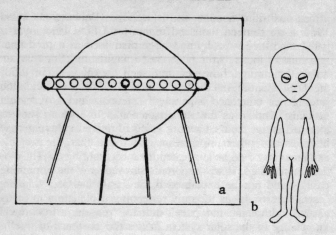

Figure 97

small mouth and their eyes were large. There was no facial hair, no head hair, no pubic hair. They were nude. I think the tallest one could have been about three-and-a-half feet, maybe a little taller.'' The witness added that he saw no genitals and no breasts, although some humanoids looked male and some female.

The multitude of people reporting sightings or contacts come from every geographical or occupational background. President Jimmy Carter, for example, disclosed in a campaign speech in 1976 that he had seen a UFO. He moved to "make every piece of information this country has about UFO sightings available to the public and the scientists''; but for reasons that were never given, his campaign promise was not kept.

Besides the official U.S. policy of "debunking" UFO reports, what has irked UFO believers in the United States is the official tendency to give the impression that government agencies have lost interest even in investigating UFO reports, whereas it has repeatedly come to light that this or that agency, including NASA, is keeping a close eye on the subject. In the Soviet Union, on the other hand, the Institute of Space Research published in 1979 an analysis of "Observations of Anomalous

Atmospheric Phenomena in the USSR" ("anomalous atmospheric phenomena" is the Russian term for UFOs), and in 1984 the Soviet Academy of Sciences formed a permanent commission to study the phenomena. On the military side, the subject came under the jurisdiction of the GRU (Chief Intelligence Directorate of the Soviet General Staff); its orders were to discover whether UFOs were "secret vehicles of foreign powers," unknown natural phenomena, or "manned or unmanned extraterrestrial probes engaged in the investigation of Earth."

Numerous reported or purported sightings in the Soviet Union included some by Soviet cosmonauts. In September 1989, the Soviet authorities took the significant step of having Tass, the official news agency, report a UFO incident in the city of Voronezh in a manner that made front pages worldwide; in spite of the usual disbelief, Tass stood by its story.

The French authorities have also been less "debunkative" (to coin a word) than U.S. officials. In 1977 the French National Space Agency (CNES), headquartered in Toulouse, established the Unidentified Aerospace Phenomena Study Group (GEPAN); it was recently renamed the *Service d'Expertise des Phenomenes de Rentrée Atmospherique*, with the same task of following up and analyzing UFO reports. Some of the more celebrated UFO cases in France included follow-up analyses of the sites and soils where the UFOs were seen to have landed, and the results showed the "presence of traces for which there is no satisfactory explanation." Most French scientists have shared the disdain of their colleagues from other countries for the subject, but among those who did get involved and voiced an opinion, the consensus has been to see in the phenomena "a manifestation of the activities of extraterrestrial visitors."

In Great Britain, the veil of secrecy over the UFO phenomenon has held tight in spite of such efforts as the inquiring UFO Study Group of the House of Lords initiated by the Earl of Clancarty (a group I had the privilege to address in 1980). The British experience, as well as that of many other countries, is reported in some detail in Timothy Good's book *Above Top Secret* (1987). The wealth of documents quoted or reproduced in Good's book leads to the conclusion that at first the various governments "covered up" their findings because UFOs were suspected of being advanced aircraft of another superpower, and admission of the enemy's superiority was not in the national interest. But once the extraterrestrial nature of the UFOs became the primary guess (or knowledge), the memory of such panics as was caused by Orson Welles' "War of the Worlds" radio broadcast was used as the rationale for what so many UFO enthusiasts call a cover up.

The real problem many have with UFOs is the lack of a cohesive and plausible theory to explain their origin and purpose. Where do they come from? Why?

I myself have not encountered a UFO, to say nothing of being abducted and experimented upon by humanlike beings with elliptical heads and bulging eyes—incidents witnessed and experienced, if such claims be true, by many others. But when asked for my opinion, whether I "believe in UFOs," I sometimes answer by telling a story. Let us imagine, I say to the people in the room or the auditorium in which I am speaking, that the entrance door is thrust open and a young man bursts in, breathless from running and obviously agitated, who ignores the proceedings and just shouts, "You wouldn't believe what happened to me!" He then goes on to relate that he was out in the countryside hiking, that it was getting dark and he was tired, that he found some stones and put his knapsack on them as a cushion, and that he fell asleep. Then he was suddenly awakened, not by a sound but by bright lights. He looked up and saw beings going up and down a ladder. The ladder led skyward, toward a hovering, round object. There was a doorway in the object through which light from inside shone out. Silhouetted against the light was the commander of the beings. The sight was so awesome that our lad fainted. When he came to, there was nothing to be seen. Whatever had been there was gone.

Still excited by his experience, the young man finishes the story by saying he was no longer sure whether what he had seen was real or just a vision, perhaps a dream. What do we think? Do we believe him?

We should believe him if we believe the Bible, I say, because what I had just related is the tale of Jacob's vision as told in Genesis, chapter 7. Though it was a vision seen in a dreamlike trance, Jacob was certain that the sight was real, and he said,

> Surely Yahweh is present in this place,
> and I knew it not. . . .
> This is none other but an abode of the gods,
> and this is the gateway to heaven.

I once pointed out at a conference where other speakers delved into the subject of UFOs that there is no such thing as Unidentified Flying Objects. They are only unidentified or unexplainable by the viewer, but those who operate them know very well what they are. Obviously, the hovering craft that Jacob saw was readily identified by him as belonging to the *Elohim*, the plural gods. What he did not know, the Bible makes clear, was only that the place where he had slept was one of their lift-off pads.

The biblical tale of the heavenward ascent of the Prophet Elijah describes the vehicle as a Fiery Chariot. And the Prophet Ezekiel, in his well-documented vision, spoke of a celestial or airborne vehicle that operated as a whirlwind and could land on four wheeled legs.

Ancient depictions and terminology show that a distinction was made even then between the different kinds of flying machines and their pilots. There were the rocketships (Fig. 98a) that served as shuttle craft and the orbiters, and we have already seen what the Anunnaki astronauts and the orbiting Igigi looked like. And there were the "whirlbirds" or "sky chambers" that we now call VTOLs (Vertical Take-Off and Landing aircraft) and helicopters; how these looked in antiquity is depicted in a mural at a site on the east side of the Jordan, near the place from which Elijah was carried heavenward (Fig. 98b). The goddess Inanna/Ishtar liked to pilot her own "sky chamber," at which time she would be dressed like a World War I pilot (Fig. 98c).

But other depictions were also found—clay figurines of human-looking beings with elliptical heads and large, slanting eyes (Fig. 99)—an unusual feature of whom was their bisexuality (or lack of it): their lower parts depicted the male member overlaid or dissected by the opening of a female vagina.

Now, as one looks at the drawings of the "humanoids" by those who claim to have seen the occupants of UFOs, it is

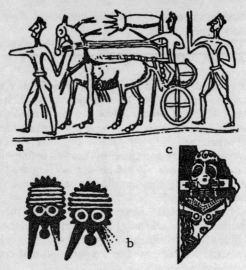

Figure 98

obvious they do not look like us—which means they do not
look like the Anunnaki. Rather, they look like the odd humanoids depicted by the ancient figurines.

This similarity may hold an important clue to the identity
of the small creatures with smooth skins, no sex organs, no
hair, elliptical heads, and large odd eyes that are supposed to
be operating the purported UFOs. *If the tales be true, then
what the "contactees" have seen are not the people, the intelligent beings, from another planet—but their anthropoid
robots.*

And if even a tiny percentage of the reported sightings is
true, then the relatively large number of alien craft visiting
Earth in recent times suggests that they could not possibly
come, in such profusion and frequency, from a distant planet.
If they come, they must come from somewhere relatively close
by.

And the only plausible candidate is Mars—and its moonlet
Phobos.

* * *

Figure 99

The reasons for the use of Mars as a jumping-off base for spacemen's visits to Earth should be clear by now. The evidence for my suggestion that Mars had served in the past as a space base for the Anunnaki has been presented. The circumstances in which *Phobos 2* was lost indicate that *someone is back there on Mars*—someone ready to destroy what to them is an "alien" spacecraft. How does Phobos, the moonlet, fit into all this?

Simply put, it fits very well.

To understand why, we ought to backtrack and list the reasons for the 1989 mission to Phobos. All present Mars has two tiny satellites named Phobos and Deimos. Both are believed to be not original moons of Mars but asteroids that were captured into Mars orbit. They are of the carbonaceous type (see the discussion of asteroids in chapter 4) and therefore contain water in substantial amounts, mostly in the form of ice just under the moonlets' surfaces. It has been proposed that with the aid of solar batteries or a small nuclear generator, the ice could be melted to obtain water. The water could then be separated into oxygen and hydrogen, for breathing and as fuel. The hydrogen could also be combined with the moonlets' carbon to make hydrocarbons. As do other asteroids and comets, these planetisimals contain nitrogen, ammonia, and other organic molecules. All in all, the moonlets could become self-supporting space bases, the gift of nature.

Deimos would be less convenient for such a purpose. It is only nine by eight by seven miles in size and orbits some 15,000 miles away from Mars. The much larger Phobos (seventeen by thirteen by twelve miles) is only some 5,800 miles away from Mars—a short hop for a shuttlecraft or transporter from one to the other. Because Phobos (as does Deimos too) orbits Mars in the equatorial plane, Phobos can be observed from Mars (or observe goings on upon Mars), between the sixty-fifth parallels north and south—a band that includes all the unusual and artificial-looking features on Mars except "Inca City." Moreover, because of its proximity, Phobos completes about 3.5 orbits around Mars in a single Martian day—an almost constant presence.

Further recommending Phobos as a natural orbiting station around Mars is its minuscule gravity, compared with that of Earth and even of Mars. The power required for take-off from Phobos is no greater than that required to develop an escape velocity of fifteen miles an hour; conversely, very little power is needed to brake for a landing on it.

These are the reasons the two Soviet spacecraft, *Phobos 1* and *2*, were sent there. It was an open secret that the mission was a scouting expedition for the intended landing of a "robotic rover" on Mars in 1994 and the launching of a manned mission to Mars after that, with a view to establishing a base thereon within the following decade. Prearrival briefings at mission control in Moscow revealed that the spacecraft carried equipment to locate "the heat-emitting areas on Mars" and to obtain "a better idea of what kind of life exists on Mars." Although the provision, "if any," was quickly added, the plan to scan both Mars and Phobos not only with infrared equipment but also with gamma-ray detectors hinted at a very purposeful search.

After scanning Mars the two spacecraft were to turn their attention entirely to Phobos. It was to be probed by radar as well as by the infrared and gamma-ray scanners and was to be photographed by three television cameras. Apart from such orbital scanning, the spacecraft were to drop two types of landers to the surface of Phobos: one, a stationary device that would have anchored itself to the surface and transmitted data over the long term; the other, a "hopper" device with springy legs that was meant to hop and skip about the moonlet and report its findings from all over it.

There were still other experiments in the bag of tricks of *Phobos 2*. It was equipped with an ion emitter and a laser gun that were to shoot their beams at the moonlet, stir up its surface dust, pulverize some of the surface material, and enable equipment aboard the spacecraft to analyze the resultant cloud. At that point the spacecraft was to hover a mere 150 feet above Phobos, and its cameras were to photograph features as small as six inches.

What exactly were the mission planners expecting to discover at such close range? It must have been an important objective, because it later transpired that the "individual scientists" from the United States who were involved in the mission's planning and equipping included Americans with experience in Mars research whose roles were officially sanctioned by the United States government within the framework of the improvement in U.S.-Soviet relations. Also, NASA had put at the mission's disposal its Deep Space Network of radio telescopes which has been involved not only in satellite communications but also in the Search for Extraterrestrial Intelligence (SETI) programs; and scientists at the JPL in Pasadena, California, were helping track the Phobos spacecraft and monitor their data transmissions. It also became known that the British scientists who were participating in the project were in fact assigned to the mission by the British National Space Centre.

With the French participation, guided by its National Space Agency in Toulouse; the input by West Germany's prestigious Max Planck Institute; and the scientific contributions from a dozen other European nations, the Phobos Mission was nothing short of a concerted effort by modern science to lift the veil from Mars and enlist it in Mankind's course on the road to Space.

But was someone there, at Mars, who did not welcome this intrusion?

It is noteworthy that Phobos, unlike the smaller and smooth-surfaced Deimos, has peculiar features that have led some scientists in the past to suspect that it was artificially fashioned. There are peculiar "track marks" (Fig. 100) that run almost straight and parallel to each other. Their width is almost uniform, some 700 to 1,000 feet, and their depth, too, is a uniform 75 to 90 feet (as far as could be measured from the Viking orbiters). The possibility that these "trenches," or tracks, were caused by flowing water or by wind has been ruled out, since neither exist on Phobos. The tracks seem to lead to or from a crater that covers more than a third of the moonlet's diameter and whose rim is so perfectly circular that it looks artificial (see Fig. 94).

What are these tracks or trenches, how did they come about, why do they emanate from the circular crater, and does the crater lead into the moonlet's interior? Soviet scientists have thought that there was something artificial about Phobos in general, because its almost perfect circular orbit around Mars at such proximity to the planet defies the laws of celestial motion: Phobos, and to some extent Deimos, too, should have elliptical orbits that would have either thrown them off into space or made them crash into Mars a long time ago.

The implication that Phobos and Deimos might have been placed in Mars orbit artificially by "someone" seemed preposterous. In fact, however, the capture of asteroids and towing them to where they would stay in Earth orbit has been deemed a technologically achievable feat; so much so that such a plan was presented at the Third Annual Space Development Conference held in San Francisco in 1984. Richard Gertsch of the Colorado School of Mines, one of several presenters of the plan, pointed out that "a startling variety of materials exist" out in space; "asteroids are particularly rich in strategic minerals such as chromium, germanium and gallium." "I believe that we have identified asteroids that are accessible and could be exploited," stated another presenter, Eleanor F. Helin of JPL.

Have others, long ago, carried out ideas and plans that modern science envisions for the future—bringing Phobos and Deimos, two captured asteroids, into orbit around Mars to burrow into their interiors?

In the 1960s it was noticed that Phobos was speeding up its

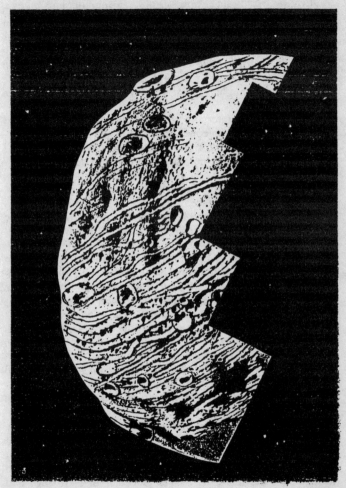

Figure 100

orbit around Mars; this led Soviet scientists to suggest that Phobos was lighter than its size warrants. The Soviet physicist I. S. Shklovsky then offered the astounding hypothesis that Phobos was hollow.

Other Soviet writers then speculated that Phobos was an "artificial satellite" put into Mars orbit by "an extinct race of humanoids millions of years ago." Others ridiculed the idea of a hollow satellite and suggested that Phobos was accelerating because it is drifting closer to Mars. The detailed report in *Nature* now includes the finding that Phobos is even less dense than has been thought, so that its interior is either made of ice or is hollow.

Were a natural crater and interior faults artificially enlarged and carved out by "someone" to create inside Phobos a shelter, shielding its occupants from the cold and radiation of space? The Soviet report does not speculate on that; but what it says regarding the "tracks" is illuminating. It calls them "grooves," reports that their sides are of a brighter material than the moonlet's surface, and, what is indeed a revelation, that in the area west of the large crater, "new grooves can be identified"—grooves or tracks that were not there when *Mariner 9* and the *Vikings* took pictures of the moonlet.

Since there is no volcanic activity on Phobos (the crater in its natural shape resulted from meteorite impacts, not volcanism), no wind storms, no rain, no flowing water—how did the new grooved tracks come about? Who was there on Phobos (and thus on Mars) since the 1970s? Who is on it *now*?

For, if there is no one there now, how to explain the March 27, 1989, incident?

The chilling possibility that modern science, catching up with ancient knowledge, has brought Mankind to the first incident in a War of the Worlds, rekindles a situation that has lain dormant almost 5,500 years.

The event that parallels today's situation has come to be known as the Incident of the Tower of Babel. It is described in Genesis, chapter 11, and in *The Wars of Gods and Men* I refer to Mesopotamian texts with earlier and more detailed accounts of the incident. I have placed it in 3450 B.C. and construed it as the first attempt by Marduk to establish a space base in Babylon as an act of defiance against Enlil and his sons.

In the biblical version, the people whom Marduk had gotten to do the job were building, in Babylon, a city with a "tower

Figure 101

whose head shall reach the heaven" in which a *Shem*—a space rocket—was to be installed (quite possibly in the manner depicted on a coin from Byblos; see Fig. 101). But the other deities were not amused by this foray of Mankind into the space age; so

> Yahweh came down to see the city
> and the tower which the humans were building.

And he said to unnamed colleagues:

> This is just the beginning of their undertakings;
> From now on, anything that they shall scheme to do
> shall no longer be impossible for them.
> Come, let us go down and confuse their language
> so that they should not understand each other's speech.

Almost 5,500 years later, the humans got together and "spoke one language," in a coordinated international mission to Mars and Phobos.

And, once again, someone was not amused.

13

IN SECRET ANTICIPATION

Are we unique? Are we alone?

These were the central questions posed in *The 12th Planet* back in 1976, and the book proceeded to present the ancient evidence regarding the Anunnaki (the biblical Nefilim) and their planet Nibiru.

Scientific advances since 1976, reviewed in previous chapters, have gone a long way in corroborating ancient knowledge. But what about the two pillars of that knowledge and that ancient answer to the central questions? Has modern science confirmed the existence of one more planet in our Solar System, and has it found other intelligent beings outside Earth?

That a search has been going on, both for another planet and for other beings, is a matter of record. That it has intensified in recent years can be gleaned from publicly available documents. But now it is also evident that when the mists of leaks, rumors, and denials are pierced, if not the public, then *the world's leaders have been aware for some time first, that there is one more planet in our Solar System and second, that we are not alone*.

ONLY THIS KNOWLEDGE CAN EXPLAIN THE IN-CREDIBLE CHANGES IN WORLD AFFAIRS THAT HAVE BEEN TAKING PLACE WITH EVEN MORE INCREDIBLE SPEED.

ONLY THIS KNOWLEDGE CAN EXPLAIN THE AC-TUAL PREPARATIONS BEING MADE FOR THE DAY, WHICH IS SURELY COMING, WHEN THE TWO FACTS WILL HAVE TO BE DROPPED LIKE BOMBSHELLS ON THE PEOPLE OF THIS PLANET EARTH.

Suddenly, all that had divided and preoccupied the world powers for decades seems not to matter anymore. Tanks, air-craft, armies are withdrawn and disbanded. One regional conflict after another is unexpectedly settled. The Berlin Wall, a symbol of Europe's division, is gone. The Iron Curtain that has divided West from East militarily, ideologically, and economically is being dismantled. The head of the atheistic Communist empire visits the Pope—with a medieval painting of a UFO as the centerpiece of the room's decoration. An American president, George Bush, who began his presidency in 1989 with a cautious wait-and-see policy, has by year's end thrown all caution to the winds and has become an ardent partner of his Soviet counterpart, Mikhail Gorbachev, in clearing the desks of the old agendas; but clearing them for what?

The Soviet president, who a few years ago made any progress in disarmament absolutely dependent on the United States dropping its Strategic Defense Initiative (SDI)—the so-called Star Wars defense in space against enemy missiles and spacecraft—agreed to unprecedented troop withdrawals and reductions a week after the same U.S. president, amidst reductions in the American military spending, asked the Congress to *increase* funds for SDI/Star Wars by 4.5 billion dollars in the next fiscal year. And before the month was out, the two superpowers and their two major wartime allies, Great Britain and France, have agreed to let German unification proceed. For forty-five years the vow never to see a unified, resurgent Germany again was a basic tenet of European stability; now, suddenly, that seemed to matter no more.

Suddenly, inexplicably, there seem to be more important, more urgent subjects on the agenda of the world's leaders. But what?

As one looks for answers, the clues point in one direction: Space. Surely, the turmoil in Eastern Europe has long been building up. Certainly, economic failures have necessitated long-overdue reforms. But what is astounding is not the outbreak of change, but the unexpected lack of almost any resistance to it in the Kremlin. Since about the middle of 1989, all that had been vigorously defended and brutally suppressed no longer seemed important; and after the summer of 1989, a reticent and go-slow American government shifted into high-gear cooperation with the Soviet leadership, rushing a previously take-our-time summit meeting between President Bush and President Gorbachev.

Was it only a coincidence that the *Phobos 2* incident in March 1989 was conceded in June to have been the result of spinning caused by an impact? Or that it was in that same June that Western audiences were shown the enigmatic television pictures from *Phobos 2* (minus the last frame or frames) revealing the heat-emitting pattern on the surface of Mars and the "thin, elliptical shadow" for which there was no explanation? Was it a mere coincidence in timing that the hurried change of U.S. policy occurred after the *Voyager 2*'s flyby of Neptune, in August 1989, which relayed back pictures of mysterious "double tracks" on Neptune's moon Triton (see Fig. 3)—tracks as enigmatic as those photographed on Mars in previous years and on Phobos in March 1989?

A review of world events and space-related activities after the March/June/August series of space discoveries in 1989 traces a pattern of bursts of activity and course changes that bespeak the impact of these discoveries.

After the loss of *Phobos 2* on the heels of the misfortune with *Phobos 1*, Western experts speculated that the USSR would give up its plans to proceed with their reconnaisance mission to Mars in 1992 and the plan to land rovers there in 1994. But Soviet spokesmen brushed such doubts aside and reaffirmed strongly that in their space program they "have given priority to Mars." They were determined to go on to Mars, and to do it jointly with the United States.

Was it mere coincidence that within days of the *Phobos 2* incident the White House took unexpected steps to reverse a Defense Department decision to cancel the 3.3-billion-dollar National Aero-Space Plane program, under which NASA was to develop and build, by 1994, two *X-30* hypersonic planes that could take off from Earth and soar into orbit, becoming self-launching spaceships for military space defense? This was one of the decisions made by President Bush together with Vice President Dan Quayle, the newly appointed chairman of the National Space Council, at the very first NSC meeting in April 1989. In June, the NSC instructed NASA to accelerate the Space Station preparations, a program funded in fiscal year 1990 at 13.3 billion dollars. In July of 1989 the Vice President briefed Congress and the space industry on the specific proposals for the manned missions to the Moon and to Mars. It was made clear that of five options, that of "developing a lunar base as a stepping-stone to Mars is receiving the greatest attention.'' A week later it was disclosed that instruments lofted by a military rocket successfully fired a ''neutral-particle beam''—a ''death ray''—in space as part of the SDI space-defense program.

Even an outside observer could sense that the White House, the President himself, was now in charge of the direction of the space program, its links with SDI, and their accelerated timetable. And so it was that immediately after his hurried summit meeting with the Soviet leader in Malta, President Bush submitted to Congress his next annual budget, with its increase of billions of dollars for ''Star Wars.'' The media wondered how Mikhail Gorbachev would react to this ''slap in the face.'' But rather than criticism from Moscow, there was accelerated cooperation. Evidently, the Soviet leader knew what SDI is all about: President Bush, in their joint press conference, acknowledged that SDI was discussed, both ''defensive'' and ''offensive''—''rockets as well as people . . . a wide discussion.''

The budget proposal also asked 24 percent more funds for NASA, specifically for carrying out what by then had become the President's ''commitment'' to ''return astronauts to the Moon and to the eventual exploration of Mars by humans.'' That commitment, it should be recalled, was made in the President's speech in July 1989 on the occasion of the twentieth anniversary of the first landing on the Moon—a commitment puzzling by its timing. When the *Challenger* shuttle was accidentally destroyed in January 1986, all space work was put on hold. But in July 1989, just a few months after the *Phobos* 2 loss, the United States, rather than pull in its horns, reiterated a determination to go to Mars. There must have been a compelling reason. . . .

Under the Human Exploration Initiative part of the proposed budget, an Administration official said, space efforts would be expanded in accordance with a program developed by the White House's National Space Council; that program included the development of new launch facilities, ''opening up new frontiers for manned and unmanned exploration'' and ''insuring that the space program contributes to the national military security.'' Human exploration of the Moon and Mars were defined assignments.

Concurrently with these developments, NASA has been expanding its network of space telescopes, both ground based and orbital, and has equipped some of the shuttles with sky-scanning devices. The Deep Space Network of radio telescopes was expanded by the reactivation of unused facilities as well as by arrangements with other nations, with stress on observation of the southern skies. Up to 1982, the U.S. Congress has grudgingly allocated funds for SETI programs, reducing them from year to year until they were completely cut off in 1982. But in 1983—again that pivotal year, 1983—the funding was abruptly restored. In 1989 NASA managed to have the funding for the "Search for Extra-Terrestrial Intelligence" doubled and tripled, in part due to the active support of Senator John Garn of Utah, a former shuttle astronaut who became convinced of the existence of extraterrestrial beings. Significantly, the funding was sought by NASA for new scanning and search devices to analyze emissions in the microwave band and *in the skies above Earth*, rather than only (as SETI had done before) listening in for radio emissions from distant stars or even galaxies. In its explanatory brochure, NASA quotes, in regard to the "Sky Survey," the formulation by Thomas O. Paine, its former Administrator:

A continuing program to search for evidence that life exists—or has existed—beyond Earth, by studying *other bodies of the Solar System*, by searching for planets circling other stars, and by searching for signals broadcast by intelligent life elsewhere in the Galaxy.

Commenting on these developments, a spokesman for the Federation of American Scientists in Washington said, "The future is starting to arrive." And *The New York Times* of February 6, 1990, headlined the report of the invigorated SETI programs "HUNT FOR ALIENS IN SPACE: THE NEXT GENERATION." A small but symbolic change: no longer a search for an extraterrestrial "intelligence," but for *Aliens*.

A search in secret anticipation.

The 1989 shock was preceded by a marked change at the end of 1983.

In retrospect it is evident that the diminution of superpower adversity was the other side of the coin of cooperation in space efforts and that from 1984 on, the only joint effort that was paramount in all minds was "Going to Mars, Together."

We have already reviewed the extent of the U.S. endorsement of, and participation in, the Phobos mission. When the role of American scientists in this mission became known, it was explained that it was "officially sanctioned due to the improvement in Soviet-American relations." It was also revealed that American defense experts were concerned about the Soviet intent to use a powerful laser in space (to bombard the surface of Phobos), fearing it would give the Soviets an advantage in their own "Star Wars" program of space defense; but the White House overruled the defense experts and gave its consent.

Such cooperation was quite a change from what had been the norm before then. In the past the Soviets not only guarded their space secrets zealously but also made every effort to upstage the Americans. In 1969 they launched *Luna 15* in a failed attempt to beat the Americans to the Moon; in 1971 they sent to Mars not one but three spacecraft intending to put orbiters on Mars just days ahead of *Mariner 9*. When the two superpowers paused for détente, they signed a space cooperation agreement in 1972; its only visible result was the *Apollo-Soyuz* linkup in 1975. Ensuing events, such as the suppression of the Solidarity movement in Poland and the invasion of Afghanistan, renewed cold war tensions. In 1982 President Reagan refused to renew the 1972 agreement, and launched instead a massive U.S. rearmament effort against the "Evil Empire."

When President Reagan, in a televised address in March 1983, surprised the American people, the world's nations (and, it later became known, most top officials of his own administration) with his Strategic Defense Initiative (SDI)—the concept of a protective shield in space against missiles and spaceships—it was natural to assume that its sole purpose was to attain military superiority over the Soviet Union. That was the Soviet reaction, and it was vehement. When Mikhail Gorbachev followed Konstantin Chernenko as Soviet leader in 1985, he adhered to the position that any improvement in East-

West relations depended first and foremost on the abandonment of SDI. But, as it now seems clear, before the year was out, a new mood began to take hold as the true reasons for SDI were communicated to the Soviet leader. Antagonism was replaced by an attitude of "Let's Talk"; and the talk was to be about cooperation in space and, more specifically, about going together to Mars.

Observing that the Soviets suddenly "shed their habit . . . of being obsessively secretive about their space program," the *Economist* (June 15, 1985) remarked that recently Soviet scientists had been astonishing Western scientists by their openness, "talking frankly and enthusiastically about their plans." The weekly noted that the prime subject was the missions to Mars.

The marked change was even more puzzling, since in 1983 and 1984 the Soviet Union appeared to be moving far ahead of the United States in space achievements. It had by then lofted a series of *Salyut* space stations into Earth orbit, manned them with cosmonauts who achieved record long stays in space, and practiced linking to these stations a variety of service and resupply spacecraft. Comparing the two national programs, a U.S. Congressional study reported, at the end of 1983, that they were like an American tortoise and a Soviet hare. Still, by the end of 1984, the first sign of renewed cooperation was given when a U.S. device was included in the Soviet *Vega* spacecraft that was launched to encounter Halley's comet.

There were other manifestations, semiofficial and official, of the new spirit of cooperation in space, despite SDI. In January 1985 scientists and defense officials, meeting in Washington to discuss SDI, invited a top Soviet space official (later a key adviser to Gorbachev), Roald Sagdeyev, to attend. At the same time then U.S. Secretary of State George Shultz met his Soviet counterpart in Geneva, and they agreed to renew the defunct U.S.-Soviet space cooperation agreement.

In July 1985 scientists, space officials, and astronauts from the United States and the Soviet Union met in Washington, ostensibly to commemorate the *Apollo-Soyuz* linkup of 1975. In reality, it was a seminar held to discuss a joint mission to Mars. A week later Brian T. O'Leary, the former astronaut who became active in the Aerospace Systems Group of Science

Applications International Corporation, told a meeting of the Society for the Advancement of Science in Los Angeles that Mankind's next giant step should be to one of the moons of Mars: "What would be a better way to celebrate the millennium's end than with a return human trip from Phobos and Deimos, especially if it was an international mission?" And in October of that same year, 1985, several American Congressmen, government officials, and former astronauts were invited by the Soviet Academy of Sciences to visit, for the first time ever, Soviet space facilities.

Was it all just an evolutionary process, part of new policies by a new leader in the USSR, changing conditions behind the Iron Curtain—deepening restlessness, mounting economic hardships that had increased the Soviet need for Western help? No doubt. But did it necessitate the rush to unveil the plans and secrets of the Soviet space program? Was there perhaps also some other cause, some significant occurrence that suddenly made a major difference, that changed the agenda, that called for new priorities—that necessitated the revival of a World War II alliance? But if so, who was now the common enemy? Against whom were the United States and the USSR aligning their space programs? And why the priority, given by both nations, to going to Mars?

For sure, there have been objections, in both nations, to such coziness. In the United States many defense officials and conservative politicians opposed "lowering the guard" in the Cold War, especially in space. In the past President Reagan agreed; for five years he refused to meet the leader of the "Evil Empire." But now there were compelling reasons to meet and to confer—in private. In November 1985 Reagan and Gorbachev met and emerged as friendly allies, pronouncing a new era of cooperation, trust, understanding.

How could he explain this U-turn, Reagan was asked. His answer was that what made a common cause was space. More specifically, *a danger from space to all the nations on Earth.*

At the first opportunity to elaborate publicly, President Reagan said, in Fallston, Maryland, on December 4, 1985:

As you know, Nancy and I returned almost two weeks ago from Geneva, where I had several lengthy meetings with General Secretary Gorbachev of the Soviet Union.

I had more than fifteen hours of discussions with him, including five hours of private conversation just between the two of us. I found him to be a determined man, but one who is willing to listen. And I told him about America's deep desire for peace and that we do not threaten the Soviet Union and that I believe the people of both our countries want the same thing—a safer and better future for themselves and their children. . . .

I couldn't but—one point in our discussion privately with General Secretary Gorbachev—when you stop to think that we're all God's children, wherever we may live in the world—I couldn't help say to him,

"Just think how easy his task and mine might be in these meetings that we held if suddenly there was a threat to this world from some other species from another planet outside in the universe. We'd forget all the little local differences that we have between our countries and we would find out once and for all that we are all human beings here on this earth together."

I also stressed to Mr. Gorbachev how our nation's commitment to the Strategic Defense Initiative—our research and development of a non-nuclear, high-tech shield that would protect us against ballistic missiles, and how we are committed to that. I told him that SDI was a reason to hope, not to fear.

Was this statement an irrelevant detail or a deliberate disclosure by the U.S. President that in his private session with the Soviet leader he had brought up the "threat to this world from some other species from another planet" as the reason for bringing the two nations together and the cessation of Soviet opposition to SDI?

Looking back, it is clear that the "threat" and the need for a defense in space against it preoccupied the American President. In *Journey Into Space*, Bruce Murray, who was Director of the NASA/Caltech Jet Propulsion Laboratory from 1976 to 1982 (and cofounder with Carl Sagan of The Planetary Society), recounts how at a meeting at the White House in March 1986 with a select group of six space scientists to brief President

Reagan on the discoveries of *Voyager* at Uranus, the president inquired, ''You gentlemen have investigated a lot of things in space; have you found any evidence that there may be other people out there?'' When they answered negatively, he concluded the meeting by saying he hoped they would have ''more excitement as time went on.''

Were these ruminations of an aging leader, destined to be dismissed with a grin by the youthful and ''determined man'' now leading the Soviet empire? Or did Reagan convince Gorbachev, in their private five-hour meeting, that the threat of aliens from space was no joke?

What we know from the public record is that on February 16, 1987, in a major address to an international ''Survival of Humanity'' forum at the Grand Kremlin Palace in Moscow, Gorbachev recalled his discussion with President Reagan in words almost identical to those the American President had used. ''The destiny of the world and the future of humanity have concerned the best minds from the time man first began thinking of the future,'' he said at the very beginning of his address. ''Until relatively recently these and related reflections have been seen as an imaginative exercise, as other-worldly pursuits of philosophers, scholars, and theologians. In the past few decades, however, these problems have moved onto a highly practical plane.'' After pointing to the risks of nuclear weapons and the common interests of ''human civilization,'' he went on to say,

> **At our meeting in Geneva, the U.S. President said that if the earth faced an invasion by extraterrestrials, the United States and the Soviet Union would join forces to repel such an invasion.**
> **I shall not dispute the hypothesis, though I think it's early yet to worry about such an intrusion.**

In choosing ''not to dispute this hypothesis,'' the Soviet leader appeared to define the threat in starker terms than President Reagan's smoother talk: he spoke of *''an invasion by extraterrestrials''* and disclosed that in the private conversation at Geneva President Reagan did not merely talk philosophically about the merits of a united Mankind but proposed that *''the*

United States and the Soviet Union would join forces to repel such an invasion.''

Even more significant than this confirmation, at an international forum, of the potential threat and the need to "join forces" was its timing. Just one year earlier, on January 28, 1986, the United States suffered its terrible setback when the space shuttle *Challenger* exploded soon after launch, killing its seven astronauts and grounding America's space program. On the other hand, on February 20, 1986, the Soviet Union launched its new space station *Mir*, a substantially more advanced model than the previous *Salyut* series. In the following months, rather than taking advantage of the situation and asserting Soviet independence of U.S. space cooperation, the Soviets increased it; among the steps taken was the invitation to U.S. television networks to witness the next space launch from their hitherto top-secret spaceport at Baikonur. On March 4 the Soviet spacecraft *Vega 1*, having swung by Venus to drop off scientific probes, kept its date with Halley's comet; Europeans and Japanese were also up there, but not the United States. Still, the Soviet Union, through Roald Sagdeyev, the director of the Institute for Space Research who had been invited to Washington in 1985 to discuss SDI, insisted that going to Mars be a joint effort with the United States.

Amid the gloom of the *Challenger* disaster, all the space programs were suspended except those pertaining to Mars. To remain on the road to the Moon and Mars, NASA appointed a study group under the chairmanship of astronaut Dr. Sally K. Ride to reevaluate the plans and their feasibility. The panel strongly recommended the development of celestial ferryboats and transfer ships to carry astronauts and cargoes for "human settlement beyond Earth orbit, from the highlands of the Moon to the plains of Mars.''

This eagerness to go to Mars, as evidence at Congressional hearings made clear, necessitated joint U.S.-Soviet efforts and cooperation between their space programs. Not everyone in the United States was for it. In particular, defense planners considered the setback to the manned shuttle program to mean a change to greater reliance on ever more powerful unmanned rockets; and to gain public and Congressional support, some data about the Air Force's new booster rockets to be used in the "Star Wars" defenses was released.

Overriding objections, the United States and the USSR signed, in April 1987, a new agreement for cooperation in space. Immediately after signing the agreement, the White House ordered NASA to suspend work on the *Mars Observer* spacecraft that was to be launched in 1990; thenceforth, there were to be joint efforts with the Soviet Union in support of its Phobos mission.

In the United States opposition to sharing space secrets with the Soviet Union nevertheless continued, and some experts viewed the repeated Soviet invitations to the United States to join in their missions to Mars simply as attempts to gain access to Western technology. Prompted, no doubt, by such objections, President Reagan once again spoke up publicly of the extraterrestrial threat. The occasion was his address to the General Assembly of the United Nations on September 21, 1987. Speaking of the need to turn swords into plowshares, he said:

In our obsession with antagonisms of the moment we often forget how much unites all the members of humanity. Perhaps we need some outside, universal threat to recognize this common bond.

I occasionally think how quickly our differences would vanish if we were facing an alien threat from outside this world.

As reported at the time in *The New Republic* by its senior editor Fred Barnes, President Reagan, during a White House luncheon on September 5, sought confirmation from the Soviet foreign minister that the Soviet Union would indeed join the United States against an alien threat from outer space; and Shevardnadze responded, "Yes, absolutely."

While one can only guess what debates might have taken place in the Kremlin in the next three months that led to the second Reagan-Gorbachev summit meeting in December 1987, some of the conflicting views current in Washington were publicly known. There were those who questioned Soviet motives and found it difficult to draw a clear distinction between sharing scientific technology and sharing military secrets. And there were those, like the chairman of the House of Representatives' Science, Space and Technology Committee, Rep. Robert A. Roe, who believed that the common effort to explore Mars would shift the international focus from "Star Wars" to "Star Trek." He and others encouraged President Reagan to stay the course of going together to Mars at the forthcoming Summit meeting. In fact, the American President authorized five NASA delegations to discuss the Mars projects with the Russians.

The bitter debate in Washington did not die, however, even after the December 1987 Summit. It was reported that the American Secretary of Defense, Casper Weinberger, was among those who accused the Soviet Union of clandestinely developing a "Star Wars" satellite-killer system and that of conducting laser-weapon experiments from their *Mir* orbiting station. So, once again, President Reagan raised the issue of the secret threat. Meeting in Chicago in May 1988 with members of the National Strategy Forum, he told them of wondering,

> What would happen if all of us in the world discovered that we were threatened by an outer—a power from outer space—from another planet.

It was no longer a vague threat from "outer space" but from "*another planet*."

At the end of that month the two superpower leaders met for their third summit in Moscow, and the joint missions to Mars were agreed upon.

Two months later the *Phobos* spacecraft were launched. The die was cast: the two superpowers on Earth had launched challengers to probe "the outer—a power from space—from another planet."

They sat back in secret anticipation. They ended up with the *Phobos 2* incident.

What happened in 1983 that brought about these monumental changes in superpower relations and caused their leaders to focus on a "threat" from "another planet"?

It is noteworthy that in his February 1987 address, the Soviet leader, in raising the issue of such a threat and choosing not to dispute it, could reassure his audience with the thought that "It's early yet to worry about such an intrusion."

Until the *Phobos 2* incident, and certainly before 1983 was over, the whole question of "Extraterrestrials" was viewed in two parallel yet separate ways. On the one hand there were those who assumed, simply by the sheer logic and probability of numbers, that an "Extraterrestrial Intelligence" ought to be "out there." Known among these theorists is the formula developed by Frank D. Drake of the University of California at Santa Cruz and president of the SETI ("Search for Extra-Terrestrial Intelligence") Institute in Mountain View, California. The formula leads to the conclusion that in the Milky Way, our own galaxy, there ought to be between 10,000 to 100,000 advanced civilizations. SETI projects have been using various radio telescopes to listen in on radio emissions from distant space in an attempt to discern among the cacophony of natural emissions by stars, galaxies, and other celestial phenomena some coherent or repetitive signal that would indicate artificiality. Such "intelligent" signals have been encountered a few times, but scientists have been unable to further pinpoint or recapture them.

The SETI search, besides being unproductive so far, raises two questions. The first (which was the reason Congress kept cutting down and finally cut off funding until the resumption in 1983) is whether there is any point in trying to discover an intelligent signal that may have taken light years to reach us and will take as long to respond (light travels 186,000 miles per *second*). Second (and this is my question): why expect advanced civilizations to use radio for communication? Would we have expected them to use bonfires if we had conducted the search centuries ago, when one mountaintop village signaled another by such means? What about all the advances we on Earth have attained—from electricity to electromagnetism to fiber optics, to laser pulses and proton beams and crystal oscillators, as well as new methods yet to be discovered?

Unexpectedly but perhaps inevitably, the SETI searches were forced to concentrate closer to Earth (and to focus not on extraterrestrial "intelligences" but on "beings") by scientists dealing with the origin of life on Earth. The two groups were brought together at Boston University in July 1980 on the initiative of Philip Morrison of the Massachusetts Institute of Technology. After a discussion of the Panspermia (deliberate seeding) theories, a leading physicist from the Los Alamos National Laboratory, Eric M. Jones, "supported the view that if extraterrestrials exist, they should already have colonized the galaxy and reached the Earth." The interlocking of the search for the origin of life on Earth and the search for extraterrestrials became even more evident at the 1986 international Life on Earth conference at Berkeley. "The hunt for signs of extraterrestrial intelligence" is the "crowning research effort, in the minds of many" who look for the origins of life, Erik Eckholm reported in *The New York Times*. The chemists and biologists were now looking to the exploration of Mars and Titan, Saturn's moon, for answers to the mystery of life on Earth.

While tests of the Martian soil remained inconclusive regarding life there, it would be naive to assume that NASA and other sensitive agencies did not wonder what all the enigmatic features on Mars mean (even if officially they have debunked the "speculations"). As early as 1968 the U.S. National Security Agency, in a study dealing with the UFO phenomenon, analyzed the consequences of a "confrontation between a technologically advanced extraterrestrial society and an inferior one on Earth." Surely, someone had to have a theory regarding the home planet of such an extraterrestrial society.

Was it Mars? That might have been the only plausible (even if incredible) answer until another line of search—for one more planet in our Solar System—merged with the issue of Extraterrestrials.

For some time astronomers who have been puzzled by perturbations in the orbits of Uranus and Neptune considered the possibility of the existence of one more planet farther out from the Sun. They designate it *Planet X*, meaning both "unknown" and "tenth." In *The 12th Planet* it was explained that Planet X and Nibiru would be one and the same, because the Sumerians considered the Solar System to have twelve members: the Sun, Moon, the original nine planets, and the planet that became the twelfth member, the Invader, Nibiru/Marduk.

It was, in fact, due to perturbations in their orbits that the discovery of Uranus led to the discovery of Neptune, and thence to that of Pluto (in 1930). Working in 1972 on the anticipated trajectory of Halley's comet, Joseph L. Brady of the Lawrence Livermore Laboratory in California discovered that Halley's orbit was also perturbed. His computations led him to suggest the existence of Planet X at a distance of 64 AU with an orbital period of 1,800 Earth-years. Since he, and all other astronomers looking for Planet X, assume it orbits the Sun as the other planets do, they measure the planet's distance from the Sun by half of its major axis (Fig. 102, distance "a"). But according to Sumerian evidence Nibiru orbits the Sun like a comet, with the Sun at an extreme focus, so that the distance from the Sun would be almost the whole major axis, not just half of it (Fig. 102, distance "b"). Could the fact that the Nibiru is on its way back toward its perigee account for the fact that Brady's 1,800-year orbit is exactly half the 3,600 Earth-years orbit the Sumerians recorded for Nibiru?

There were other conclusions by Brady that were in significant accord with the Sumerian data: that the planet has a retrograde orbit, and that this orbit is not in the same plane (the ecliptic) as that of the other planets (except Pluto) but at an inclination to it.

For a while astronomers wondered whether Pluto might be the cause of the perturbations in the orbits of Uranus and Neptune. But in June 1978 James W. Christie of the U.S.

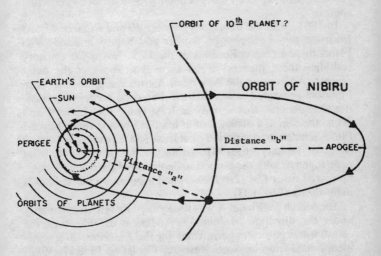

Figure 102

Naval Observatory, Washington, D.C., discovered that Pluto has a moon (he named it Charon) and that Pluto is much smaller than had been thought. This ruled out Pluto as the cause of the perturbations. Moreover, Charon's orbit around Pluto also revealed that Pluto, like Uranus, was lying on its side. This and its odd orbit strengthened the suspicion that a single outside force—an Intruder—had tipped over Uranus, dislodged and tipped over Pluto, and caused Triton (a moon of Neptune) to have a retrograde orbit.

Intrigued by these findings, two colleagues of Christie at the U.S. Naval Observatory, Robert S. Harrington (who collaborated with Christie on the Charon identification) and Thomas C. Van Flandern, concluded after a series of computer simulations that there had to be an Intruder, a planet two to five times the size of Earth, in an inclined orbit, with a semi-axis of "less than 100 AU" (*Icarus*, vol. 39, 1979). This was another step in the confirmation by modern science of ancient knowledge: the whole concept of an Intruder that had caused all the oddities was in accord with the Sumerian tale of Nibiru; and the distance of 100 AU, if doubled due to the Sun's focal position, would place Planet X about where the Sumerians had sited it.

In 1981, with the data from *Pioneer 10* and *Pioneer 11* and from the two *Voyagers* on Jupiter and Saturn in hand, Van Flandern and four colleagues at the U.S. Naval Observatory restudied these planets' orbits as well as those of the outer planets. Addressing the American Astronomical Society, Van Flandern presented new evidence, based on complex gravitational equations, that a body at least twice the size of Earth orbits the Sun at a distance of at least 1.5 billion miles beyond Pluto, with an orbital period of at least 1,000 years. *The Detroit News* of January 16, 1981, published the news on its front page together with the Sumerian depiction of the Solar System, borrowed from *The 12th Planet*, and a summary of the book's main thesis (Fig. 103).

The search for Planet X was then joined by NASA, primarily under the direction of John D. Anderson of JPL, then the celestial-mechanics experimenter for the *Pioneers*. In a statement issued from its Ames Research Center on June 17, 1982, and headlined *"Pioneers* May Find Tenth Planet," NASA

— Friday —
January 16, 1981
108th YEAR NO 147

The Detroit News

MICHIGAN'S LARGEST NEWSPAPER

15¢

with geysers of water shooting skyward from many manholes,

more stranded people and to prevent

Continued on Page 2A

auto maker in late 1979.

Continued on Page 4A

— Lesson from history —
10th planet? Pluto's orbit says 'yes'

By HUGH McCANN
News Staff Writer

If new evidence from the U.S. Naval Observatory of a 10th planet in the solar system is accurate, it could prove that the Sumerians, an ancient eastern Mediterranean civilization, were far ahead of modern man in astronomy.

Astronomer Thomas Van Flandern told a meeting of the American Astronomical Society in Albuquerque this week that irregularities in the orbit of Pluto, the farthest known planet from the sun, indicates that the solar system contains a 10th planet.

Pluto was the last planet discovered, in 1930. Since then, astronomers have been searching unsuccessfully for planets farther out. Indeed, Pluto had unknowingly been photographed but remained unrecognized for a long time because it was so difficult to see. Presumably, any other new planets would be easy to miss visually.

BUT THE heavenly body suspected by Van Flandern is making its presence felt in the same way that Pluto's presence was suggested — from the bulges that Pluto's gravitational field causes in the elliptical orbit of its closet neighbor, Neptune.

Now, says Van Flandern, subtle bulges detected in Pluto's orbit mean that there must be still another planet. He calculates that the unseen

Sumerian tablet in East Berlin shows a solar system with sun, moon and 10 planets.

planet is four times the size of Pluto and 1.5 times its distance from the sun..

Van Flandern's announcement comes as no surprise to Zecharia Sitchin, whose book, *The 12th Planet*, came out three years ago.

SITCHIN, WHO describes himself as a Russian-born linguist and archeologist, says that the Sumerians, who date back 6,000 years, knew of a planet beyond Pluto. They counted it the 12th planet, he explains, because, in their system of reckoning, the sun and moon are also counted as planets. Its Sumerian name was Nibiru.

Continued on Page 12A

Figure 103

disclosed that the two spacecraft had been enlisted in the search for Planet X. "Persistent irregularities in the orbits of Uranus and Neptune strongly suggest that some kind of mystery object is really there—far beyond the outermost planets," the NASA statement said. Because the *Pioneers* were traveling in opposite directions, they would be able to determine how far away that body is: if one of them sensed a stronger pull, the mystery body is near and must be a planet; if both sensed the same pull, the body must be between 50 and 100 billion miles away and might be a "dark star" or "brown dwarf," but not another member of the Solar System.

In September of that year, 1982, the U.S. Naval Observatory confirmed that it was "seriously pursuing" the search for Planet X. Dr. Harrington said his team has "narrowed themselves to a fairly small portion of the sky," and added that the conclusion by then was that the planet "was moving much more slowly than any of the planets that we now know."

(Needless to say, all the above-mentioned astronomers leading the search for Planet X soon received long letters from me, accompanied by copies of *The 12th Planet*; their responses have been equally long and detailed as well as gracious).

The transformation of the search for Planet X from an academic pursuit to one principally involving the U.S. Naval Observatory (an entity of the U.S. Navy) and overseen by NASA took place concurrently with the intensified use of manned spacecraft for the search. It is known that on various secret missions of the U.S. space shuttles, new telescopic devices for scanning the distant skies were employed, and that Soviet cosmonauts aboard the *Salyut* space station were equally engaged in secret searches for the planet.

Among the myriad dots of light in the heavens, planets (as well as comets and asteroids) are distinguished from fixed stars and galaxies because they move. The technique is to take photographs of the same portion of the sky several times and then "blink" the photos on a comparing viewer; to the trained eye this reveals whether some point of light has moved. Clearly, this method would not work too well for Planet X if it is so distant and if it moves very slowly.

Even when the role of the *Pioneer* spacecraft in the search for Planet X was announced in June 1982, John Anderson himself, in a review prepared for the Planetary Society, stressed that in addition to the answers the *Pioneer* spacecraft might provide, the enigma of the unknown planet might be resolved through the "infrared search of the solar neighborhood" by the "all-sky survey of the *Infrared Astronomical Satellite* (IRAS)." He explained that IRAS "will be sensitive to the heat trapped in the interiors of substellar bodies"—heat that is slowly lost to space in the form of infrared radiation.

This heat-sensing satellite, IRAS, was launched into orbit 560 miles above the Earth at the end of January 1983 as a joint U.S.-British-Dutch endeavor. It was expected to be able to sense a planet the size of Jupiter at a distance of 277 AU. Before it ran out of the liquid helium that cooled it, it observed some 250,000 celestial objects: galaxies, stars, interstellar dust clouds, and cosmic dust, as well as asteroids, comets, and planets. The search for a tenth planet was one of its declared objectives. Reporting on the satellite and its mission, *The New York Times* of January 30, 1983, headlined the article "Clues Get Warm in the Search for Planet X." It quoted astronomer Ray T. Reynolds of the Ames Research Center as saying, "Astronomers are so sure of the 10th planet that they think there's nothing left but to name it."

Did IRAS find the tenth planet?

Although specialists admit it will take years to sift through and "blink" the more than 600,000 images transmitted by IRAS in its ten months of operation, the official response to the question is no—no tenth planet was found.

But that, to put it mildly, is not a correct answer.

Having scanned the same part of the heavens at least twice, IRAS did make it possible to "blink" images; and, contrary to the impression given, *moving objects* were discovered. These included five previously unknown comets, several comets that astronomers had "lost," four new asteroids—and "*an enigmatic cometlike object.*"

Was it perhaps Planet X?

In spite of the official denials, a disclosure did leak out at the end of the year. It came in the form of an exclusive interview of the key IRAS scientists by Thomas O'Toole of the science service of the *Washington Post*. The story, generally ignored—suppressed, perhaps—was carried by several dailies, which variously headlined it "Giant Object Mystifies Astronomers," "Mystery Body Found in Space," and "At Solar System's Edge Giant Object is a Mystery" (Fig. 104). The opening paragraphs of the exclusive story began thus:

WASHINGTON—A heavenly body possibly as large as the giant planet Jupiter and possibly so close to Earth that it would be part of this solar system has been found in the direction of the constellation Orion by an orbiting

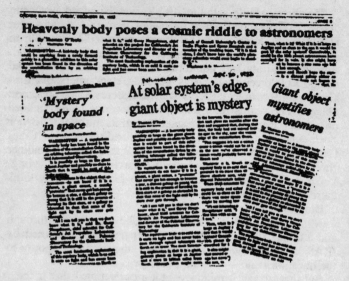

Heavenly body poses a cosmic riddle to astronomers

'Mystery' body found in space

At solar system's edge, giant object is mystery

Giant object mystifies astronomers

Figure 104

telescope called the Infra-red Astronomical Observatory (IRAS).

So mysterious is the object that astronomers do not know if it is a planet, a giant comet, a "protostar" that never got hot enough to become a star, a distant galaxy so young that it is still in the process of forming its first stars, or a galaxy so shrouded in dust that none of the light cast by its stars ever gets through.

"All I can tell you is that we don't know what it is," said Gerry Neugebauer, chief IRAS scientist.

But could it be a planet—another member of our Solar System? That possibility seemed to have occurred to NASA. According to the *Washington Post*,

When IRAS scientists first saw the mystery body and calculated that it could be as close as 50 billion miles, there was some speculation that it might be moving toward Earth.

"The mystery body," the report went on, "was seen twice by IRAS." The second observation took place six months after the first and suggested that the body had hardly moved from its spot in the sky. "This suggests it's not a comet because a comet would not be as large as we've observed and a comet would have probably moved," said James Houck of Cornell's Center for Radio Physics and Space Research and a member of the IRAS science team.

Could it be a slow-moving and very distant planet, if it is not a faster-moving comet?

"Conceivably," the *Washington Post* reported, "it could be the 10th planet that astronomers have searched for in vain."

So, what did IRAS discover, I inquired of the Public Information Office of JPL in February 1984. This is the response I received:

> The scientist quoted in the press reports used a statement reflecting his lack of ranging data on the object seen by IRAS.
>
> In true scientific fashion he carefully noted that if the object were close it would have to be Neptune-size. But if distant, an entire galaxy.

Gone, then, is the Jupiter-sized comparison: now it was a Neptune-sized planet "if the object were close"—but a galaxy (!) if distant.

So, did IRAS spot, by heat sensing, the Tenth Planet? Many astronomers believe so. As an example, let us quote William Gutsch, chairman of the American Museum-Hayden Planetarium in New York (and science editor of WABC-TV). Writing about the IRAS discoveries in his syndicated column "Skywatch," he said: "A tenth planet may have already been spotted and even catalogued," although it is yet to be seen with optical telescopes.

Was this also the conclusion reached at the White House, as witness the developments that have followed in superpower relations as of 1983 and the repeated "hypothetical" statements by the two leaders concerning aliens from space?

When Pluto was discovered in 1930 it was a great astronomical and scientific discovery, but no earthshaking event. The same would have applied to the discovery of Planet X;

but not anymore—not if Planet X and Nibiru are one and the same. For if Niburu exists, then the Sumerians were also right about the Anunnaki.

If Planet X exists, we are not alone in this Solar System. And the implications for Mankind, its societies, its national divisions, and its arms races are indeed so profound that the American president was right to apply the consequences to the superpowers' confrontation on Earth and cooperation in space.

The strong indication that what IRAS had spotted was not "a distant galaxy" but a "Neptune-sized planet" is further corroborated by the intensified efforts to scan certain parts of the heavens with optical telescopes and by the sudden stress on conducting these searches in the southern skies.

On the very day that the *Washington Post*'s story was published in several newspapers, NASA let it be known that it had begun an optical scan of not one but nine "mystery sources" of infrared radiation. The purpose was, the statement said, to find these "unidentified objects" in "parts of the sky where there is no obvious source of radiation, such as a distant galaxy or large assemblage of stars." This would be done with some of the world's "most powerful telescopes"—two on Mt. Palomar in California—one a giant and one smaller; the extremely powerful telescope at Cerro Tololo in the Chilean Andes, "and every other major telescope" in the world, including the one atop Mount Mauna Kea in Hawaii.

In their optical searches for Planet X, astronomers pay heed to the negative results of the search conducted by Clyde Tombaugh, the discoverer of Pluto, during more than a decade after that discovery. His conclusion was that the tenth planet has a "highly elliptical and highly inclined orbit and is now far from the Sun." Another noted astronomer, Charles T. Kowal, the discoverer of several comets and asteroids, including Chiron, concluded in 1984 that there is no other planet within a celestial belt reaching 15 degrees above and below the ecliptic. But since his own calculations convinced him that such a tenth planet must exist, he has suggested looking for it at about a 30-degree inclination to the ecliptic.

By 1985 numerous astronomers were intrigued with the "Nemesis theory," first proposed by geologist Walter Alvarez of the University of California at Berkeley and his father, the

Nobel-prize-winning physicist Luis Alvarez. Noticing a regularity in the extinctions of species of Earth (including the dinosaurs), they proposed that a "death star" or planet with a highly inclined and immense elliptical orbit periodically stirs up a shower of comets that then bring death and havoc to the inner Solar System, including Earth. As it happened, the more astronomers and astrophysicists (such as Daniel Whitmire and John Matese of the University of Southwestern Louisiana) analyzed the possibilities, the more they ended up not with a "death star" but with Planet X. Working with Thomas Chester, chief of the IRAS data team, to sift through the infrared transmissions, Whitmire announced in May 1985: "There's a chance Planet X has already been recorded and is awaiting discovery right now." Jordin Kare, a physicist at the Lawrence Berkeley Laboratory, has suggested that the Schmidt telescope in Australia be used with a computer scanning system called "Star Cruncher" to survey the southern skies. If it cannot be located there, Whitmire said, "astronomers might have to wait for the year 2600" to locate it when it crosses the ecliptic.

Meanwhile, the two *Pioneers* were cruising in opposite directions beyond the realm of the known planets, dutifully reporting their sensors' observations. What were they reporting regarding Planet X? On June 25, 1987, NASA issued a press release headlined "NASA Scientist Believes a Tenth Planet May Exist." It was based on a news conference at which John Anderson reported that the *Pioneers* had found nothing. That, he explained, was good news, for it ruled out once and for all the possibility that the perturbations of the outer planets were caused by a "dark star" or "brown dwarf." But the perturbations were there; he told the media that the data had been checked and rechecked and there was no doubt about it; indeed, the perturbations were more pronounced a century ago, when Uranus and Neptune were on the other side of the Sun. This led Dr. Anderson to conclude that Planet X does exist; its orbit is much more inclined than that of Pluto, and it has about five times the mass of Earth. But these, he said, were guesses which may not be proven right or wrong until such time as the planet is actually observed.

Commenting on the NASA news conference, *Newsweek* (July 13, 1987) reported: "NASA held a press conference last week to make a rather strange announcement: an eccentric 10th planet may—or may not—be orbiting the Sun.'' But unnoticed went the fact that the news conference was called under the auspices of the Jet Propulsion Laboratory, the Ames Research Center, and NASA headquarters in Washington. This meant that whatever had to become known bore the stamp of approval of the topmost space authorities. The message was hidden in a final comment by Dr. Anderson. Asked when Planet X would be found, he said, ''I wouldn't be surprised if it is found in 100 years, or it may never be found . . . and *I wouldn't be surprised if it's found next week.*''

That, no doubt, was why three NASA agencies had sponsored the news conference: *That* was the news.

It is evident from all these developments that whoever is in charge of the search for Planet X has been convinced that it is undoubtedly out there, but it still must be observed ''the old-fashioned way,'' visually, with telescopes, before its existence, position, and precise orbit can be ascertained. It is noteworthy that since 1984, after the enigmatic IRAS disclosure, there has been a spate of rushed construction of new or enhancement of older powerful telescopes by the United States, the Soviet Union, and European entities. Telescopes in the southern hemisphere have received the most attention. In France, for example, the Paris Observatory has formed a special team to search for Planet X, and a New Technology Telescope (NTT) was activated by the European Southern Observatory in Cerro La Silla in Chile. At the same time the two superpowers turned to outer space for the same search. The Soviets are known to have equipped, in 1987, their new space station *Mir* with several powerful telescopes when they attached to it an eleven-ton ''science module'' called *Kvant*, which has been described as a ''high-energy astro-physics facility.'' Four of the telescopes, it was disclosed, were to search the southern skies. NASA had planned to loft the most powerful space telescope ever built, the *Hubble*, when the shuttle program went awry after the 1986 *Challenger* accident; there is reason to believe that the expectation of the discovery of Planet X in June 1987 was based on the hope that *Hubble* would be lofted at that time (it was finally put into orbit at the beginning of 1990 only to be found defective).

In the meantime, the most systematic and increasingly pre-

cise land-based search for Planet X continued to be that of the
U.S. Naval Observatory. A series of comprehensive articles
in the scientific journals in or about August 1988 reaffirmed
the calculations of the planetary perturbations and the conviction by leading astronomers of the existence of Planet X. By
then, many scientists also subscribed to Dr. Harrington's assumption that the planet is inclined at about 30 degrees to the
ecliptic and has a semimajor axis of about 101 AU (or a full
major axis of more than 200 AU). Its mass, he believes, is
probably four times that of Earth.

With an orbit that emulates that of Halley's comet, Planet
X spends part of its time above the ecliptic (in the northern
skies) and most below it (in the southern skies). Increasingly,
the U.S. Naval Observatory team decided that the search for
Planet X at present should focus on the southern hemisphere,
at a distance about 2.5 times farther away than Neptune and
Pluto are now. Dr. Harrington presented his latest findings in
a paper published in *The Astronomical Journal* (October 1988)
titled "The Location of Planet X." A sketch of the heavens
indicating the best location "fits" (of where Planet X may be
now) in both the northern and southern skies accompanied the
paper. But since its publication, data from *Voyager 2*, which
had flown by Uranus and Neptune and detected such ongoing
perturbations—minute yet discernible—in their present orbits,
left no doubt in Harrington's mind that Planet X must be now
in the southern skies.

Sending me a reprint of the paper, he marked alongside the
northern portion of the sketch "Not consistent with Neptune,"
and alongside the southern portion of the skies he wrote, "Best
area now" (Fig. 105).

On January 16, 1990, Dr. Harrington reported at the American Astronomical Society meeting in Arlington, Virginia, that
the U.S. Naval Observatory has narrowed its search for the
tenth planet to the southern skies and has announced the dispatch of a team of astronomers to the Black Birch Astronomic
Observatory in New Zealand. The data from *Voyager 2*, he
disclosed, now lead his team to believe that the tenth planet
is about five times larger than Earth and about three times
farther from the Sun than Neptune or Pluto.

These are exciting developments, not only because they
bring modern science to the verge of announcing what the

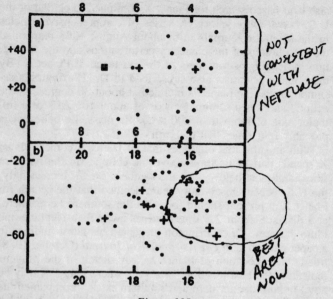

Figure 105

Sumerians already knew so long ago—that there is one more planet in our Solar System—but also because they go a long way toward confirming the details of the planet's size and orbit.

Sumerian astronomy envisaged the heavens surrounding Earth as divided into three bands or "Ways." The central band was the "Way of Anu," ruler of Nibiru, and it extended from 30 degrees north to 30 degrees south. Above it was the "Way of Enlil," and below it, "The Way of Ea/Enki" (Fig. 106). This division seemed to make no sense to modern astronomers studying the Sumerian texts; the only explanation I could find for it was the reference in those texts to the orbit of Nibiru/Marduk as it became visible from Earth:

> Planet Marduk:
> Upon its appearance: Mercury.
> Rising 30 degrees of the celestial arc: Jupiter.
> When standing in the place of the celestial battle:
> Nibiru.

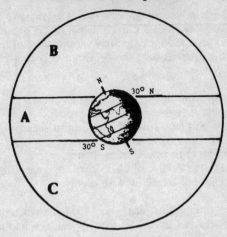

Figure 106

These instructions for observing the incoming planet clearly
refer to its progression from an alignment with Mercury to an
alignment with Jupiter by *rising 30 degrees*. This could happen
only if the orbit of Nibiru/Marduk is inclined 30 degrees to the
ecliptic. Appearing 30 degrees above the ecliptic and disappearing (to a viewer in Mesopotamia) 30 degrees below it,
creates the "Way of Anu," which forms a band extending 30
degrees above and below the equator.

The thirtieth parallel north, it was pointed out in *The Stairway to Heaven*, was a "sacred" line along which the spaceport
in the Sinai peninsula, the great pyramids of Giza, and the
gaze of the Sphinx were located. It seems plausible that the
alignment had to do with Nibiru's position, 30 degrees in the
northern skies, as it reached the perihelion in its orbit. By
concluding that the inclination of Planet X might be as high
as 30°, modern astronomers corroborate Sumerian astronomical
data.

So does the most recent determination that the planet is
orbiting toward us from the southeast, the direction of the
constellation Centaurus. Nowadays we see there the zodiac
constellation Libra; but in Babylonian/biblical times that was
the place of Sagittarius. A text quoted in R. Campbell Thomp-

son's *Reports of the Magicians and Astronomers of Nineveh and Babylon* describes the movements of the incoming planet as it curves around Jupiter to arrive at the place of the Celestial Battle in the asteroid belt, the"Place of Crossing" (and hence the name *Nibiru*):

> When from the station of Jupiter
> the Planet passes toward the west,
> there will be a time of dwelling in security. . . .
> When from the station of Jupiter
> the Planet increases in brilliance
> and in the Zodiac of Cancer will become Nibiru,
> Akkad will overflow with plenty.

It can be simply illustrated (Fig. 107) that when the planet's perihelion was in Cancer, its first appearance had to be from the direction of Sagittarius. In this regard it is pertinent to quote the biblical verses from the Book of Job that describe the appearance of the Celestial Lord and its return to its distant abode:

> Alone He stretches out the heavens
> and treads upon the farthest Deep.
> He arrives at the Great Bear, Orion and Sirius
> and the constellations of the south. . . .
>
> He smiles his face upon Taurus and Aries;
> From Taurus to Sagittarius He shall go.

It is not just an arrival from the southeast (and the return thereto) but also a description of a retrograde orbit.

If Extraterrestrials exist, should Earthlings try to reach them? If they can journey in space and reach Earth, will they be benign, or—as H. G. Wells depicted in *The War of the Worlds*—will they come to destroy, conquer, annihilate?

When *Pioneer 10* was launched in 1971, it carried an engraved plaque intended to tell Extraterrestrials who may come upon the spacecraft or its remains where it came from and who had sent it. When the *Voyagers* were launched in 1977, they

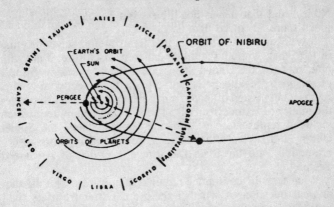

Figure 107

carried a golden disk similarly engraved, an encoded digital message and a recording of spoken messages by the Secretary General of the United Nations and delegates from thirteen nations. "If inhabitants of other worlds have the technology to intercept one of these records," Timothy Ferris of NASA told the U.N. at the time, "they should be able to figure out how to play the record."

Not everyone thought it was a good idea. In Britain, the Astronomer Royal, Sir Martin Ryle, counseled against any attempt by people on Earth to make their existence known. His concern was that another civilization might see Earth and Earthlings as a tempting source of minerals, food, and slaves. He was criticized not only for paying too little heed to the possibility of gain from such contacts but also for creating unnecessary fears: "Given the immensity of space" (*The New York Times* editorialized), "the nearest intelligent beings are not likely to exist closer than hundreds or thousands of light years away."

But, as the chronology of discoveries and superpower relations indicates, it was realized by the time the first U.S.-Soviet summit was held that such intelligent beings are much closer to us than that; that there indeed exists one more planet in our own Solar System; that it was known in antiquity as

Nibiru; and that it was not lifeless but peopled, with beings much more advanced than us.

It was some time after that first Reagan-Gorbachev meeting in 1985 that, without fanfare or untimely disclosure, if not with utter secrecy, the United States convened a "working group" of scientists, legal experts, and diplomats to meet with NASA representatives and officials from other U.S. agencies to ponder the matter of Extraterrestrials. The working committee, which included representatives from the United States, the Soviet Union, and several other nations, conducted its work in co-ordination with the State Department's Office of Advanced Technology.

What was the committee required to consider? Not the theoretical question of whether there are Extraterrestrials light years away; not how to go about searching for such Extraterrestrials on the chance they might exist. The task before the committee was much more urgent and ominous: *What should be done as soon as their existence is discovered.*

Little is publicly known of the deliberations of that Working Committee, but from what could be gleaned it is evident that its main concern was how to maintain authoritative control over an extraterrestrial contact and prevent unauthorized, premature, or damaging disclosure of the event. How long could the information be kept secret? How should the information be released to the public? How to handle the anticipated escalation from rumors to worldwide panic? Who should be in charge of answering the deluge of questions, and what should be said?

In April 1989, immediately after the *Phobos 2* incident at Mars, the international team hammered out a set of guidelines. It was a two-page document titled DECLARATION OF PRINCIPLES CONCERNING ACTIVITIES FOLLOWING THE DETECTION OF EXTRATERRESTRIAL INTELLIGENCE. It has ten clauses and an Annex; and it is clear that its principal purpose was to maintain the control by certain authorities of the news *following* the "detection of extraterrestrial intelligence."

The "Principles" set out guidelines that seek to minimize, as some close to the document have put it, the "potentially panicky public reaction to the first evidence that humankind is not alone in the universe." The *Declaration of Principles* opens with the statement that "we, the institutions and individuals participating in the search for extraterrestrial intelligence, recognizing that the search for extraterrestrial intelligence is an integral part of space exploration and is being undertaken for peaceful purposes and for the common interest of all mankind," and pledges the participants "to observe the following principles for disseminating information about the detection of extraterrestrial intelligence."

The Principles are to apply to "any individual, public or private research institution, or governmental agency that believes it has detected a signal from or other evidence of extraterrestrial intelligence." They prohibit "the discoverer" from making "a public announcement that evidence of extraterrestrial intelligence has been detected" without first promptly informing those who are parties to the declaration, so that "a network could be established to enable continuous monitoring of the signal or phenomenon."

The Principles then elaborate on the procedures to be followed regarding the evaluation, recording, and protection of the signals and the frequencies on which they were transmitted, and in Clause 8 prohibit unauthorized response:

No response to a signal or other evidence of extraterrestrial intelligence should be sent until appropriate international consultations have taken place. The procedures for such consultations will be the subject of a separate agreement, declaration or arrangement.

The Working Committee considered the possibility that the "signal" might be not simply one that indicates its intelligent origin but an actual "message" that may need decoding, and assumed that scientists would have no more than one day to decode it before the word would get out, rumors would fly, and the situation would become uncontrollable. The committee envisaged a buildup of pressure from the media, from the public in general, and from "politicians" for an authoritative and calming announcement.

Why should there be pandemonium and worldwide panic if, say, the authorities were to announce the possibility of intelligent life in some star system several light years away? If they were thinking, for example, that such a signal might come from the first star system *Voyager* might come upon after it left the Solar System, the encounter would take place forty thousand years in the future! Surely, that is not what has worried the Committee. . . .

Clearly, then, the Principles were drawn up in anticipation of a message or phenomenon closer to home, from within the Solar System. Indeed, the legal basis for the Principles the Declaration invokes is the United Nations treaty governing activities by states in the "exploration and use" of the Moon and other celestial bodies in the Solar System. Accordingly, the Secretary General of the U.N. was also to be notified—after the national governments had been informed and had had a chance to examine the evidence and decide what to do about it.

Seeking.to allay the concern by various international astronomical, astronautical, and other organizations that had "demonstrated interest in and expertise concerning the question of the existence of extraterrestrial intelligence" that the discovery would become a purely political or national matter, the signatories to the Declaration agreed to the formation of an "international committee of scientists and other experts" that would not only help examine the evidence but would also "provide advice on the release of information to the public." The SETI Office of NASA referred, in July 1989, to this group as "the *special post-detection committee*." Subsequent documents disclose that the formation and activities of this special post-detection committee will be handled by the Chief of the SETI Office of NASA.

In July 1989 the superpowers became aware that what had occurred at Phobos was not a malfunction; forthwith the mechanism for the "Activities Following the Detection of Extraterrestrial Intelligence" was set in place.

Modern science has indeed caught up with ancient knowledge—of Nibiru and the Anunnaki. And Man knows, once again, that he is not alone.

AND ITS NAME SHALL BE . . .

It is customary for the discoverer of a new celestial body to have the privilege of naming it.

On January 31, 1983, the author of this book wrote to the Planetary Society the following letter:

Ms. Charlene Anderson
The Planetary Society
110 S. Euclid
Pasadena, Calif. 91101

Dear Ms. Anderson:

In view of very recent reports in the press concerning the intensified search for the 10th planet, I am forwarding to you copies of my exchanges on the subject with Dr. John D. Anderson.

According to the New York Times of this Sunday (see enclosure) ''astronomers are so sure of the 10th planet, they think there's nothing left but to name it.''

Well—the ancients had already named it: *Nibiru* in Sumerian, *Marduk* in Babylonian; and I believe I have the right to insist that it so be called.

                                        Sincerely,

                                        Z. Sitchin

INDEX

Zecharia Sitchin's
The Earth Chronicles

BOOK I: THE 12TH PLANET
39362-X/$6.99 US/$9.99 CAN

This revolutionary work brings together lost, antediluvian texts, ancient cosmologies, and newly discovered celestial maps to reach the shocking conclusion that we are descendants of a superior race from the 12th planet.

BOOK II: THE STAIRWAY TO HEAVEN
63339-6/$6.99 US/$8.99 CAN

BOOK III: THE WARS OF GODS AND MEN
89585-4/$6.99 US/$8.99 CAN

BOOK IV: THE LOST REALMS
75890-3/$6.99 US/$8.99 CAN

BOOK V: WHEN TIME BEGAN
77071-7/$6.99 US/$8.99 CAN

BOOK VI: THE COSMIC CODE
80157-4/$6.99 US/$9.99 CAN

And Don't Miss the Companion Volumes:
GENESIS REVISITED
76159-9/$6.99 US/$8.99 CAN
DIVINE ENCOUNTERS
78076-3/$6.99US/$8.99 CAN